4, 17, 157, 161
12-13
25-29
28
129-30
142

CONFLICT IN NORTHWEST AFRICA

HOOVER INTERNATIONAL STUDIES
Peter Duignan, general editor

Publications in the Hoover International Studies series of the Hoover Institution on War, Revolution and Peace are concerned with U.S. involvement in world and regional politics. These studies are intended to represent a contribution to the discussion and debate of major questions of international affairs.

Conflict in Northwest Africa: The Western Sahara Dispute
John Damis

CONFLICT IN NORTHWEST AFRICA

The Western Sahara Dispute

John Damis

HOOVER INSTITUTION PRESS
Stanford University | Stanford, California

Hoover Press Publication 278
Copyright © 1983 by the Board of Trustees of the
    Leland Stanford Junior University

Library of Congress Cataloging in Publication Data
Damis, John.
    Conflict in northwest Africa.

    (Hoover international studies)
    Bibliography: p.
    Includes index.
    1. Western Sahara—Politics and government.
I. Title.   II. Series.
DT346.S7D44 1983   964'.8   82-21168
ISBN 0-8179-7781-3

Manufactured in the United States of America

With love and appreciation
to my mother
and the
memory of my father

Contents

List of Maps and Tables

Maps

Tables

List of Abbreviations

ALPS	Saharan People's Liberation Army
ALS	Army for Liberation of the Sahara
Aosario	Association of People Originating from Sakiet al-Hamra and Rio de Oro
CMRN	Military Committee for National Recovery (Mauritania)
CMSN	Military Committee of National Welfare (Mauritania)
ENMINSA	Empresa Nacional Minera del Sáhara SA
FLN	National Liberation Front
FLU	Liberation and Unity Front
Fosbucraa	Fosfatos de Bou Craa
Frolinat	Chad National Liberation Front
GPRA	Provisional Government of the Algerian Republic
ICJ	International Court of Justice
Miferma	Mines de Fer de Mauritanie
MLS	Saharan Liberation Movement
Morehob	Mouvement de Résistance des Hommes Bleus
MPAIAC	Movement for the Self-Determination and Independence of the Canary Archipelago
NAC	Non-Aligned Conference
Nidam	Saharan Youth Organization
OAU	Organization of African Unity
OCP	Office Chérifien des Phosphates
OPEC	Organization of Petroleum Exporting Countries
PLO	Palestine Liberation Organization
Polisario	Popular (Front) for the Liberation of Sakiet al-Hamra and Rio de Oro
PSOE	Socialist Workers Party (Spain)
PUNS	Saharan National Unity Party
SDAR	Saharan Democratic Arab Republic
SNIM	Société Nationale d'Industrialisation Minière (Mauritania)
SWAPO	South West Africa People's Organization
UCD	Central Democratic Union (Spain)
UNGA	United Nations General Assembly
UNHCR	United Nations High Commission for Refugees
USFP	Socialist Union of Popular Forces

Editor's Foreword

Northwest Africa is a troubled portion of the world. Since 1975, conflict over the disposition of the Western Sahara has upset the politics of Morocco, Algeria, Mauritania, and — to a lesser extent — Libya. The Western Sahara is a dry and inhospitable region, yet the struggle continues over the sovereignty of this former Spanish territory, absorbing much of the energies and resources of Morocco and producing a highly dedicated liberation front, the Polisario.

According to Dr. Damis, the Western Sahara conflict represents more than a struggle between Morocco and the Polisario; it is part of a wider struggle for dominance in northwest Africa between Morocco and Algeria. Furthermore, the Polisario survives largely because of this antagonism between Rabat and Algiers. The Polisario has virtually no material resources of its own and, without support from Algeria and Libya, would cease to exist in any significant sense. Within the Organization of African Unity (OAU), divisions over the admission of the Polisario's Saharan Democratic Arab Republic have created the most serious crisis in the organization's history.

Dr. Damis first began work on northwest Africa in 1964, but his interest in the Sahara conflict intensified between 1975 and 1977, when he served as the U.S. State Department's foreign affairs analyst for North Africa. He has visited the area several times since then. As a result of his many visits and study of the dispute for seven years, he concludes that the Polisario conflict in northwest Africa will persist for many years.

Dr. Damis is surely correct in this surmise. It is, however, in the U.S. interest to continue supporting King Hassan of Morocco. The United States requires a friendly ruler in control of the Strait of Gibraltar with a foothold both in the North Atlantic and the western Mediterranean. The United States has used Moroccan territory for air bases and communications and will need to do so again if the Rapid Deployment Force is to become a reality. If Hassan were to lose the Western Sahara, his regime would probably be toppled. An unstable or unfriendly Morocco will hurt the interests of Israel, Egypt, and Zaire. Morocco has been a moderate voice in Middle Eastern politics, and Hassan's support is still necessary in efforts to make the Egyptian-Israeli peace treaty work. The United States will have to provide money, arms, and food to help Morocco in the struggle against the Polisario. It is worth the price to keep Morocco friendly and stable.

Peter Duignan

Coordinator, International Studies
Hoover Institution

Acknowledgments

It is a pleasure to acknowledge the contributions of several individuals and one institution to the preparation of this study. The project was undertaken at the invitation of the Hoover Institution on War, Revolution and Peace, whose Publications Committee awarded me two grants to support my research and writing during the summer of 1980, spent as a visiting scholar at the institution, and the winter of 1981. I am grateful for the cooperation and assistance provided by members of the Hoover Institution, especially Peter Duignan and Helen Berman. Since 1977, a number of U.S. Foreign Service Officers have helped to clarify for me various aspects of the Western Sahara issue. Charles Daris, Grant Smith, and Brian Flora deserve special mention; the last of these patient diplomats collected for me a wide variety of relevant articles from the international press for the period 1975–1979 that proved extremely useful in the drafting of the manuscript. Within the Polisario Front, Majid Abdullah hosted my visit to the Tindouf region and kept me informed of subsequent developments in the movement during 1979–1980. Lewis Ware and William Zartman read the entire manuscript and provided many helpful comments and suggestions. The manuscript was typed and occasionally retyped cheerfully and efficiently by Ilse Dignam and Susan Hammond of the Hoover Institution and Karen Kosmas, Paulette Sanders, and Mary Dozark of Portland State University. Finally, my wife, Maria Wulff, offered many helpful stylistic suggestions, prepared three of the maps, and was supportive and patient when the demands of work became burdensome.

Introduction

It is not unusual for a single issue or dispute to dominate an entire region. In the Middle East, for example, the Arab-Israeli conflict has been a very high priority for several states of the area since the late 1940s, although in the past decade other problems like the Lebanese conflict, inter-Arab rivalries, the Iranian revolution, and the Iraq-Iran war have destroyed large amounts of human and material resources. In northwest Africa the politics and international relations of the three states of the area—Morocco, Algeria, and Mauritania—have been dominated to an unusual degree since 1975 by the ongoing conflict over the decolonization and final disposition of the Western Sahara. The dispute over this former colonial territory has commanded a striking proportion of the energies and resources of the region and has spawned a highly dedicated and well-equipped national liberation movement, the Polisario Front.

Despite the importance of U.S. political and military relations with Morocco and economic ties with Algeria, the Western Sahara conflict is not widely understood among the American public. Apart from sporadic coverage in the press and some articles in professional journals, no more than a handful of books on this subject has appeared in English, and without exception these works have been heavily historical or highly partisan. This study, while introducing the background necessary for an understanding of the emotions involved in the Sahara issue, aims to present a balanced and concise analysis of the major factors and developments in the Western Sahara conflict since 1975.

Three working hypotheses form the analytic framework of this study. The most basic is that the Western Sahara conflict, beyond the specific issues of Saharan decolonization and self-determination, is part of a broader set of problems between Morocco and Algeria that is not limited to the regimes now in power in Rabat and Algiers. A settlement limited to the Sahara problem would not resolve basic regional issues. Ultimately, the dispute over the Western Sahara reflects a struggle between systems — a pro-Western monarchy and a liberal economy in Morocco versus an authoritarian one-party regime and a socialist economy in Algeria. Thus, the struggle for control of Saharan territory forms part of a larger geopolitical struggle for influence and dominance in northwest Africa between two competing and antagonistic political and economic systems.

Second, the viability of the Polisario Front as a serious national liberation movement able to sustain an effective military struggle against the Moroccan state and to attract international recognition results, to a significant degree, from Moroccan-Algerian regional antagonisms. There is little question that the Polisario movement is animated by a genuine core of Sahrawi nationalists, highly dedicated and committed to a long and difficult struggle for an independent Saharan state. At the same time, however, the movement has virtually no material resources of its own. Unlike the National Liberation Front in Vietnam or the Popular Movement for the Liberation of Angola, the Polisario Front is heavily dependent on outside sources of support. While many observers have been struck by the ideological purity of the Polisario's cause, few have noted that the front would be rendered ineffective if Algeria and Libya ceased to supply military and economic aid as well as the necessities of daily life. It is one thing to capture weapons; it is quite another to produce food and purchase gasoline.

The third working hypothesis is that outside powers have only marginal influence on the Western Sahara conflict. The underlying dynamics of the dispute can be found within northwest Africa. The decisions critical to the evolution of the conflict were made in Rabat, Algiers, and Nouakchott, not Paris, Washington, or Moscow. Least of all is the Sahara conflict a proxy war fought by local armies on behalf of the superpowers. Neither the United States nor the Soviet Union has anything to gain from a continuation or escalation of the military struggle in northwest Africa.

A few words on the organization of the study may be useful to the reader. The first chapter presents, in broad strokes, the salient features of the land, population, and historical background of the Western Sahara. Chapter Two analyzes, in more detail, the positions and interests of the four major parties to the conflict — Morocco, Mauritania (until 1979), Algeria, and the Polisario Front. The third chapter describes and analyzes at some length the major stages in the evolution of the Saharan conflict since the diplomatic maneuvering of the mid-1960s. Chapter Four assesses the roles of major third parties to the dispute—Spain, Libya, France, the United States, and the Soviet Union. The concluding chapter analyzes previous, unsuccessful mediation attempts, suggests a new approach, and stresses the regional context of a settlement.

The problem of rendering Arabic and Berber words and names into English is compounded by variations among English, French, and Spanish spellings used by scholars and journalists who write about northwest Africa. Since no single system of transliteration is satisfactory to everyone, I have adopted a somewhat arbitrary approach by spelling any given word or name according to my own preference for simplicity, with proper consideration for accepted spellings. For example, I have used the simplified English spelling of Sakiet al-Hamra and Sahrawis, from the Arabic al-Sāqia al-Hamrā' and Sahrāwā, rather than the Spanish Saguia el-Hamra and Saharauis or the French Saguiet El Hamra and Sahraouis/Sahraouies (fem.). Lengthening macrons and most other diacritical marks have been omitted.

My work on North Africa began in 1964, and I made the first of many trips to the area three years later. My exposure to, and knowledge of, the Western Sahara conflict began in earnest when I served from 1975 to 1977 as the Department of State's foreign affairs analyst for North Africa. In November 1975, at the time of the Moroccan Green March, I visited Morocco and Algeria, which provided an excellent opportunity to assess the very different emotional components of the dispute in each country. During the fall of 1978, a visit to Morocco allowed me to travel to the Western Sahara; and during a visit to Algeria in the winter of 1979, a trip was arranged to the Polisario camps in the Tindouf region. More recently, I visited Morocco, the Western Sahara, and Algeria in the summer of 1981.

The combination of visits to North Africa and study of the dispute over a period of seven years has reinforced my belief that the Sahara conflict will persist, in one form or another, for some time to come. Though frustrating to the statesman, the persistent nature of the conflict makes more urgent the work of the political analyst. The history of international relations is punctuated with examples of local festering wars that, left unresolved, eventually escalated into regional—and occasionally international—conflicts.

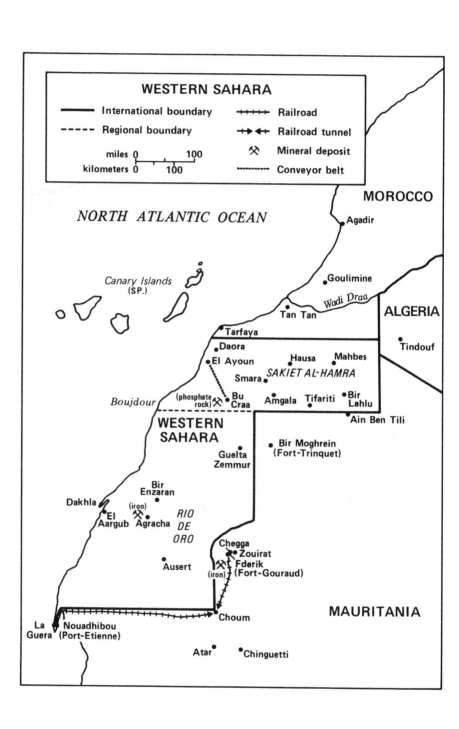

WESTERN SAHARA

— International boundary   ┼┼┼┼ Railroad
--- Regional boundary   ⇥ ⇤ Railroad tunnel

miles 0 ———— 100   ⚒ Mineral deposit
kilometers 0 —— 100   ⋯⋯⋯ Conveyor belt

MOROCCO

NORTH ATLANTIC OCEAN   •Agadir

Canary Islands   •Goulimine
(SP.)
   Wadi Draa
○ ▷ ⌢   Tan Tan•   ALGERIA

   •Tarfaya   •Tindouf
   •Daora
   •El Ayoun   •Hausa   •Mahbes
      Smara•   *SAKIET AL-HAMRA*
Boujdour   (phosphate⚒•Bu   •Amgala   •Tifariti   •Bir
   rock)   Craa   Lahlu
      •Ain Ben Tili
   WESTERN
   SAHARA   •Bir Moghrein
   Guelta•   (Fort-Trinquet)
   Zemmur

   Bir
   Enzaran•
Dakhla   (iron)   *RIO*
•El   ⚒•   *DE*
Aargub   Agracha   *ORO*
      •Chegga
      •Zouirat
   •Ausert   ⚒†Fderik
      (iron)┤(Fort-Gouraud)

         MAURITANIA
   ┼┼┼┼┼┼┼┼┼┼┼⇥•Choum
La ▸Nouadhibou
Guera (Port-Etienne)
      Atar•   •Chinguetti

1 | The Land and the People

The 1975 Green March of 350,000 Moroccans into the Western Sahara drew international attention to this largely unknown area. A Spanish colony from 1884 to 1976 (known in the West after 1962 as Spanish Sahara), the territory was described by a journalist a few years ago as a "God forsaken scorching desert tract half the size of France with little water and less people."[1] Located in northwest Africa, the Western Sahara is bordered on the north by Morocco, on the west by the Atlantic Ocean, on the south and east by Mauritania, and in the northeast for 26 miles by Algeria.

Since 1975, however, the Western Sahara has received considerable attention as the scene of an unresolved armed conflict over the disposition of this former colony. This conflict has dominated the politics of the neighboring northwest African states and has become a familiar issue at international diplomatic forums. Claimed and partially occupied by Morocco, partially claimed and occupied by Mauritania from 1976 to 1979, and indirectly defended by Algeria through its support of a war of national liberation, the once obscure Western Sahara has become since 1975 one of the world's better known trouble spots. With an ever present danger of escalated fighting, this conflict carries the double risk of superpower involvement and severe regional destabilization.

The Land

The Western Sahara has never been an inviting area. A French traveler in the seventeenth century described the land as a "Sandy Plain...Inhabited only by Wild Beasts."[2] Rainfall is so meager that before 1964 Villa Cisneros (now Dakhla) had to import drinking water from the nearby Canary Islands, located in the Atlantic off the coast of southern Morocco. Visitors to the Western Sahara are often struck by two features of the land: the vastness of the territory and the absence of sand throughout most of the desert terrain.

The Western Sahara's territory comprises 102,703 square miles, an area comparable to that of Colorado or New Zealand and a little larger than that of the United Kingdom. Territorial distances are 429 miles from north to south and 362 miles at the widest point from east to west. From the northeast corner to La Guera in the extreme southwest is over seven hundred miles — most of the distance from New York to Chicago. The coastline runs for about six hundred miles along the Atlantic Ocean on a northeast to southwest axis. The Spanish divided the territory in 1962 along the twenty-sixth parallel into two parts. The northern panhandle, with 31 percent of the land, is called Sakiet al-Hamra (or Saguia el-Hamra in Spanish) after the river that runs across that region, while the larger southern area, with 69 percent of the land, is named Rio de Oro ("river of gold"). Prior to 1962, all of Spain's Saharan territory was known in the West by the name of Rio de Oro.

Although the Western Sahara itself comprises a sizable area, when viewed from a larger geographical perspective the territory is only a small part of an enormous body of land — the Sahara, known to Arabs and medieval cartographers alike as the Great Desert. Together with southern Morocco below the Anti-Atlas Mountains, the Western Sahara forms the northwest edge of the Great Desert, whose 3.5 million square miles extend across the northern third of the African continent to the Red Sea in the east and constitute the largest continuous desert area in the world.

Travelers in the Sahara are familiar with a salient feature of the Great Desert — most of its surface is not covered with sand. This feature is particularly noticeable in the Western Sahara. The great sand dune areas (comprising the Erg Iguidi and Erg Chech) that cover most of northern Mauritania and western Algeria barely extend into the Western Sahara and form only a narrow strip in Rio de Oro running from Guelta Zemmur northward for about one hundred miles.

The Atlantic coastline of the Western Sahara consists of alternating stretches of rugged cliffs and sandy beaches. Classic sand dunes are present near much of the coast, extending inland for ten to twenty miles. Along the central coastline, between Boujdour and Dakhla, the beaches are backed by escarpments rising as high as six hundred feet. Although extensive sandy zones can be found scattered throughout the Western Sahara, most of the rest of the territory consists of vast rocky plains that rise gradually from the coast to a maximum height of about thirteen hundred feet in the interior.

The flat desert surface makes a gradual transition from dried alluvial plains covered with stones (*reg*) nearer the coast to sterile rocky plateaus (*hammada*) in the interior. In Sakiet al-Hamra in the north, the sandstone plateau forms a geographical continuum with the Tindouf and Draa hammadas in southwest Algeria. Isolated mountain ranges rise up to twenty-seven hundred feet above the plateau in the area around Guelta Zemmur and up to seventeen hundred feet in the Adrar Sutuf mass in the southeast corner of Rio de Oro.

The desert plains of the Western Sahara are near enough to the ocean to capture some of the moisture carried by the Atlantic winds. These winds are the source of a meager rainfall, which averages from two to eight inches per year depending on the region and the distance from the coast. Though seemingly insignificant, this rainfall is many times greater than the levels received by totally arid desert regions to the east in Mauritania and Algeria and is sufficient to support seasonal vegetation. Thus, despite an arid soil, the slopes of depressions that punctuate the rocky plains are relatively fertile and can nurture occasional acacia, jujube, and gum trees. Other vegetation includes scattered scrub brush, thorn trees, an esparto grass, clover, and small flowers. In the southern desert steppe area, Tiris al-Gharbiyya, considerable vegetation appears following the rainy season, adequate to support abundant game, including hare, gazelle, antelope, and ostriches.

The territory contains only one river of any importance, the Sakiet al-Hamra ("the red rivulet," named for the color of its muddy clay riverbed). Even this watercourse is intermittent and rarely reaches the sea. The river's source is in the mountainous Guelta Zemmur region. Typical of rivers in the Sahara, the Sakiet al-Hamra runs underground for some distance before rising to ground level at Farsia in the northern panhandle; it then flows directly westward for about two hundred miles before emptying into the Atlantic near El Ayoun, the capital of the Western Sahara. With a bed over two miles wide as it nears the coast, this river supplies enough water for year-round cultivation of date trees and other vegetation on the fertile lands bordering its banks. Other permanent sources of water are limited to a few small springs and scattered wells. Although the Western Sahara contains no major oases, soundings have indicated the existence of large underground lakes, including one of the world's largest, some twenty-four thousand square miles in area, discovered at a depth of about fourteen hundred feet in the Dakhla area in 1963.[3]

These various water sources nurture enough seasonal vegetation to support migrant grazing on a widespread scale. In 1973, for example, despite the forbidding desert climate of scorching summer days and cold winter nights, the herds of the Western Sahara numbered 76,000 camels and 120,000 goats.[4]

If the Western Sahara suffers from a harsh desert climate, a bleak land-scape, and an arid soil, it is at least blessed with a variety of natural resources, mineral and otherwise. Some of these resources are proven and utilized, some are proven but not yet exploited, while the presence of other resources is thus far only suggested by inconclusive tests.

The most notable resource in the first category is the much discussed phosphate wealth located in Sakiet al-Hamra. Preliminary tests by the Spanish in 1961 revealed the existence of very high grade phosphate at Bu Craa, about sixty miles southeast of El Ayoun. In 1963, this deposit was estimated at 1.7 billion metric tons, making the Bu Craa vein the world's largest deposit of phosphate rock. By 1976, estimates of the reserves had risen to 1.715 billion tons in the southern part of the Bu Craa basin plus another deposit of 500 million tons in the north.[5] The phosphate is particu-larly valuable because of its location—less than twenty feet below the sur-face—and its quality—80 percent bone phosphate of lime. During 1975, the last full year and also the peak year of production at the Bu Craa mines, the Spanish extracted an impressive 5.6 million tons of raw phosphate.[6]

The fertile fishing grounds off the Atlantic coast constitute another valu-able natural resource. The two-thousand-mile coastal zone from northern Morocco to southern Mauritania contains some of the richest fishing in the world. The waters off the coast of the Western Sahara may possess as much as two billion tons of fish. During the last years of Spain's presence, about 1.5 million tons of fish were harvested from these waters annually, much of it by U.S., Soviet, Japanese, and South Korean boats.[7]

Iron deposits, estimated at seventy million tons, were discovered at Agracha in the middle of Rio de Oro, but no attempt has been made to mine them. Indications of varying reliability have surfaced suggesting the ex-istence of a variety of other mineral resources in unknown quantities in the Western Sahara, including titanium, vanadium, zinc, uranium, potassium, copper, gold, natural gas, magnetite, and petroleum. In the early 1960s, several joint U.S.-Spanish companies, granted concessions by the Spanish government, carried out extensive prospecting for petroleum. These ex-plorations revealed many traces of oil but no viable deposit. There is con-flicting evidence about the presence of the other minerals. Some may not exist in commercial quantities, while others may not be present at all.

The People

For purposes of this study, two questions about the indigenous (Sahrawi) population of the Western Sahara need to be addressed. First, who are the Sahrawis and where did they come from? And second, how numerous is the native Sahrawi population? Curiously enough, it is easier to ascertain the origin of the Sahrawis than their present numbers. While the Western Sahara probably was populated by blacks in prehistoric times, the first known inhabitants of the territory were Berber tribes of the Sanhaja, one of the three larger Berber confederations of northwest Africa during the Roman period. The Sanhaja Berbers pushed the original black population southward across the Senegal River, which now forms the southwest border of Mauritania. These Sanhaja tribes were often sedentary, engaging in agriculture and raising animals. Over the course of the first millennium of the Christian era, however, the Western Sahara continued to experience the progressive desiccation that had begun around 3000 B.C. The desert Berbers, in turn, gradually became nomadic raiders who preyed on caravans, depended on camels, engaged in extortion and robbery, and feuded with rival tribes.[8] By the ninth century, these nomads were known for their warlike qualities and were feared and disdained by the agriculturalists and urban dwellers beyond the desert. In Fez, an Idrisid ruler of that time characterized the desert Berbers as "warriors, caravan raiders, a marauding and ferocious people."[9] The major descendants of the Berbers in the present-day Western Sahara are the Tekna.

It was not until the fourteenth century that Arab tribes began to settle in the Western Sahara. These Arabs were part of the Maqil, a large Bedouin tribe from the Arabian peninsula that had immigrated into Egypt before crossing North Africa as part of the Hilalian invasion. Between the eleventh and thirteenth centuries, the Maqil first followed the great tribal group of the Beni Hilal and Sulaim into North Africa and then gradually migrated westward across the Maghreb and settled mostly in Morocco. Forced out of southern Morocco by the Merinides (a Berber dynasty centered in Fez), a Maqil tribe—the Ulad Delim—gradually moved in and forcefully established itself in the southern Sahara. From about 1400 to 1700, a gradual accommodation took place between the Ulad Delim and the Berbers, smoothed by intermarriage and tribal alliances, in which the Berbers assimilated Arab blood and culture. During this period, the Hassaniyya Arabic dialect of the Ulad Delim largely replaced Berber, and the conversion of Berbers to Islam accelerated. Since the end of the seventeenth century, all Berber tribes of the territory have claimed Arab descent—a telling measure of the acceptance and predominance of Maqil Arab culture.[10]

The third major component of the Western Saharan population is composed of Reguibat, a large Bedouin tribe whose vast grazing lands extend far outside the territory. The tribe is of Arab origin, and all its members trace their ancestry to the pious Sidi Ahmed al-Reguibi, who settled in southern Morocco in 1503. Beginning in the late nineteenth century, the population of the Reguibat expanded very rapidly, in part by assimilating weaker or defeated individuals or groups. Estimates of the Reguibat's population range from fifty thousand to three hundred thousand. The tribe is divided into two broad units whose territorial bases overlap: the Sahel (coastal) Reguibat and the Sharg (eastern) Reguibat. These nomadic Bedouins roam over a large area that includes southern Morocco, the eastern part of the Western Sahara, northern and central Mauritania, and parts of Mali and western Algeria. The Reguibat have been called the "Blue People" because the indigo dye used in their clothing rubs off on their skin. The members of this tribe are known for their fierce fighting qualities, remarkable tracking ability, pride in their own traditions, and a very high degree of social and structural cohesion.[11]

In this century, the most important tribes of the Western Sahara have been the Eastern Reguibat, the Tekna group (especially the Izarguien), and the Tidrarin in Sakiet al-Hamra, and the Ulad Delim, the Coastal and Eastern Reguibat, and the Tidrarin in Rio de Oro[12] (see Map 2 for the territorial distribution of the tribes). The major tribes are known for certain traits of behavior—the Tekna for their peaceful disposition, commercial proclivities, and pro-Moroccan sympathies, the Reguibat for their antipathy toward Morocco and their fierce resistance to European colonialism, and the Ulad Delim for their readiness to serve in the Spanish colonial administration and their pro-Moroccan sympathies. This is not to suggest, however, that the three major tribes in the Sahara presently function as political units. While most of the Reguibat, for example, have supported the Polisario Front, various individual members of the tribe have not. It may be more accurate to suggest that fractions of the major tribes are political units, but even here there is a lack of clear evidence. In some cases immediate families have been divided by competing political loyalties.

Only the northern Tekna tribes now speak Berber. The great majority of the territory's population speak Hassaniyya Arabic, which is much closer to classical Arabic than are the dialects spoken in Morocco and Algeria. With minor variations Hassaniyya Arabic is the dialect spoken from Tarfaya in southern Morocco to Nouakchott in southern Mauritania. Language, in combination with shared ethnicity, cultural tradition, and religion, thus is one of the major affinities linking the Sahrawis of the Western Sahara to Sahrawis in southern Morocco and western Algeria and to the Moors (of mixed Arab-Berber background) of northern and central Mauritania. These same shared affinities, in turn, distinguish this larger population grouping and set it apart from the Berbers of the Moroccan Anti-Atlas to the north, the Berber-speaking Tuaregs of southern Algeria to the east, and the blacks in the Senegal River valley in southern Mauritania.

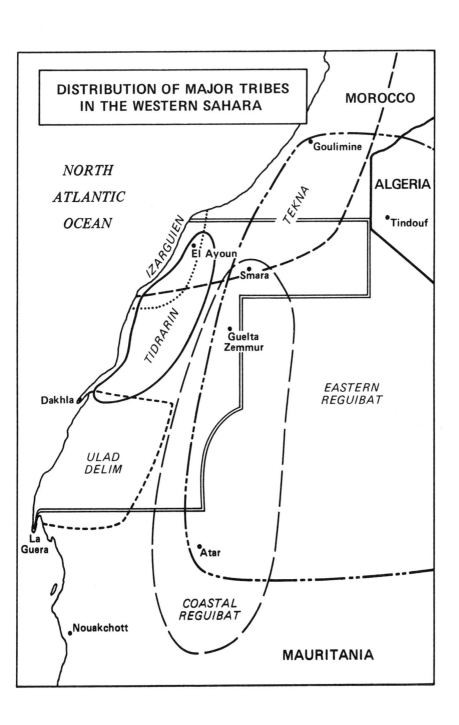

DISTRIBUTION OF MAJOR TRIBES
IN THE WESTERN SAHARA

MOROCCO

NORTH

ATLANTIC

OCEAN

ALGERIA

Goulimine

TEKNA

•Tindouf

IZARGUIEN

El Ayoun
•Smara

TIDRARIN

•Guelta
Zemmur

EASTERN
REGUIBAT

Dakhla

ULAD
DELIM

La
Guera

•Atar

COASTAL
REGUIBAT

•Nouakchott

MAURITANIA

The difficulties of accurately assessing the size of the indigenous population of the Western Sahara are both practical and political. Most of the Sahrawis are nomadic herders who frequently move from one area to another in search of water and grazing land for their animals. They shift location without regard for international frontiers — lines on a map that represent political boundaries imposed by colonial powers. Bedouins, like the camel-herding Reguibat, are settled only by force, either human (military) or climatic (drought). At any given time, their numbers within a fixed territory may fluctuate considerably. In addition, in the wake of armed resistance against Spanish and French forces in the late 1950s, a sizable number of Sahrawis left or were forced out of the territory; most of these people resettled in southern Morocco. Because of the frequent movement of nomads, because many Sahrawis left the territory (even before 1975) for economic or other reasons to live temporarily or permanently among their tribal kinfolk beyond the frontier, and because of the close affinity between Sahrawis of the territory and those in neighboring countries, it is very difficult to determine which Sahrawis are indigenous to the Western Sahara. For political reasons, supporters of an independent Saharan state find it useful to inflate the size of the population, while those opposed to such a state try to minimize the number of Sahrawis.

Estimates of the Sahrawi population range from 31,500 by the Spanish in 1954 (based on a count of the 6,300 tents then in the territory) to about 70,000 by Spanish counts in 1970 and 1974 to a figure of 150,000 put forward by Morocco in 1966[13] all the way to the implausible figure of 750,000–850,000 claimed by the Polisario Front, the national liberation movement currently fighting for an independent Saharan state. A thorough census taken by the Spanish in the fall of 1974 counted a total of 73,497 Sahrawis. The census was done by Spanish specialists, aided by bilingual Sahrawi students, utilizing Land Rovers and helicopters to reach isolated areas of the territory.[14] Polisario officials argue that this census significantly undercounted the Sahrawi population since it missed many nomads or counted only the one male member of a family who had an identity card and normally had contact with the Spanish administration. While this may account for some omissions, it is important to note that as a result of the severe drought that persisted throughout the Sahel from the late 1960s to 1974, the Spanish administration was in close contact with the vast majority of Sahrawi nomads through the provision of essential food subsidies that were given only to persons formally registered with the government.

The 1974 Spanish census is the most reliable and documented survey and must be taken at least as a starting point. To its total of 73,497 should be added the 20,000–35,000 Sahrawis who left the territory in the late 1950s and resettled mostly in Morocco. Beyond these two figures are the unknown numbers of Sahrawis who were refugees in Mauritania or Algeria (prior to 1975), temporarily beyond the frontier (the nomadic movement factor), or simply missed the census. Considering these various factors, it is most likely that the population of the Western Sahara is at least 100,000 but well below 200,000 — perhaps a working estimate of 120,000–150,000 is as close as one can come to the actual figure.

Historical Sketch

Prior to the twentieth century, the Western Sahara usually remained outside the control of any central authority. Roman administration was never established south of the Atlas Mountains. The rule of the first great Arab dynasty in Morocco, the Idrisids (788–974), did not penetrate the desert, and it was Berber traders who carried Islam to the territory. Only rarely did the Western Sahara form part of a larger political and administrative organization, as occurred under the Almoravids (1061–1147), a Berber dynasty driven by a crusading Islamic puritanism that originated in southern Mauritania and established Marrakesh as its capital. The period from the thirteenth to the late nineteenth century was highlighted by the gradual subjugation of the desert Berbers by the Ulad Delim (noted earlier), coastal incursions by Portuguese and Spanish slave traders, merchants, and fishermen, and periodic military expeditions sent by Moroccan-based dynasties — the Saadians (1554–1659) and the Alawites (1666–present). During these centuries, Sahrawi life revolved around nomadism based on camels. Frequent tribal feuding made the territory an area of endemic warfare. An important source of livelihood came from raiding the trans-desert caravans that followed the western route between Marrakesh or Sijilmassa in Morocco in the north and Mali in the south.

A new and quite different chapter in the Western Sahara's history began in the late nineteenth century when much of Africa was divided up by the competing colonial powers of Europe. Militarily weak and financially drained, Spain was not a strong competitor in the scramble for colonial territories. As much by default as by design, Spain obtained the Western Sahara after Britain, France, Germany, and Belgium had taken or staked claims on more desirable parts of Africa. Spain had a historical interest in the territory as a strategic area for the support of the Canary Islands, where the Spanish were firmly entrenched, and as a commercial asset linked to the Canaries' fishing industry. An additional motivation was the prestige attached to colonial possessions.

In 1884, Spain sent a mission with a modest military force to establish three coastal trading stations at Villa Cisneros (now Dakhla), Cintra, and Cape Blanc. In December of that year, the Madrid government claimed a

"Spanish protectorate of the African coast" of Rio de Oro and announced its claim in an international declaration: "Considering the importance of the Spanish installations... and in view of the documents signed by the independent tribes... who have on various occasions asked for and obtained the protection of the Spanish... the King has decided... to take under his protection the territories... between Bahia del Oeste [now La Guera] and C[ape] Bojador [Boujdour]."[15] This declaration was transmitted in writing to the European powers in January 1885. Embellished by treaties with local Saharan rulers, the Spanish claim was recognized by the European powers at the 1884-1885 Berlin Conference. The Berlin Conference adopted the principle that the effective occupation of a territory's coast entitled a colonial power to the interior of that territory. Spanish claims to the interior, however, were limited by French colonial designs on Mauritania, which France created in 1904 as a territory of French West Africa. Accordingly, in a series of negotiations and treaties between 1900 and 1904, Spain and France defined the territory's northern, eastern, and southern borders, with the northern boundary formally established in the Franco-Spanish Convention of November 27, 1912.

It was one thing for Spain to lay claim to the Western Sahara, but quite another matter to occupy and control it. The Spanish were quite content for half a century to maintain a small presence within a series of coastal enclaves, and even there they were obliged to fend off periodic attacks by the Ulad Delim. Spain ultimately reaped the benefits of the long and patient French pacification of southern Morocco and Mauritania between 1900 and 1934, a military effort that necessarily spilled over into the Spanish territory.

An important part of the resistance to foreign domination was played by Shaikh Ma al-Ainain from Chinguetti in central Mauritania, a political-religious leader who rallied a dedicated following and in the 1890s established the city of Smara in Sakiet al-Hamra as his stronghold. For many years, acting ás the representative of the sultan of Morocco, Ma al-Ainain led the resistance against the French pacification. When the Moroccan sultan showed signs of capitulating to French authority, Ma al-Ainain asserted his own claim to religious leadership shortly before his death in 1910. The resistance was carried on by Ma al-Ainain's son El Hiba, who was proclaimed sultan in 1912 by tribes opposed to the signing of the protectorate treaty by Morocco. That same year, the French Army defeated El Hiba's forces near Marrakesh and went on to sack Smara in 1913. Other members of Ma al-Ainain's family relentlessly carried on the struggle under the banner of an Islamic jihad ("holy war") until the French finally eliminated the last pocket of resistance in the Anti-Atlas Mountains in southern Morocco in 1934.

Within the territory the Spanish slowly extended their occupation — to La

Guera on the southern coast in 1920 and finally to the ruins of Smara in 1936. In 1934, after 50 years of occupation, Spain divided the territory into two administrative parts, Sakiet al-Hamra in the north and Rio de Oro in the south. Between 1934 and 1958, the two parts of Spanish Sahara, along with Spanish South Morocco (the present Tarfaya province of Morocco) and the small coastal enclave at Ifni (between Tarfaya and Agadir), were governed as parts of Spanish West Africa under the centralized administration of a military governor in Ifni.

During the late 1950s, armed resistance to Spanish control in the Sahara erupted again. After obtaining independence from France in March 1956, Morocco laid claim to all Spanish possessions in northwest Africa (plus all of Mauritania, which was a French overseas territory from 1946 to 1958). Although Spain returned its protectorate in the north to Morocco in April 1956, it refused to relinquish Tarfaya, Ifni, and especially Spanish Sahara. In late 1957, Moroccan irregular forces, numbering from three thousand to five thousand and supported by Reguibat and Tekna nomads, attacked the Spanish military forces in the territory (and in Ifni) and forced them back to the coastal cities—Dakhla, Boujdour, and El Ayoun. The irregulars, called the Army for Liberation of the Sahara (ALS), were former resistance fighters from the Moroccan Army of Liberation who had kept their weapons and had not been incorporated into the post-independence Moroccan military; the ALS was organized mainly by Morocco's Istiqlal party but was not fully controlled by the Istiqlal. In February 1958, France and Spain responded with a sizable combined military offensive that retook Smara and defeated the irregular forces by the end of the year.[16]

Against the background of the 1957–1958 fighting, Spain made two political decisions. In January 1958, the Spanish government issued a decree making the Western Sahara a Spanish African province and incorporating the territory into metropolitan Spain. Control of the Saharan province was assigned to the director-general of African provinces in Madrid. The captain-general of the Canaries commanded the military forces in Spanish Sahara (and in Ifni), and a governor-general stationed in El Ayoun exercised local administrative responsibilities. Three deputies were subsequently elected to represent the Sahara in the Spanish Cortes (parliament) in Madrid. In April 1958, Spain retroceded to Morocco the region of Tarfaya, which extended from the Wadi Draa in southern Morocco to the northern border of Spanish Sahara. This area of about ten thousand square miles, which Spain had administered superficially since 1912 as a protectorate under the name of Spanish South Morocco, became the Moroccan province of Tarfaya. More than a decade later, in June 1969, Spain ceded the small coastal enclave of Ifni back to Morocco.

The Spanish never seriously assumed possession of their Saharan territories until shortly before World War II, and even then their presence was only slightly felt until Moroccan independence in 1956. It was not until 1963 that Madrid set up a formal administration in the territory. Spain did not attempt to build up a substantial presence in the Sahara, and its administration made little effort to work for the benefit of the Sahrawi population. In 1925, there were fewer than seven hundred Spanish troops in the territory, although this military presence increased to about fifteen thousand in the early 1970s. The number of Spanish civilians in the Sahara was only 1,330 in 1950, 5,304 in 1960, and 16,648 in 1970.[17] By 1973, the Spanish population in the Western Sahara was about thirty-five thousand. Perhaps half of the Spaniards were soldiers, while the remainder were mainly civilian administrators, technicians, and businessmen and their families.

Virtually no Spaniards lived outside the towns or the military garrisons. There is evidence of open cultural and social discrimination during the last phase of Spain's colonial presence, and contact between the Spanish and Sahrawi populations was reduced to a minimum. The Spanish built just three hundred miles of paved road in the Sahara and no railroad; freshwater sources were developed only at El Ayoun and the main military garrisons. Although Spain did engage in some public works (wells, local primary and secondary schools plus university education in Spain, loans, food subsidies, monthly stipends for the needy) during the last decade of its rule, these uncoordinated eleventh-hour efforts were intended mainly to encourage the Sahrawis to think well of Spain when it came time to decolonize the territory. A telling measure of Spanish concern for the native population is that by 1975 the literacy rate was under 5 percent, only two Sahrawis had higher university degrees, and only twelve had advanced technical diplomas.

The one area in the Sahara where the Spanish did invest substantially was the phosphate industry—with the obvious motive of exploiting fully a rich mineral resource. In addition to the revenues to be gained from phosphate exports, Spain had a domestic need for phosphate that otherwise had to be met by imports from Morocco. To exploit this resource, the Spanish National Institute of Industry in 1962 created an operating company, ENMINSA, which in 1969 became Fosfatos de Bou Craa (Fosbucraa). An estimated $400–500 million from Spanish and international sources provided the necessary investment to acquire mining equipment and to construct treatment, storage, dock, and port facilities. This investment includes the world's longest conveyor belt, a $72 million system built by the German firm Krupp, to transport the pale-yellow phosphate rock 62 miles from Bu Craa to El Ayoun port. In 1973, after several years of preparation, Fosbucraa began to mine the phosphate in significant quantities. In 1975, the last full year of operations, production reached 2.8 million tons and exports totaled 2.6 million tons, with Spanish plans calling for expansion to 10 million tons annually in each category by 1980.

Finally, a word should be said about the Jemaa ("general assembly") established by the Spanish to provide the Sahrawis a means of participation in government — or at least to give the outside world the impression of an institution of self-government. As originally set up in 1967, the Jemaa (Yema'a in Hispano-Arabic) had 43 members, mostly elected representatives of tribal chiefs; it amounted to an assembly of traditional notables with purely advisory powers. The Jemaa was progressively enlarged and strengthened: by 1973, it had 103 members, 96 of whom were elected either directly or indirectly, and its power allowed a considerable margin for independent expression. The U.N. Visiting Mission that observed the Jemaa in 1975 judged that it represented mostly the older and more conservative element of Sahrawi society. If correct, this judgment is at least consistent with Spain's intention of creating an assembly whose organization followed traditional Saharan institutions.

By the 1960s, Spanish colonialism had made an uneven impact on the Western Sahara and its native population. In some sectors of Sahrawi life, the Spanish presence had cut deeply, while in others it had hardly made a ripple. In the economic realm, Spain's colonization of the territory greatly undermined the commercial caravan economy that was an important feature of traditional Sahrawi society. Spanish policy significantly reduced nomadism in the Western Sahara, a trend that was reinforced by the severe and lengthy drought that began in the Sahel in the late 1960s.

Politically, however, the small number of Spaniards, living in a few coastal cities or stationed at military garrisons, did not affect Sahrawi life in any significant way. Some young Sahrawi students who had received a modern education outside the territory began to assert opinions independent of those of their more conservative fathers. But with the exception of these students and the few thousand Sahrawis who worked as laborers on Spanish projects or served in the territory's security forces, the population continued to follow traditional Saharan social patterns, little touched by the Spanish presence. Political loyalty was to the family, the tribe, and Islam. There was very little allegiance to a Spanish Saharan entity. And apart from the traditional Sahrawi resistance to any authority or government imposed from the outside, there were very few indications of a developing national consciousness.

2 | The Parties to the Conflict

The conflict over the Western Sahara essentially has involved a dispute about the decolonization and future disposition of a colonial territory—Spain's Saharan province. As the colonizing power, Spain was obviously a key participant in the decolonization of the territory. Since 1976, however, Spain has played only a peripheral role in the conflict. Spain's important role in the decolonization of the Western Sahara is discussed in Chapter Three, and its marginal role in the conflict since 1976 is treated in Chapter Four.

The major parties to the conflict have been three northwest African states—Morocco, Algeria, and Mauritania—and a national liberation movement—the Polisario Front. For Morocco and Algeria, the Western Sahara conflict is only the most immediate manifestation of a prolonged antagonism between different, competitive political and economic systems, both symptom and cause of a natural power rivalry between the two leading states of the Maghreb. The third state, Mauritania, withdrew from the conflict when it signed an agreement in August 1979 with the Polisario. Nevertheless, Mauritania played an important role in the evolution of the conflict (detailed in Chapter Three), and its position deserves careful attention. Finally, for the Polisario Front, the conflict is an unavoidable part of its struggle to establish an independent Saharan state.

Morocco

Morocco claims the Western Sahara as an integral part of its national territory. For the overwhelming majority of Moroccans, the validity of this claim is self-evident and not subject to serious questioning. The Moroccan position rests on long-standing ties to the Western Sahara before and during Spain's colonization of the territory, which began in 1884. These ties involved varying degrees of political, legal, and especially religious authority, which, in the Moroccan historical context, constituted effective sovereignty. This claim to the Western Sahara has been asserted vigorously by most elements of the Moroccan political spectrum since independence in 1956. The Moroccan historical claim takes precedence over the discovery of Saharan mineral wealth, both in time and in domestic political impact, and a clear understanding of the historical factors is necessary before considering the significance of the phosphate deposits.

Historical Ties to the Western Sahara

At a more general level, the Moroccan claim to the Western Sahara forms part of larger claims to territories that once were controlled by various dynasties based in Morocco. In its extreme form, this irredentism has expressed itself in the concept of Greater Morocco. As shown in Map 3, Greater Morocco corresponds to the area ruled by the Almoravid dynasty in the eleventh and twelfth centuries — an area that covered not only Morocco and the Western Sahara but also all of Mauritania, northwest Mali, and much of western Algeria. The Almoravids were a Berber dynasty that originated in southern Mauritania. Under their great leader Yusuf ibn Tashfin, they expanded their authority rapidly and established the city of Marrakesh as their seat of power. By the time of Yusuf ibn Tashfin's death in 1106, the Almoravids had achieved the religious and political unification of Morocco and the Western Sahara.[1]

At the time Morocco gained its independence from France and Spain in 1956, the Istiqlal party — the leading organizational force in the independence struggle — propagated and popularized the concept of Greater Morocco. The champion of this extreme form of Moroccan irredentism and its most effective spokesman was Allal al-Fassi, the highly respected leader of the Istiqlal party. Al-Fassi, who died in 1974, was a deeply religious man, a charismatic political leader, and a keen student of Moroccan history. He argued that the Moroccan nation, serving as the successor state to the great Berber empires of North Africa, had a legitimate right to exercise its sovereignty over former territories of those empires.[2]

According to Allal al-Fassi, Greater Morocco constituted a national, historical, geographic, and social entity. To bring all of this entity back under Moroccan control, al-Fassi called for the liberation of the Sahara and Mauritania; until the territories from the Wadi Draa to the Senegal River were liberated, Morocco's decolonization would not be completed. In a speech in June 1956, just two months after independence, he declared: "If

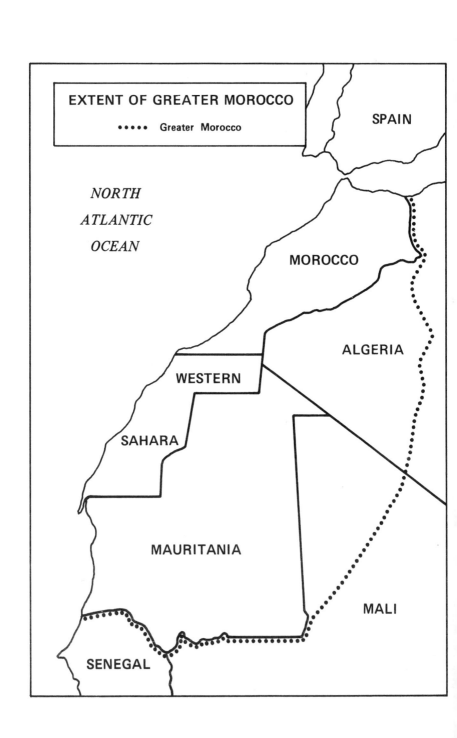

EXTENT OF GREATER MOROCCO

••••• Greater Morocco

SPAIN

NORTH
ATLANTIC
OCEAN

MOROCCO

ALGERIA

WESTERN

SAHARA

MAURITANIA

MALI

SENEGAL

Morocco is independent, it is not completely unified. The independence of Morocco must be completed. The frontiers of Morocco end in the south at Saint Louis, Senegal. The struggle must continue until total union."[3] In April 1957, al-Fassi founded a weekly Arabic newspaper, *Sahra al-Maghrib* (The Moroccan Sahara), to help "our Mauritanian brothers to free themselves and rejoin Morocco, our common fatherland";[4] this newspaper argued forcefully for the unification of all the territories once controlled by Morocco. New cells of the Istiqlal party spread this message among the Moroccan public, and a map showing the frontiers of Greater Morocco was distributed widely throughout the country.

In the years since Moroccan independence, the concept of Greater Morocco has had to be reconciled with the realities of the newly independent states of Mauritania, Mali, and Algeria, each with its internationally recognized borders. Morocco strongly resisted Mauritania's independence, granted by France in 1960, and opposed the new state's admission to the United Nations on the grounds that it was an artificial creation of French colonialism. Throughout the 1960s, the Moroccan cabinet included a minister for Saharan and Mauritanian affairs. It was not until 1969 that Morocco finally recognized Mauritania as an independent state; ambassadors were exchanged between the two countries the following year. Morocco never seriously pushed the historical claim to northwest Mali. This claim has not been a visible issue among any domestic political group. Mali's independence in 1960 went almost unnoticed within Morocco, and little has been heard about the matter in the past twenty years.

The irredentist claim to parts of western Algeria, particularly to the Tindouf region, however, remains a live issue in Moroccan politics. France, during most of its long occupation of Algeria (1830–1962), saw little reason to establish a precise frontier with Morocco since the border territory was largely uninhabited. After taking over Morocco in 1912, the French administered the Tindouf region from Agadir in Morocco until 1952, when they transferred it to Algeria. Moroccan troops were at Tindouf until about 1950, and the payment of troops at Tindouf was done with Moroccan money until 1960.[5]

Saharan territories, including Touat and Tindouf, were transferred from Morocco to Algeria during the 1930s and 1940s, when Morocco came out on the short end of a power and influence struggle between French officials in Rabat and Algiers.[6] Moroccans argue that it was only when France decided to grant independence to Morocco and consolidate its position in Algeria that the present border was adopted. Considerable territory was in dispute among several conflicting frontier lines. In the Moroccan view, the French adopted the westernmost frontier, arbitrarily shifting three provinces from Morocco to Algeria, on the assumption that France would remain indefinitely in Algeria. Moroccans consider that most of their eastern border with Algeria does not conform to historical reality—that is, it is too favorable to Algeria.[7] During the Algerian war of independence, from 1954 to 1962, France offered to shift the frontier eastward if Morocco would end its active support of the Algerian revolution, which included cross-border sanctuaries. The Moroccan government refused this offer and insisted that it would discuss the border question only with Algerian authorities. Morocco received promises in 1960, 1961, and 1962 from the two presidents of the Provisional Government of the Algerian Republic (GPRA) that the border question would not be settled until Algeria had attained its independence and that the French colonial boundary between the two countries would have no validity.

Upon attaining independence in 1962, the new Algerian government announced that its western frontier with Morocco, as established by France, was permanent and not subject to negotiation. This announcement caused resentment, if not bitterness, in Morocco. After consistently supporting their Algerian brothers during the revolutionary struggle against French colonialism, Moroccans felt betrayed by the rulers of independent Algeria. Tension over the disputed frontier led to a three-week border war in the fall of 1963. The Moroccans' superior military organization and equipment at that time enabled their forces to penetrate into the disputed territory and to advance to within a few miles of Tindouf in southwest Algeria. To counterbalance this advance, Algerian forces surrounded Figuig, a Moroccan town northeast of Bechar. This brief desert war ended when an Organization of African Unity (OAU) mediation effort persuaded King Hassan II to order a withdrawal of his forces across the border—an unpopular decision among the Moroccan public and one that evoked considerable resentment among the king's top military commanders.[8]

The Moroccan-Algerian frontier question remained a contentious issue between the two countries throughout the 1960s. One of the reasons the Algerian Army overthrew Ahmed Ben Bella in June 1965 was that he had considered giving up Algerian territory in his agreement with King Hassan at Saidia a month earlier.[9] Efforts to resolve the frontier issue through bilateral negotiations produced the Treaty of Solidarity and Cooperation, signed at Ifrane on January 15, 1969. A joint Moroccan-Algerian boundary commission recommended the acceptance of the frontier line adopted by the French during their final years in Algeria, and agreement was reached on the demarcation of this border at a meeting in Tlemcen on May 27, 1970. King Hassan accepted the de facto frontier as the legal boundary in the Rabat agreements of June 15, 1972, signed at the time of an OAU summit meeting. The second of these two agreements called for joint exploitation of the large iron ore deposits at Gara Jebilet, one hundred miles southeast of

Tindouf in Algeria, and joint development of a steel complex at Nador, near Melilla on the Mediterranean coast of eastern Morocco. Algeria ratified the Rabat agreements in 1973; Morocco has yet to do so.

According to King Hassan, Morocco could not ratify the agreements because it did not have a parliament from 1972 to 1977. While some outside observers found this explanation disingenuous, the question now has become academic. Since 1975, the Western Sahara conflict has so embittered Moroccan-Algerian relations that no Moroccan parliament could even consider ratifying an agreement with Algeria, especially one that concedes disputed national territory. Moroccan maps, whether from the government or private publishers, continue to show an eastern border for only the first one hundred miles south from the Mediterranean coast, usually ending at Teniet El Sassi. For the remaining several hundred miles to the south and west, there is no frontier line—a symbolic reminder that for many Moroccans most of the border with Algeria remains an unresolved issue.

Beyond the larger irredentist claims involved in the Greater Morocco concept, Morocco has a specific and much more substantial claim to the Western Sahara. This claim is based on historical ties of a political-religious nature to the Sahrawi population. A premise of the claim is that the Moroccan state was founded on the religious bond of Islam and the tribal allegiance of various tribes to the ruling head of the state, the sultan. In this view, to look for a territorial foundation or well-defined frontiers for the Moroccan state prior to the twentieth century is to misunderstand the Moroccan historical context.

A salient feature of Islamic history has been the close ties between religious and political life; during the first centuries of Islam, there was little separation between the two. This connection between religion and politics is basic to the Moroccan state and is a crucial part of Morocco's claim to historical and legal ties to the Western Sahara. Sovereignty in Islam is conferred by a pledge of allegiance (*bai'a*) of a population to a ruler. Often the allegiance is given by a leader—tribal, communal, or religious—in the name of the community. Throughout the nineteenth and early twentieth centuries, several of the tribes in the Western Sahara offered their allegiance to Moroccan sultans.[10] In Moroccan (Islamic) law, this allegiance signifies, and always has signified, sovereignty. The Moroccan sultan was commander of the faithful, the steward of God on earth for all matters, religious or secular. Since the sultan personified both state and church, Moroccans argue that ties of personal allegiance from certain tribes to the sultan cannot be differentiated from ties of territorial sovereignty.

A further factor is the overlapping of the populations of several tribes between Morocco and the Western Sahara. An example of this is the Ulad Delim. While most of this important Arab tribe established itself in the southern Sahara, one part settled in the Sidi Kacem region and in the Gharb, northeast of Rabat,[11] and another branch settled in the regions of Marrakesh and Essaouira. Other examples include the Eastern Reguibat, some of whom migrate in southern Morocco as far north as Goulimine; the Tekna group, of which several tribes, including the Izarguien, the Arrusiyyin, and the Filala, live partially in Morocco; and the Ulad Bu Sba, some of whom live in the Essaouira region. These tribal overlappings create north-south currents that link the Western Sahara to Morocco. These currents appear dramatically in the person of Sultan Moulay Ismail (1672–1727), a powerful early ruler of Morocco's present Alawite dynasty. Moulay Ismail was the son of a Sahrawi woman from the Filala tribe, and he married a Sahrawi, Khenata bint Shaikh Bekkar al-Maghfiri, who was the mother of his successor.

While accepting the religious authority of the sultan, it was common for tribes not only in the Western Sahara but also in many parts of Morocco to resist the political control of the central government. The Moroccan state historically included both a core area under the sultan's control and a peripheral area, usually larger, outside his political, military, or administrative control. These two areas, known as *bilad al-makhzan* ("lands of the government") and *bilad al-siba* ("lands of dissidence"), were in a never ending state of flux. During periods of cohesion and strength at the center, the sultan would consolidate power and expand the *makhzan* lands through military expeditions against dissident tribes. During periods of central weakness or instability, tribes near the periphery would rise up in revolt, enlarging the *siba* lands and encroaching on the area under the sultan's control. At the same time, there were tribes that submitted partly to central control, thus forming areas of semidissidence. A tribe in this middle ground might receive the sultan's officials and obey their directives but refuse to pay taxes.

The *siba* lands of the Moroccan state, by definition, included only areas in which the tribes accepted the spiritual authority of the sultan. The test of this acceptance was whether a tribe gave its oath of allegiance (*bai'a*) to the sultan, accepted him as commander of the faithful, and had the Friday sermon said in his name. In the areas of dissidence, the tribes recognized the sultan's suzerainty but refused to submit to central administrative control. There was no contradiction in the Moroccan historical context for the same *siba* tribes that recognized the religious authority of the sultan to reject his officials, refuse to pay his taxes, and revolt against his political control.[12]

Moroccans admit that only rarely did the sultan's control extend to the Western Sahara. The sheer distance between the Sahara and the seats of central power in Fez, Meknes, or Marrakesh posed one obvious obstacle. Even more important, the geography of the Sahara made it virtually impossible to exercise administrative control over the nomadic tribes. Administration requires population centers, and the Western Sahara has no major oases or other natural centers from which administrative control could be exercised. Nevertheless, while the political and administrative control of the sultan did not extend to the Western Sahara, his religious authority was widely accepted, and thus the territory remained part of the Moroccan *siba* lands. The Sahara was as much a part of the Moroccan state as those areas of the Middle and High Atlas Mountains that were in a perennial state of dissidence. Moroccans argue that the European concept of the ruler's domains—a realm limited to those areas well controlled by a central government—simply does not apply to the case of Morocco, where there were frequent instances of requests from *siba* areas for concessions by the sultan.[13]

Although Moroccans trace their ties to the Western Sahara back to the Almoravid dynasty in the eleventh century, the critical period in question is the late nineteenth and early twentieth centuries—that is, the time of Spain's colonization of the territory. During this period, a variety of leaders of Western Sahara tribes received their appointments or instructions (or both) from the Moroccan sultan.[14] Thus in 1886, the sultan appointed *caids* (royal officials at the tribal level) over the Ait Lhassen and Yaggout tribes of the Tekna group and several Tekna subtribes, plus a third caid to watch the southern coasts for Spanish incursions. In 1890, a caid was appointed over the Tidrarin tribe. In 1901, the sultan appointed two caids to watch the coastline between Tarfaya and Boujdour for foreign landings. In 1906, a caid was appointed over the Ait Lhassen and Izarguien tribes of the Tekna group. And in 1909, the sultan appointed a caid over the Ait Moussa, Reguibat, and Tidrarin tribes. These appointments of caids, along with various instructions given by the sultan, strongly support the Moroccan claim of ties to the Sahara during the critical period of Spanish colonization.

Moroccans point to the role of Shaikh Ma al-Ainain (see Chapter One) as further evidence of their country's ties to the Western Sahara in the late nineteenth and early twentieth centuries. Ma al-Ainain led the resistance to French military incursions not only in the Sahara but also in southern Morocco and Mauritania. He was a powerful local leader in his own right, and Moroccan sultans often used important local leaders to solidify the central authority of the state. Thus, Sultan Moulay Hassan received Ma al-Ainain in 1890 and assigned him several missions involving the English economic station at Cape Juby (now Tarfaya) and the Spanish presence in Rio de Oro. In 1894, Ma al-Ainain swore allegiance to the new sultan. In 1896 and 1900, Ma al-Ainain met with the sultan in Marrakesh. During the first visit, he requested and received material support to build his stronghold in Smara; on his second visit, he assisted in the nomination of a new Moroccan grand vizir (prime minister).

In 1904, Ma al-Ainain met with the sultan in Fez to discuss the French military threat in the Sahara. The sultan authorized him to police all Saharan areas of the Moroccan state and to generate a holy war. In 1905, the sultan sent a delegation to Smara to deliver imperial edicts for the nomination of caids. Ma al-Ainain cooperated with this delegation by sending emissaries throughout Mauritania and the Western Sahara to gather tribal leaders for a meeting to launch the holy war under the sultan's banner. The Izarguien and Ait Lhassen tribes of the Tekna group accepted Moroccan administrative control at this time. From 1905 to 1910, the sultan sent large quantities of arms, which greatly added to Ma al-Ainain's influence and regional prestige. Finally, in 1907, Ma al-Ainain went to Fez with a delegation of Saharan leaders for consultations with and investiture by the sultan.[15] Because of these links and close cooperation between Ma al-Ainain and the sultan and the frequency with which Ma al-Ainain carried out imperial instructions, Moroccans argue that this important resistance leader acted as a representative of the sultan, at least until 1910, the last year of his life, when he broke with the sultan. They point out that even in revolt, Ma al-Ainain and his son El Hiba claimed to be Moroccan, to represent Morocco, and to aspire to its throne.

Moroccans also argue that their country's historical ties to the Western Sahara were recognized by the major foreign powers during the period of colonization. Several nations concluded agreements and exchanged diplomatic correspondence with the Moroccan government in the decades prior to March 30, 1912, when Morocco lost its independence after the sultan signed the Treaty of Fez with France. Some of these agreements entail clear international recognition of Moroccan sovereignty in the Western Sahara and especially in the northern Sakiet al-Hamra region. While the diplomatic record is too extensive and complex to be summarized briefly, a few selected international agreements can be cited to illustrate the thrust of the Moroccan claim in this area.[16]

In the Spanish-Moroccan Treaty of November 20, 1861, for example, the sultan agreed to use his authority to obtain the release of sailors from Spanish vessels wrecked on Saharan coasts. This treaty indicates that the Spanish recognized that the sultan possessed sufficient authority along the Saharan coasts to obtain the safe return of shipwrecked, and presumably captured, Spanish crews. The Anglo-Moroccan Treaty of March 13, 1895, involved the sale to Morocco of the English trading station at Tarfaya (then Cape Juby), established in 1879 by the enterprising Donald MacKenzie. This agreement clearly recognized the southern limit of Morocco at Boujdour, thus including Sakiet al-Hamra — the northern portion of the Western Sahara — within Moroccan territory. In the two interpretive letters appended to the Franco-German agreement of November 4, 1911, Germany agreed not to interfere with French actions in Morocco. The text of these letters clearly recognized Morocco as extending to the Spanish colony of Rio de Oro, that is, once again to Boujdour. The terms of the 1911 Franco-German convention were accepted formally by Great Britain, Italy, Austro-Hungary, Russia, Sweden, the Netherlands, Belgium, and Portugal—all the signatories of the 1906 Act of Algeciras except Spain.

Although every Moroccan may not know the specific details of the country's historical ties to the Western Sahara, there is a very wide belief among the public in the validity of the general claim. As mentioned earlier, the Moroccan claim to the Sahara was popularized at the time of independence in 1956 by the nationalist Istiqlal party as part of a broader claim to Greater Morocco. The claim to the Western Sahara was given official sanction at the highest levels of the Moroccan government in 1957: by Prime Minister M'Barak al-Bekkai in September and by Foreign Minister Ahmed Balafrej in November; in the latter month, the palace created an office (which later became a ministry) of Saharan and frontier affairs within the Ministry of Interior.[17] At a time when the Moroccan monarchy was just one of several competing forces within the country's political system, the palace was obliged to take up the Saharan claim as its own—lest the monarchy be outflanked by the Istiqlal party as the standard-bearer of Moroccan nationalism. In February 1958, King Mohammed V (the father of King Hassan), in a much noted speech at M'Hamid, south of Zagora along the Wadi Draa at the gateway to the Sahara, committed the monarchy to the recovery of the Western Sahara. Addressing a tribal assembly called together from distant regions of the Sahara, Mohammed V assured his "faithful subjects" "of his determination to work untiringly, by all means and with all his energy, for the recovery of the Sahara and all the territory belonging historically to the kingdom."[18]

In the generation after independence, the claim to the Western Sahara quickly became, and has remained, an unquestioned and integral part of Moroccan nationalist ideology. All prominent political figures have repeated this claim frequently in the media, in public declarations, and in interviews with the foreign press. For Moroccans national liberation has always meant the twin goals of independence and the reunification of national territories—an ongoing historical process that began with the independence of the French and Spanish protectorates and the restoration of Tangier from international status in 1956, continued with the retrocession by Spain of Tarfaya in 1958 and Ifni in 1969, and most recently involved the recovery of the Saharan provinces in 1976. Moreover, this process is not yet completed. According to the official Moroccan government position (presently muted), national territories still to be recovered comprise Ceuta (Sebta) and Melilla, two small Spanish enclaves on the Mediterranean coast, and the small Chaffarine (Zaffarine) Islands near the mouth of the

Moulouya River. For much of the Moroccan public, the national patrimony also includes parts of western Algeria.

Moroccans are well aware that their independence was achieved and Tangier, Tarfaya, and Ifni were returned through successive negotiations. There was never any question of a referendum or formal exercise of self-determination. Accordingly, they saw no need for, nor did they expect to see, a referendum or act of self-determination take place in the Western Sahara, a territory they consider no less Moroccan than Tarfaya or Ifni. In Moroccan eyes the proper route to Saharan decolonization was through negotiations with Spain. While a majority of United Nations members have supported the right of self-determination for the Sahrawi population, King Hassan has preferred the decolonization precedent of West Irian, which became part of Indonesia in 1969 through collective consultations held with the indigenous population.[19] In response to the international demand for the exercise of self-determination in the Western Sahara, Moroccans point to various expressions of popular will: the pledge of allegiance given by the president of the Jemaa, Khatri Ould al-Joumani, to King Hassan in November 1975; the February 1976 vote of the Jemaa to become part of Morocco (and Mauritania); and the participation of the Sahrawi population in Morocco's 1976–1977 local, professional, and parliamentary elections and in two constitutional referendums in May 1980.[20]

For all shades of Moroccan opinion, from King Hassan down to the common man, the Western Sahara question is now closed — or at least it should be closed. Moroccans blame Algeria for the ongoing conflict in the Sahara and see the Polisario Front as an artificial creation staffed by and composed of Algerian mercenaries. Moroccans argue that Algerian support for Saharan self-determination is pragmatic and opportunistic, pointing out that during the 1961 Evian negotiations the GPRA categorically rejected a French proposal to organize a referendum in the Algerian Sahara.[21] In the Moroccan view, Algeria first supported Moroccan (and Mauritanian) claims to the Sahara in 1974 and 1975, but then, in pursuit of long-held ambitions to dominate North Africa, reversed its position and opposed Morocco. The charge of Algerian hegemony is a frequent theme of the Moroccan press and is illustrated by an April 1979 editorial from the pro-government Casablanca daily *Le Matin du Sahara*:

> Everybody is perfectly aware of the fact that — aside from the intransigents in the Algerian regime — there is no liberation movement in the Sahara, that the whole affair is simply an aggression perpetrated by Algiers to seize part of our Saharan provinces in order to encircle Morocco and cut it off from Mauritania, which would form an easy prey for Algerian expansionism, and finally separate Morocco once and for all from black Africa.[22]

Moroccans view their conflict in the Sahara as a struggle not against a phantom national liberation movement but rather against a rival state in northwest Africa. It follows, in this view, that the Western Sahara conflict must be settled in the framework of a larger Moroccan-Algerian settlement.

The Phosphate Factor

Many outside observers have attached considerable importance to the Bu Craa phosphates in explaining Morocco's interest in the Western Sahara. According to this view, Morocco's campaign to take over the Sahara has been motivated largely by a desire to gain control of the territory's large deposits of high-grade phosphate.[23] Because this view has received wide international attention (press references often speak of the mineral-rich Western Sahara), it is important to assess the actual impact of the phosphate factor on Morocco's Saharan policy.

One element of this question is the considerable time lag between the assertion of Morocco's claim to the Western Sahara and the revelation of phosphate deposits of a commercial nature in the territory. The Istiqlal party began agitating for the recovery of the Sahara in November 1955, when negotiations were completed with France for Moroccan independence. Spain did not announce publicly the size of the Bu Craa deposits until a decade later in 1965.[24] By the time of the Spanish announcement, the recovery of the Sahara had been a basic tenet of Moroccan politics for several years. Given this commitment "to reintegrate the despoiled Saharan provinces," which dates from the late 1950s, it is probable that Moroccan policy toward the Western Sahara would have evolved in much the way it did even in the absence of the discovery of sizable phosphate deposits in Sakiet al-Hamra.

The other major question in assessing the importance of the phosphate factor is the relation of the Saharan deposits to Morocco's own considerable phosphate reserves. Within the internationally recognized borders of Morocco are located the largest reserves of phosphate rock in the world. Commercially viable deposits were estimated at 16.2 billion tons at 1978 costs and prices. These deposits represent about half of the total world reserves of 34.5 billion tons and dwarf the reserves of the other major phosphate-producing countries: the Soviet Union (4.5 billion tons), South Africa (3.0 billion tons), and the United States (1.8 billion tons). If one includes estimates made with different assumptions about prices and technology—that is, assuming higher prices and improved technology—Moroccan reserves increase to 55.2 billion tons out of a world total of 129.5 billion tons.[25]

Morocco's phosphate industry dates back to the first decade of the protectorate period when France established the Office Chérifien des Phosphates (OCP) in 1921. Since independence, OCP has operated as a state-owned monopoly. Moroccan phosphate production increased from 5.6 million tons in 1956, the year of independence, to 7.5 million tons in 1960 to 14.5 million tons in 1972. During the twenty years leading up to the 1973–1974 energy crisis, the price of phosphates on the world market maintained a remarkable stability, fluctuating modestly from $14.20 a ton in 1952 to $11.75 a ton during the 1960s to $14.15 a ton in 1973.[26]

Milled phosphate rock is the basic ingredient in the manufacture of phosphatic fertilizer, which, along with nitrogenous and potassic fertilizers, is widely used in agriculture. There are no known substitutes for phosphate, nor is there any known way of recovering or recycling this commodity—a valuable substance that is found only in limited locations. The use of phosphate in fertilizer is essential for the production of particular crops, especially many high-yield hybrids. Phosphatic fertilizer also increases the yields of many crops and hastens the ripening of grain, a factor of great importance in areas with short growing seasons.

World demand for fertilizer has grown almost continuously in the past two decades and will continue to grow. Despite an excess of phosphate production over world demand from 1969 to 1972, Morocco continued to increase its productive capacity. When world demand began to catch up with supply in 1973, Morocco was in a much better position than were the other major phosphate producers to meet the increased demand. In addition, the 1973–1974 Arab oil embargo created a shortfall in the supply of hydrocarbon feedstocks used in the manufacture of nitrogenous fertilizer.

Given strongly increasing demand and inspired by OPEC's spectacularly successful oil-pricing policy, Morocco moved dramatically in 1974 to push up the price of its phosphates. In January 1974, Morocco tripled the export price of its high-grade rock from $14 a ton to $42 a ton; in July, the price jumped to $63 a ton and again to $68 a ton by the end of the year, making a total increase of nearly 400 percent in less than twelve months.[27] As it turned out, the particular market conditions of cartel solidarity and limited supply that sustained OPEC's massive price increases simply did not exist in the international phosphate market. Morocco's dramatic price increases had the effect of attracting new sources of phosphate onto the world market, especially independent U.S. producers—which were willing to sell at export prices that undercut Morocco's. The additional phosphate production, which soon produced a surplus of supply on the world market, plus competitive pricing policies by U.S. producers, forced Morocco to lower the prices of its high-quality phosphates from $68 a ton at the beginning of 1976 to $37 a ton by the end of the year. In 1977, Moroccan phosphate sold for as little as $24 a ton; the price has since varied between $33 and $54 a ton.[28]

The Parties to the Conflict | 27

Moroccan phosphate production has increased to meet the greater world demand for fertilizer, even as phosphate prices have fallen or leveled off. OCP's production rose from 14.5 million tons in 1972 to 19.7 million tons in 1974 before dropping to 13.5 million tons the following year in the face of surplus world supply. Beginning in 1976, Moroccan phosphate production rose steadily and reached the total of 20.2 million tons in 1979 before declining modestly to just under 19 million tons in 1980. Morocco is the world's third largest phosphate producer, behind the United States and the Soviet Union, and will replace the USSR in the next few years as the second leading producer. The yearly totals for major phosphate producers from 1975 to 1981 are shown in Table 1.

Table 1

WORLD PHOSPHATE PRODUCTION, 1975–1981

(millions of metric tons)

	1975	1976	1977	1978	1979	1980	1981
United States	44.3	44.7	47.3	50.0	51.6	54.4	53.6
Soviet Union	24.5	24.2	24.2	24.8	25.0	26.1	25.2
Morocco	13.5	15.5	17.3	19.7	20.2	18.8	19.7
Tunisia	3.5	3.3	3.6	3.8	4.0	4.6	4.6
China	3.0	3.7	4.1	4.4	5.5	6.7	11.5
Togo	1.2	2.1	2.9	2.8	2.9	2.9	2.2
Western Sahara	2.7	–	–	–	–	–	–
Senegal	1.9	1.8	1.9	1.8	1.6	1.5	1.9
Jordan	1.4	1.7	1.8	2.2	2.8	4.2	4.2
Others	11.7	10.3	12.7	15.4	14.6	17.7	14.9
World Total	107.7	107.3	115.8	124.9	128.2	136.9	137.8

SOURCE: ISMA Ltd. (International Phosphate Industry Association) statistics.

Morocco occupies a unique place in the world phosphate industry because of its strength as an exporter. Whereas the United States and the Soviet Union must retain 74 to 82 percent of their phosphate production for domestic consumption, Morocco, with much more modest domestic needs, can export nearly 90 percent of its production. Moroccan exports make up one-third of the total international phosphate trade, which gives Morocco an important, though by no means commanding, position in the world phosphate industry. The yearly totals for major exporters of phosphate rock from 1975 to 1981 are shown in Table 2.

Table 2

MAJOR EXPORTERS OF PHOSPHATE ROCK, 1975–1981

(millions of metric tons)

	1975	1976	1977	1978	1979	1980	1981
Morocco	13.1	14.7	15.8	17.7	18.0	16.5	15.6
United States	10.7	9.1	13.2	13.4	14.4	14.4	10.5
Soviet Union	5.8	4.9	4.2	4.0	4.1	4.6	5.0
Tunisia	1.7	1.9	1.9	1.7	1.5	1.4	1.0
Togo	1.1	2.0	2.9	2.8	3.0	2.9	2.2
Western Sahara	2.7	0.3	0.03	0.5	0.5	0.01	–
Senegal	1.6	1.6	1.8	1.8	1.6	1.4	1.2
Jordan	1.1	1.6	1.8	2.2	2.7	3.6	3.5
Others	5.9	5.2	6.9	7.4	7.6	7.5	6.8
World Total	43.7	41.3	48.5	51.5	53.4	52.3	45.8

SOURCE: ISMA Ltd. (International Phosphate Industry Association) statistics. Figures for the Western Sahara for the years 1977–1980 are from Fosbucraa, El Ayoun.

Phosphate rock exports bring Morocco about $700 million a year, plus $300 million from exports of phosphate derivatives. Although these earnings are an important source of foreign exchange, as a sector of the Moroccan economy the value of the phosphate industry is only one-fourth as large as agricultural production and is on a par with tourism. Phosphate revenues thus make a noticeable but too easily exaggerated contribution to the country's $16 billion gross national product. The Moroccan economy is not based on one industry—especially in comparison to the economies of several other countries in the Arab world. Oil accounts for about half of government revenues in Algeria, two-thirds in Iraq, 85 percent in Libya, and nearly all in Saudi Arabia and the small shaikhdoms of the Persian Gulf area.

The phosphate deposits at Bu Craa in the Western Sahara, while very large, are only one-eighth the size of Morocco's own enormous reserves. Since 1975, there has been no new production at the Bu Craa mines and only limited exports since 1976 from existing stockpiles. There is sufficient production capacity at OCP's mines at Khouribga, inland from Casablanca, and Youssoufia, inland from Safi, to supply all the phosphate that Morocco is able to sell abroad. Increased production capacity to meet greater world demand in the coming decades will come from new OCP mining centers being developed at Ben Guerir, Sidi Hajjaj, and Meskala. In terms of volume, Morocco has no need in the foreseeable future for Saharan phosphates. From an economic standpoint, however, the Bu Craa phosphates are more profitable to mine and treat; they are closer to the surface and higher in quality—80 percent bone phosphate of lime compared with grades of 68 to 77 percent at the Khouribga and Youssoufia mines. Thus, the exploitation of the Bu Craa phosphates would provide Morocco a marginal economic benefit.

OCP plans to expand phosphate production from the current twenty million tons a year to an estimated forty to forty-five million tons in 1990. It hopes to add to this production five to ten million tons from the Bu Craa mines.[29] In this projection Saharan phosphates would provide from 10 to 20 percent of Morocco's total production. From a purely economic standpoint, the worst development for Morocco would be the emergence of an independent Saharan state, whose several million tons a year of high-grade phosphate would cut into Morocco's share of the export market. It is more important for Morocco, then, to deny the Saharan phosphates to a competitor than to mine them itself. Given the volume of Morocco's own reserves and the secondary importance of the phosphate industry in the Moroccan economy, however, even the loss of the Western Sahara's deposits to a competitor would not seem to entail really major economic consequences for the country. Seen in perspective, it is difficult to consider phosphates as more than a marginal factor in Morocco's Saharan policy.

Mauritania

Like Morocco, Mauritania has also asserted a claim to the Western Sahara. The Mauritanian claim, however, has been complicated by several factors. Because of its weakness as a national power in relation to neighboring Morocco and Algeria, Mauritania has been obliged to give careful attention to practical considerations of regional politics. In addition, Mauritania has shifted its Saharan policy more than once since the 1950s and at times has supported different positions simultaneously. Another factor of note in Mauritania is that, unlike in Morocco, there has never been strong national unity on the Saharan issue. Finally, because of the high cost of fighting an unwinnable armed conflict against Polisario Front forces, Mauritania opted to sign a peace agreement with the Polisario in August 1979, relinquishing all claims to the Western Sahara.

With an area twice as large as France and three-fourths desert, a population of less than two million, and a gross national product of only $500 million, Mauritania is a large, underpopulated, poor, and militarily weak country. Prior to French colonization and eventual independence in the twentieth century, there was never a Mauritanian state in the sense of a centralized government administration based in the territory. Instead, there existed confederations of tribes that formed emirates, like the Adrar emirate, which functioned as local power bases.

During the 1950s, as the territory moved toward independence in 1960, politically conscious Mauritanians were acutely aware of the Istiqlal party's concept of Greater Morocco, which included all of Mauritanian territory in its irredentist claim. The Moroccan claims received much support both within Mauritania and internationally among Arab countries. The founder (in 1948) and leader of the Mauritania Entente party, Hurma Ould Babana, urged the members of his party to support union with Morocco. Ould Babana argued that such a union would protect the rights of Mauritania's Moors (of Arab-Berber origin) against encroachments by the country's black population. In addition, Morocco carried out armed subversion within Mauritania from 1957 to 1962 in an attempt to bring Mauritania under its control.[30]

Largely as a counterweight to the threat of Greater Morocco, a competing claim of Greater Mauritania arose in the late 1950s. In a July 1957 speech at Atar, Mokhtar Ould Daddah, then vice-president of the government council and future president of the Islamic Republic of Mauritania, asserted that Mauritania regarded the Sahrawis as "brethren." That same year, Ould Daddah called for the "unity of the Moors from the Wadi Draa to the Senegal River." Unlike Morocco's claim, which rested on ties of allegiance to the sultan as political-religious head of the Moroccan state, the Greater Mauritania concept rested on shared ethnicity among the population in the territory of the Moors—*ard al-bidan* ("the land of the whites"). Ould Daddah argued that the Moorish population of nomadic tribes that inhabited Mauritania, the Western Sahara, southern Morocco, and parts of northern Mali and western Algeria shared common ties of race (Arab-Berber), language (Hassaniyya Arabic), religion (Islam), culture (Arab-Berber-Islamic), and economy (nomadism). Supporters of a Greater Mauritania also invoked history by recalling that the Almoravid dynasty, whose control in the eleventh and twelfth centuries extended over Morocco and Spain, was created by tribes based in Mauritania.

Although granted independence by France in November 1960, Mauritania was not accepted immediately as an independent state by all members of the international community. Morocco, which refused to recognize Mauritania's independent sovereignty, posed a serious national security threat. Morocco's claim to Mauritania was initially supported by most of the Arab League states, the Soviet Union, and several progressive African states. The new Mauritanian state was backed by most African states, virtually all Western countries, and especially France. During its first struggling years of independence, Mauritania adopted a cautious foreign policy and aligned itself with France and the more conservative neighboring African states that had been part of French West Africa. Ould Daddah's government stressed the country's role as a bridge between Arab North Africa and black sub-Saharan Africa. By the mid-1960s, in an effort to gain acceptance in the Arab world and thereby neutralize Morocco's opposition, Mauritania shifted its foreign alignments away from black Africa and toward the progressive Arab states, especially Algeria. This foreign policy realignment culminated in 1972–1974, when Mauritania withdrew from defense treaties with France, left the franc zone and established its own national currency, nationalized the large French iron-mining company Miferma, and joined the Arab League.

Morocco's eventual recognition of Mauritania's independent existence in 1969 and the dropping of its claim to Mauritanian territory removed at least some of the rationale for pushing the concept of Greater Mauritania. Nevertheless, the Ould Daddah government continued to be concerned about possible Moroccan expansionist designs. Thus, in regard to the Western Sahara, Mauritania's preference has been for a Saharan buffer between it and Morocco, either through Mauritanian control of all or part of the Western Sahara or in the form of an independent Saharan state. This preference has led to frequent ambiguities in Mauritania's Saharan policy.

From the early 1960s until 1974, Mauritania supported self-determination for the Western Sahara by means of a referendum. The Ould Daddah government genuinely believed that if given a free choice, the Sahrawis would choose to join or federate with their Mauritanian brethren. This belief was based on the close ethnic ties between Sahrawis and Moors—the two peoples share much in common, from their physical appearance to their Hassaniyya Arabic language to their social customs. Moreover, many Sahrawi nomads migrated to Mauritania, and many Moors have family roots or ties in the Sahara. Mauritania's current prime minister, for example, Mohamed Khouna Ould Haidalla, comes from a small Reguibat tribe that was originally from Bir Enzaran in central Rio de Oro.[31] If the Sahrawi population expressed a preference for an independent state, at least Mauritania's national security would be served by a buffer between Mauritania and a potentially expansionist Morocco.

During the critical period of 1974–1975 (see Chapter Three), when Morocco made clear that it would pursue its campaign to recover the Western Sahara by whatever means necessary, Mauritania hedged its position by pursuing three different and quite contradictory policies simultaneously. For international consumption the Ould Daddah regime supported the principle of self-determination for the Sahrawi population, the same principle that had permitted Mauritania to become an independent nation in 1960 against the will of Morocco. For internal consumption the government asserted Mauritania's rights over all of the Western Sahara (plus Tarfaya in southern Morocco) in fulfillment of the Greater Mauritania concept. Finally, as a compromise policy—a tactical concession to the reality of

Moroccan power and commitment—Ould Daddah was prepared to divide the Sahara with Morocco.[32]

The Mauritanian government feared being left out of a Spanish-Moroccan or Moroccan-Algerian arrangement to decolonize the Western Sahara. As Morocco's campaign to annex the Sahara gained momentum, Ould Daddah faced the prospect of a fait accompli that would bring Moroccan power flush against Mauritania's long and weakly defended northwestern border. In this situation, and with few cards of his own to play, the Mauritanian leader opted to cast his lot with, rather than against, Morocco. The fateful policy decision to agree with Morocco to partition the Western Sahara led Mauritania into a ruinous war that ended in the overthrow of the Ould Daddah government in a military coup on July 10, 1978.

During the period from late 1975 to mid-1978, when Mauritania struggled to absorb and control the southern Saharan region of Tiris al-Gharbiyya, the government's position was almost identical to that of Morocco. According to this position, internationally recognized negotiations had enabled Mauritania to achieve a "reunification of the fatherland" that would henceforth be irreversible and nonnegotiable. Saharan popular will was expressed by the February 1976 vote of the Jemaa to join Mauritania (and Morocco) and by Sahrawi participation in the August 1976 national elections, which sent eight Sahrawi deputies from Tiris al-Gharbiyya to the Mauritanian national assembly. When Mauritania became badly bogged down in a guerrilla war against the Polisario Front, Ould Daddah blamed the conflict squarely on Algeria, which he accused of trying to destroy his nation. In his view, Mauritania was the victim of hegemonic and expansionist Algeria and mercenaries in the pay of Algeria (the Polisario Front). Ould Daddah argued that this perilous situation obliged him to seek and accept assistance from Morocco and France to help defend Mauritania. In the Mauritanian view, since Algeria created the conflict, only a change in Algeria's aggressive policy could end the problem.[33]

The Mauritanian campaign under Ould Daddah to annex the southern part of the Sahara was not supported by the kind of national unity found in Morocco. The U.N. Visiting Mission that went to Mauritania in the spring of 1975 found three main divisions among public opinion on the Western Sahara question. Some Mauritanians wanted full integration of the Sahara into their country. A second group recognized the right of the Sahrawis to self-determination, but hoped they would opt for integration. Finally, some Mauritanians supported genuine Saharan independence; this group was made up largely of individuals who thought of themselves as Sahrawi refugees rather than as citizens of Mauritania.[34]

The lack of consensus within Mauritania partially arose from, and was compounded by, racial division—a division that is typical of all the Sahelian states stretching across Africa from the Sudan to the Atlantic. The southern part of these states is inhabited mainly by peasants who belong racially and culturally to black Africa, whereas in the north are desert nomads who are oriented toward Arab North Africa. In the specific case of Mauritania, the population — estimated to be from 1.5 to 1.8 million people — is made up of three components, roughly equal in number. One-third of the population, which includes the northern nomads, is both racially and ethnically Moorish. Another third is racially black or mixed Moorish-black but ethnically Moorish — that is, they speak Hassaniyya Arabic. The remaining component of the population is both racially and ethnically black. The blacks, who belong mainly to the Toucouleur, Fulbe, and Soninke ethnic groups, live in the Senegal River basin in the south and speak African languages common to the population in neighboring Senegal.

The question of Mauritania's national identity — whether Arab or black African — has provoked periodic racial tensions since the first years of independence. In 1966, for example, there were major riots when Ould Daddah attempted to make Arabic the official language, and the blacks objected when Mauritania joined the Arab League in 1973. Blacks see the Arabic language as symbolizing the domination of administrative and commercial positions by the Arab-Moorish culture. Opposition by blacks to the imposition of Arabic as the main language in schools led to postponement of the start of the academic year in both 1979 and 1980.[35] While the Moors have thoroughly dominated the government establishment, the blacks have made up the majority of the military conscripts. Among the sedentary black population living along the Senegal River valley in southern Mauritania, there was rarely any enthusiasm for a conflict that they tended to see as an Arab war fought for more desert and more Moorish nomads. The blacks did not welcome the absorption of a population group — the Sahrawis — who would aggravate the delicate racial balance in the country.

The positions of the military regimes that have ruled Mauritania since the July 1978 coup have been no less ambiguous than those of Ould Daddah. The new regimes neither rejected nor repeated Ould Daddah's position. Instead, they spoke of the need to find a lasting peace and tried to negotiate a withdrawal from the war in a way that would not antagonize Morocco excessively. Since signing a peace agreement with the Polisario Front in August 1979, Mauritania has no longer been a party to the Western Sahara conflict. In March 1981, following an attempted coup by expatriate Mauritanian army officers allegedly supported by Morocco, Nouakchott broke relations with Rabat. The government's present position is that Mauritania is neutral on the Sahara question and maintains an equal distance from both Morocco and Algeria. While no longer an active participant in the Western Sahara conflict, Mauritania played a critical role in the Moroccan campaign to annex the disputed territory. (The twists and turns in Mauritanian policy are examined in detail in Chapter Three.)

Algeria

Unlike Morocco and Mauritania, Algeria has never asserted a claim to the Western Sahara. Despite the absence of its own claim, however, Algeria has been very much a party to the Saharan conflict. Far from being a disinterested neighbor, the Algiers government refused to accept a development — the Moroccan-Mauritanian takeover of the Western Sahara — that worked against long-term Algerian national interests. In mid-1975, Algeria reversed its earlier support of Morocco and Mauritania and came out strongly in favor of Saharan self-determination. Since that time, the governments of Houari Boumediene and, since early 1979, Chadli Benjedid have provided territorial sanctuaries and crucial military and diplomatic support to the national liberation struggle of the Polisario Front. By publicly supporting the internationally recognized principle of self-determination, Algeria is able to wage by proxy a war that is very costly for neighboring Morocco.

At the ideological level, support for Saharan self-determination is very much in keeping with Algeria's own revolutionary experience. No Algerian state with a centralized administrative authority existed prior to the French colonial presence (1830–1962). For periods during the Middle Ages, Algerian territory was part of empires based in Morocco or the Arab East; from the sixteenth to the nineteenth centuries, there were only city-states administered by Ottoman Turkish rulers or local military commanders. The Algerian nation grew out of the intensive interaction with, and opposition to, French colonialism. This struggle culminated in a bloody war of national liberation, the Algerian revolution of 1954–1962, which led to negotiations with France, a referendum, and independence. Since independence in 1962, Algeria has consistently supported national liberation movements and the principle of self-determination through referendum — popular causes in Third World politics. The Algerian government has staked out a serious claim to Third World leadership; it was especially active in this regard in the mid-1970s. With its socialist ideology and espousal of a New International Economic Order, Algeria sees itself as the standard-bearer of the progressive developing nations in their struggle against "Western imperialism." In this setting Algeria would benefit from the emergence of an independent Saharan state since such a state's ideological orientation is likely to be socialist, nonaligned, and pro-Algerian.

Algerian officials insist that the Sahrawis must be allowed to decide freely on their own future. The Algerian government claims that it is not concerned with the specific choice the Sahrawis might make, even if they opt to become part of Morocco. In private, however, Algerians stress that a genuine act of self-determination will result in independence, and their support for self-determination is closely tied to a specific outcome of the process. Thus, behind a highly principled public stance lies a clear preference for an independent Saharan state—a state that would serve Algeria's long-term interests, both economically and, more important, at the level of regional geopolitics.

An independent Saharan state, especially one that came into existence through a war of national liberation backed by Algeria, would be open to heavy Algerian influence. At the economic level, such a state could be expected to serve Algeria's interests by providing an access to the Atlantic for iron ore in southwest Algeria. Large iron deposits were discovered in 1952 at Gara Jebilet, about one hundred miles southeast of Tindouf. The deposits are estimated to contain 3.24 billion tons of medium-to-low grade ore. Since Gara Jebilet is nearly one thousand miles from Oran on Algeria's Mediterranean coast, there is a question of the economic feasibility of exploiting the iron ore. The Algerian government reportedly commissioned studies to determine the optimal method of transporting the ore to the sea. Of 84 possible routes considered to the Atlantic or the Mediterranean, the most economical was found to be a 320-mile railroad to Morocco's Atlantic coast near Tarfaya. The current hostile relations between Morocco and Algeria rule out this route. In the event of an independent Saharan state, however, a rail link could pass a few miles further south, across the Sakiet al-Hamra panhandle,[36] even though the topography there would make it more difficult to construct a railroad.

One of the June 1972 Rabat agreements (mentioned earlier) called for joint Moroccan-Algerian exploitation of the Gara Jebilet iron ore deposits. This agreement, never ratified by Morocco, remains a dead letter. The Moroccans envisioned the transport of the iron ore across southern Morocco to the Atlantic coast for export abroad. The Algerians, however, retained other options. By 1975, they said their government had decided to build a railroad from Gara Jebilet toward the Mediterranean coast, presumably to connect with the existing rail line that runs as far south as Bechar. This decision was part of a larger plan to build a steel mill in Sidi bel Abbes and to create a focus of industrialization (a "pole of development") in northwestern Algeria to balance the existing industrial complex at Annaba in the northeast.[37] The prospect of an Algerian Atlantic corridor to export the Gara Jebilet iron ore was frequently mentioned in the international press. Even if such a corridor is no longer desirable, Algeria would still benefit economically from an independent Saharan state because of the possibilities for joint exploitation of the Western Sahara's mineral resources.

At the level of regional geopolitics, the fate of the Western Sahara becomes enmeshed in the basic power rivalry between Morocco and Algeria. This rivalry, which includes sharply different political systems, has been inherent in their bilateral relations since both countries became independent. With their population of 20 million and an industrial base, Algerians aspire to be the pre-eminent power in North Africa. Morocco, with its population of 21 million, is the only Maghreb country that can challenge Algerian power. Like many states, Algeria seeks a regional balance of power that gives it a comfortable edge over its neighbors. Thus, Algeria is bound to oppose a Moroccan takeover of the Sahara because such a territorial change would enlarge, enrich, and strengthen Morocco as a rival to Algerian pre-eminence in North Africa. In addition, Moroccan annexation of the Sahara would have an encircling effect on Algeria by extending Morocco's territory several hundred miles further south along the Atlantic coast of northwest Africa. Finally, Algerians fear that the absorption of the Western Sahara by their neighbors would only encourage Moroccan expansionist tendencies and whet the Moroccans' appetite for pursuing their unfulfilled and often articulated irredentist claims to territory in western Algeria.

The emergence of a weak Saharan state would have just the reverse consequences for regional geopolitics. Such a state would be highly vulnerable to heavy Algerian influence and would look naturally to Algeria for protection against frustrated Moroccan irredentism. An Algerian foothold in an independent Saharan state would have an encircling effect on Morocco. Further, Algeria would be well placed to exert (once again) heavy influence on weak Mauritania. Both these factors would improve for Algeria the regional balance of power and would ensure Algeria's predominant position in North Africa.

Algerians say that they have supported Saharan self-determination unfalteringly since the question first surfaced in the mid-1960s. There is evidence, however, that Algerian President Boumediene gave his blessing to Moroccan-Mauritanian plans to take over the Western Sahara—privately in 1972 and October 1974 and publicly in July 1975.[38] The details of the shifts in Algerian policy are examined in Chapter Three. It is sufficient to state here that by mid-1975 the Boumediene regime adopted an unswerving policy of opposition to Moroccan and Mauritanian efforts to annex the Sahara. While stopping short of direct military intervention, Algeria has supported Saharan self-determination by providing the diplomatic clout and most of the materiel that have made the Polisario Front a viable force capable of sustaining a war of national liberation—a war that drains the resources of neighboring Morocco.

At the official level, Algerians see the Western Sahara conflict as a problem of decolonization and a war of national liberation waged by the Sahrawi people. In this view, the present warfare resulted directly from the 1975–

1976 partition, invasion, and occupation of the Sahara by Morocco and Mauritania, who have denied the Sahrawi people the exercise of their legitimate right of self-determination and independence. Algerians argue that their position is consistent with both the U.N. commitment to the principle of self-determination and the OAU positions that territories must exercise their right to self-determination within established colonial boundaries and a territory with recognized boundaries may neither be absorbed nor dismembered against the will of its inhabitants. Algeria considers as null and void the November 1975 tripartite accord in which Spain agreed to turn over administrative authority in the Western Sahara to Morocco and Mauritania. As the legitimate representative of the Sahrawi people, the Polisario Front is supported with necessary economic, military, and humanitarian assistance.

In the Algerian view, the Moroccans are squarely to blame for the Saharan conflict. From 1966 to 1974, Morocco supported the principle of self-determination for the Sahrawi population, and the principle was endorsed repeatedly by the United Nations, the OAU, and the Non-Aligned Movement. Even more important, in three regional summits with Presidents Boumediene and Ould Daddah from 1970 to 1973, King Hassan insisted on the necessity of consulting the Sahrawi population about its future. Hassan suddenly reversed his position in August 1974 when he announced that Morocco would oppose a referendum that could lead to Saharan independence. For Algeria, excluding the possibility of independence would negate the basic principle of self-determinaton, and thus Algeria cannot accept the position Morocco has adopted since 1974.[39]

Algerians deny that any bilateral conflict exists between their country and Morocco. The Algerian government considers that the frontier issue with Morocco was resolved permanently with King Hassan's signing of the 1972 Rabat agreements. It treats the present Moroccan-Algerian border as an internationally recognized frontier that must be defended against outside aggression. The Sahara dispute is between Morocco and the Polisario, not Morocco and Algeria. The conflict will end when Morocco recognizes the legitimate national rights of the Sahrawi people and withdraws from the Western Sahara. Existing tension in northwest Africa can be reduced only through political means in negotiations between Morocco and the Polisario Front.[40]

The government's position has not found strong support among the Algerian public. While there is a general recognition of the justness of the Sahrawis' right to self-determination, few Algerians would be willing to make concrete sacrifices on behalf of the Saharan cause. Algerian technocrats in particular view the Western Sahara conflict as an unfortunate obstacle to regional economic cooperation with Morocco. The government's position is passively accepted among the general public. Outside of a small number of militants, however, there are few signs in Algeria of genuine popular support for the Polisario Front's war of national liberation.

The Polisario Front

The remaining party to the Western Sahara conflict is not a country but a national liberation movement — the Polisario Front — that is strongly backed by a country — Algeria. "Polisario" is an acronym for Popular (Front) for the Liberation of Sakiet al-Hamra and Rio de Oro, or (Frente) Popular para la Liberación de Saguia el-Hamra y Río de Oro as the name appeared originally in Spanish. The front was created in 1973, although its somewhat obscure origins are the subject of partisan debate. The Polisario claims to be the legitimate representative of the Sahrawi people and in 1976 proclaimed an independent state and established a government-in-exile in Algiers. While the commitment of the front's leaders and the movement's success in instilling a sense of nationalism among large numbers of Sahrawis are widely recognized, it is also quite evident that the Polisario is heavily dependent on outside sources — namely, Algeria and Libya — for critical economic, military, and humanitarian support.

The origins of the Polisario Front can be traced to an earlier group, the Saharan Liberation Movement, or MLS from the initials of its French name. This group was founded in 1968 by Mohamed Sid Brahim Bassir, who was known as Bassiri. The MLS began with a reformist orientation and a gradualist approach that sought full autonomy and equal rights of citizenship for Sahrawis through peaceful means. Bassiri, who may have worked as a journalist in Rabat, was the prime mover behind the group's newspaper, *Our Sahara.*

Both the leaders and the program of the MLS changed significantly following a violent confrontation with Spanish authorities in El Ayoun on June 17, 1970. The colonial administration had organized on that day a demonstration by Spanish-dominated shaikhs to show support for Spain's policy of integration within the framework of a Hispanic-Saharan union. The MLS organized a much larger counterdemonstration of several thousand people in Zemla, an outlying section of El Ayoun, to show opposition to Spain's integration policy. The crowd refused to disperse, the militia's authority was challenged, and Spanish soldiers opened fire. Reports of the numbers of demonstrators killed range from twelve to sixty and the number of wounded from dozens to hundreds. The Spanish moved quickly against the MLS and arrested many of its militants, including Bassiri, whose fate remains unknown.[41]

The lesson of Zemla was clear to the MLS. Henceforth, reformist approaches and the goal of autonomy were abandoned, and a consensus gradually emerged on the need to seek full independence from Spain. Nonviolent tactics were replaced by a commitment to armed struggle. The movement went underground and regrouped its forces in the desert. The necessity of seeking outside sources of support became evident. Finally, in the absence of Bassiri, a new leader, Mustapha Sayyid El Ouali, then in his mid-twenties, emerged in 1971–1972 to head the movement. These various changes in strategy, tactics, organization, and leadership were very much in evidence by May 20, 1973, when the Polisario Front, ten days after its formation, surfaced publicly with guerrilla attacks against Spanish troops in the Sahara.

While acknowledging the vanguard role of the MLS, the Polisario Front disputes the nationalist authenticity of several other liberation movements that formed in the Sahara between 1969 and 1975. One early group, called the Saharan Youth Organization (Nidam), was formed in 1969 and probably helped to organize the June 1970 demonstration. Little is known of Nidam, but it may have been a forerunner of another group organized by Eduardo Moha in 1971. Moha, a Sahrawi educated in Morocco and France, formed a resistance movement around a group of young intellectuals, several of whom were students at Mohammed V University in Rabat. Moha's group was known as Morehob, the Mouvement de Résistance des Hommes Bleus. When Morocco found Morehob's goal of Saharan independence unacceptable, Moha transferred the group's headquarters to Algiers in 1973.[42] Within a few months, Morehob moved its main office again, this time to Brussels. By early 1975, the opportunistic Moha was again siding with Morocco, which left Algeria wary of providing further support for Saharan liberation movements. In any event, the activities of Morehob seem to have been limited to the realm of propaganda. Finally, in 1974–1975, Spain and Morocco each sponsored its own group—the Saharan National Unity Party (PUNS) and the Liberation and Unity Front (FLU). Both the PUNS and FLU were disbanded after Spain agreed in November 1975 to withdraw from the Sahara. Some of the members of these two groups later joined the Association of People Originating from Sakiet al-Hamra and Rio de Oro (Aosario), a pro-Moroccan Saharan movement created by Rabat in 1977.

The leadership and upper ranks of the Polisario Front come originally from three fairly distinct groups. One part derives from a nucleus of Western Saharan nationalists, some of whom had studied in the Canary Islands and Spain; the leading figure of this group was Bassiri. Another portion of the Polisario upper echelons is composed of young men who had studied in

Rabat between 1965 and 1970, some at Mohammed V University and others in high school. A number of those who studied in Rabat in the 1960s were members of families of the ALS irregular forces from the 1950s or members of refugee families who had gone from Mauritania to Morocco. These students, some of whom were Moroccan,[43] were active in creating the MLS in 1968. Most of the individuals in these first two groups were the educated sons of wealthier merchants and tribal leaders, the usual vanguard element in anticolonial nationalist movements. The remaining part is formed of opponents of the regime of Mokhtar Ould Daddah in Mauritania. This group includes members of the opposition Nahda party, activists in the 1971–1972 student movement, and a few former officials like Ahmed-Baba Miské, a former Mauritanian ambassador to the United Nations, and Ibrahim Hakim, who had served as a Mauritanian diplomat in West Germany and Algeria. Ideologically, the individuals from all three groups are simultaneously nationalist, revolutionary, and anti-imperialist. Mustapha Sayyid El Ouali, for example, the leading figure in the Polisario Front until his death in 1976, had read Frantz Fanon and Che Guevara in their first editions in Arabic.[44]

During the first two years of its existence, the Polisario Front was based in Mauritania, from which it launched attacks against Spanish targets in the Sahara. Ould Daddah's regime tolerated and aided the Polisario out of solidarity with its authentic Sahrawi composition and sympathy for its anticolonialist struggle. In view of the close ethnic links between Sahrawis and Moors, it is not surprising that the front turned first to Mauritania for support and cross-border sanctuaries. At the same time, the Polisario sought and received support from Libya, where Mu'ammar al-Qadhafi early on had called for an armed struggle against the Spanish.[45]

According to one account, from May 1973 to July 1975, the Polisario fought about fifty major engagements, in which 30 of their fighters were killed or taken prisoner[46] — suggesting that their sabotage and harassment operations were planned quite carefully. During this period, the front operated in highly mobile units of about a dozen people, and the group's combatant strength was estimated to be about eight hundred.[47] (The Polisario Front's growth and its escalation of military tactics since 1975 are examined in Chapter Three.)

When Morocco and Mauritania moved into the Western Sahara in late 1975 and early 1976, the Polisario Front encouraged and assisted the flight of a large number of Sahrawis out of the territory. Some, who supported the Polisario or did not want to live under the control of the new administrative authorities, left voluntarily; others left to escape the intimidation and repression of the incoming liberating armies. Within a few months, perhaps a third to a half of the Sahrawi population left the Western Sahara and was resettled in refugee camps in southwest Algeria. During the period when the camps were set up, the Polisario had to spend two-thirds of its efforts on organizing and teaching, which cut heavily into its military activities.

The number of refugees, like the size of the Sahrawi population (see Chapter One), has become a matter of partisan debate. Morocco claims there are no more than 15,000 authentic Sahrawis in the camps and argues that other Sahrawi and Tuareg nomads from Algeria, Mauritania, Mali, and perhaps even Niger, struggling to survive after years of Sahelian drought, have swelled the refugee population. Other figures range from 40,000 to 100,000 refugees, estimated by independent relief agencies, to a camp population of 100,000–150,000 claimed by the Polisario Front. Based on a count made by the author in 1979 of the tents in two camps and assuming an average of five people in each tent, a range of 17,000 to 35,000 refugees seems a reasonable estimate.[48]

The Sahrawi refugees live in 23 camps within an area stretching from 25 to 140 miles southeast of Tindouf. The camps are grouped into three clusters, called the El Ayoun, Dakhla, and Smara *wilaya*s, after the major administrative units of the Western Sahara. The camps are in an area that, even among desert regions, has a particularly inhospitable terrain. To sustain themselves in this environment, the refugees are utterly dependent on Algeria for the supply of food and water, which must be brought in by truck from considerable distances. Life in the camps is bare but not desperate. Serious health problems in 1976–1977 — kwashiorkor (a chronic children's disease caused by protein and calorie deficiencies), measles, widespread bronchitis, tuberculosis, hepatitis, trachoma, chronic diarrhea, and dehydration — have been alleviated but not eliminated.

The camps are well organized, discipline is high, and morale has not become a problem. Since almost all adult males serve in the military, the camp population consists of old men, women, and children. All adults living in the camps belong to one of five committees — justice, health, artisanat, education, and Red Crescent (food distribution). Each committee elects a chairperson, and the chairpeople form a camp council.

In the absence of men, the camps are fully managed by women. The responsibility of running the camps strengthens the traditional autonomy of Sahrawi women, who assumed family responsibilities during the prolonged absences of their husbands. The present period of struggle would seem propitious for the emancipation of Sahrawi women through new responsibilities that are forced on them.[49] But despite Polisario claims of full equality for both sexes, there is little evidence that women play an important role in the movement. Women do not receive formal military training. Instead, stress is given to the roles of child-bearing and child-rearing. Females are encouraged to marry at the age of fifteen or sixteen and to have large families—seven or eight children are typical. Since Polisario leaders would like to see a large increase in the Sahrawi population, the rhetoric of the revolution reinforces and supports traditional Sahrawi family customs.

Life in the camps is controlled to a great extent by the Polisario Front, and the population has been highly politicized. The front continuously tries to instill a sense of Saharan nationalism through chants, poetry, songs, demonstrations, frequent allusions to the just struggle, and the school curriculum. This sense of Saharan identification is constantly inculcated at the expense of tribal ties. To promote the growth of nationalist sentiment, refugees are deliberately mixed together with strangers from other areas.[50]

The development of loyalty to a national entity has been an enormous but crucial challenge for the Polisario Front. Prior to the present conflict, political loyalties among Sahrawis were essentially to families, tribes, and Islam—far below the level of nationalism or loyalty to one of the neighboring states. The Polisario has achieved considerable success among the refugees in moving from these traditional loyalties to the creation of a Saharan national consciousness. This process benefits from the correspondence of Polisario concepts of self-determination, communal sharing, and independence to traditional themes in Saharan tribal culture. In addition, some of the front's cohesion and solidarity results from the high proportion of Polisario leaders and rank-and-file members who come from the same tribe, the Reguibat.

Political organization within the camps is along lines of local democracy, similar to the popular-committees experiment in Libya. In ascending order from the local to the national level, the Polisario Front organization builds from 11-member cells to a council for each camp to a 21-member Political Bureau to a 9-member Executive Committee, the most important decision-making body. Supreme authority is vested in a 500-member National Congress, which usually meets every two years and elects the front's secretary-general and Executive Committee. In addition to this democratic structure, the conditions of a revolutionary struggle work against the development of privileges. Nevertheless, at least one sympathetic observer found in 1978 that social influence still seemed to derive from membership in tribes and castes and the power relations that they induce in the community.[51]

At its First National Congress in May 1973, the Polisario Front stated its clear goal of independence, which could come from an authentic referendum if Spain were willing to hold one. The means to be employed were pressure from the masses combined with an armed struggle. The Second Congress in

August 1974 proclaimed that "the masses guarantee the war of liberation." The political manifesto of the 1974 congress supported Algerian policies and found that mutual aid with Algeria was essential. Privately, the Polisario recognized that they would have to rely militarily on alliances, which meant Algeria.[52]

At the Third National Congress in August 1976, the Polisario countersign was "Neither peace nor stability before the return to the national territory and total independence." This slogan suggested the victory of the supporters of a national approach over the international approach of exporting the revolution to Mauritania. The 1976 congress approved a General National Program, which is the Polisario's basic ideological manifesto. According to the program, the particular characteristics of the Sahrawi people are "their Arab, African, and Islamic identity, their participation in the Third World family, their opposition to imperialism, colonialism, and exploitation." Finally, the Fourth Congress in September 1978 declared: "The struggle continues for national independence and peace" — perhaps an indication that the Polisario had adopted a somewhat longer timetable for its war of national liberation.

At the public level, the Polisario Front has postponed the detailed definition of political and economic issues. Doctrinal questions are seen as secondary to the total effort of the national liberation struggle. Once independence is achieved, these questions presumably will be decided in a democratic fashion by the Sahrawi population.

In February 1976, the Polisario proclaimed the birth of the Saharan Democratic Arab Republic (SDAR), "a free, independent, sovereign state ruled by an Arab national democratic system of progressive unionist orientation and of Islamic religion."[53] The constitution adopted at the Third National Congress in August 1976 described the state as "Sakiet al-Hamra and Rio de Oro, within their historical boundaries." The government was defined in the constitution as a democratic republic with an objective of implementing socialism. Islam was declared the state religion and the basis for law.[54] At present, the state is represented by a government-in-exile in Algiers.

The overriding goal of the Polisario is an internationally recognized, independent Saharan state and people — a general goal that the front pursues within the guidelines issued by the national congresses. In its struggle the Polisario Front remains, as it has been since the setting up of the refugee camps, heavily dependent on Algeria for the vital supply of food, fuel, and water.

The Polisario's view of the Western Sahara conflict closely resembles the Algerian position, and on many points the two are indistinguishable. In this view, the conflict arose because Morocco and Mauritania invaded and took over the Sahara and denied the Sahrawi people their inalienable right of self-determination. The conflict will continue until the Moroccan government is forced by the just struggle of the Sahrawis to realize the error of its ways, end its aggression, and negotiate a peace settlement with the front. In the Polisario's view, a settlement of the conflict must be based on the withdrawal of all foreign troops from the Western Sahara and formal recognition by Morocco and Mauritania of the national sovereignty of the SDAR.

3 | Evolution of the Conflict

The conflict over the Western Sahara has evolved through several fairly distinct phases since the mid-1960s. During the 1960s and until 1974, the parties to the conflict did little more than stake out their diplomatic positions: on one side Morocco, Algeria, and Mauritania shared a common interest in the decolonization of the Sahara; on the opposing side was Spain, the colonial master of the territory. In mid-1974, when Spain began to take steps to leave the Sahara, preparations accelerated on all sides in anticipation of a potential conflict. Between that point and October 1975, Morocco made clear its intention to take over the Sahara and reached an understanding with Mauritania to work in tandem; Algeria, after first supporting this undertaking, came out strongly in favor of Saharan self-determination.

Between October 1975 and February 1976, the Saharan conflict reached its highest point of tension. Following the World Court opinion, the Moroccan Green March, and the Madrid Tripartite Agreement, Morocco and Mauritania moved into the Western Sahara despite strong protests by Algeria. After Spain's departure from the territory in February 1976, Morocco and Mauritania tried to absorb the Sahara into their own national territories against the diplomatic opposition of Algeria and the military opposition of the Polisario Front—a phase that continued until Mauritania bowed out of the conflict in August 1979. Since that date, Morocco has continued alone to confront the Polisario Front in an ongoing struggle. This chapter analyzes the shifting aims, positions, and strategies of the various parties during the several phases of the Sahara dispute, with special emphasis on Morocco and Algeria.

Diplomatic Background, 1960–1974

During the 1960s, Spain faced an increasing demand from the world community for the decolonization of its Saharan territory. Much of this demand was voiced through the United Nations and was based on Resolution 1514, passed by the U.N. General Assembly (UNGA) on December 14, 1960. At this same time, the United Nations published a list of territories under colonial domination – including the Western Sahara – that should be decolonized in accordance with Resolution 1514, which contains the "Declaration on the Granting of Independence to Colonial Countries and Peoples." To further the implementation of this declaration, the United Nations created a special watchdog committee in 1961, known as the Committee of 24. Beginning in 1963, the question of Spanish (or the Western) Sahara was discussed at length in U.N. debates for more than a decade, both in the Fourth (Decolonization) Committee and in General Assembly plenary sessions. The first of many U.N. resolutions calling on Spain to implement the Sahara's right to self-determination was passed by the Fourth Committee on October 16, 1964.[1]

Within northwest Africa Morocco's bilateral disputes with both Algeria and Mauritania prevented any regional coordination of policy against Spain over the Sahara issue. As mentioned in Chapter Two, Morocco and Algeria fought a brief border war in 1963. The repercussions of this conflict extended to the Sahrawis, especially the population at Tindouf, whose support was clearly divided between partisans of each country. Algerian leaders, fearing that a pro-Moroccan sentiment would solidify among Sahrawis at Tindouf, imprisoned some Reguibat tribesmen and, at the same time, set up funds to assist the integration of the Reguibat into the Algerian state.[2] In the case of Mauritania (also noted earlier), Morocco refused to recognize its independence and territorial integrity on the grounds that Mauritania's territory historically formed part of the Moroccan state. When the OAU was set up in 1963, its charter contained a clear reference to the territorial integrity and the inviolability of colonial frontiers. With its disputes with both Algeria and Mauritania probably in mind, Morocco expressly stated its reservations to this OAU position.[3]

The diplomatic campaign for the decolonization of the Western Sahara accelerated in the mid-1960s. In 1965, the UNGA passed its first resolution calling on Spain to implement the Sahara's right to self-determination. Madrid's position during this period was that its African territories were Spanish provinces and, as integral parts of the Spanish state, were not entitled to self-determination. The 1965 UNGA resolution also called on Spain to negotiate with Morocco and Mauritania. Since both these countries claimed the disputed territory in its entirety, they rejected any idea of a joint treaty. That same year, Morocco's claim to the Sahara was underscored when some tribal leaders from Rio de Oro affirmed their allegiance to King Hassan. In November 1966, the General Assembly passed the first of several annual resolutions calling for Saharan self-determination through a referendum. Having failed to come to an understanding, Morocco and Mauritania both supported this U.N. resolution.[4]

The Moroccan-Mauritanian enmity over the Sahara during the 1960s played into the hands of Spain. In light of the discovery of large phosphate deposits in Sakiet al-Hamra, the Spanish government came to view Saharan self-determination as a way to create a puppet state, one that would allow the Spanish to keep control of the phosphate wealth. In 1967, Spain publicly accepted the principle of a referendum. During the next several years, the Spanish government continued to accept this principle but refused to specify a date for a referendum. In retrospect, Madrid's support for a referendum in the Sahara can be seen as a tactic for perpetuating Spain's presence in the territory.

Spain was unresponsive to Moroccan attempts to negotiate a bilateral accord on the Sahara issue, and Madrid periodically assured Mauritania of its unwillingness to make a deal with Morocco. This ploy was used, for example, in a secret meeting in August 1968 in Bordeaux between the Mauritanian and Spanish foreign ministers. Spain told Mauritania at this meeting that the Sahrawis administered by Spain, if given a choice, would clearly opt in favor of the Mauritanians because of the close tribal and geographical links between the two communities.[5] Meanwhile, the UNGA passed Resolution 2428 in December 1968, which invited Spain to organize a referendum of self-determination under U.N. auspices and after consulting with Morocco and Mauritania and "every other interested party." Algeria quickly declared itself an "interested party" without a territorial claim.

By the end of the 1960s, the three northwest African states were able to resolve, at least temporarily, several of their major regional disputes, thus laying the groundwork for a united front against Spain. Most of the initiative for this improvement in regional relations came from Morocco, which may have been seeking a free hand to pursue its interests in the Western Sahara issue. In January 1969, Morocco and Algeria signed a twenty-year Treaty of Solidarity and Cooperation at Ifrane, which heralded a "new era of friendly relations" between the two countries. This treaty was followed four months later by a meeting in Tlemcen in May at which King Hassan and President Boumediene talked about coordinating their Sahara strategy and settling their border problem; in addition, ten bilateral agreements and conventions in the economic, commercial, and judiciary fields were signed. In September 1969, Morocco recognized Mauritania at the Islamic summit conference in Rabat, and in December the two states agreed to establish formal diplomatic relations. Full diplomatic missions began operating in the respective capitals in April 1970, and in June Rabat and Nouakchott signed a friendship treaty that formally ended Morocco's claim on Mauritania. The stage was now set for a series of Moroccan-Algerian-Mauritanian summit meetings at which the Sahara issue was a major focus of attention.

The northwest African summitry began in September 1970 when King Hassan, President Boumediene, and President Ould Daddah met at Nouadhibou in northern Mauritania to plan a coordinated Saharan policy against Spain. In a joint communiqué, the three heads of state announced the establishment of a Tripartite Coordinating Committee to follow the process of Saharan decolonization. Publicly at least, the meeting achieved a rare degree of unity on the need to decolonize the Western Sahara and liberate the territory from Spanish control. Because of this unity, references were made in the following months and years to the "spirit of Nouadhibou."

During the OAU summit meeting in Rabat in June 1972, Morocco and Algeria signed two agreements (see Chapter Two) covering their common frontier and joint economic cooperation. King Hassan announced at the time that the agreements would ensure peace and security for Morocco in exchange for a border strip of land fifteen to twenty kilometers in width. It is widely believed that in return for Moroccan concessions on the disputed frontier territory and the implied renouncing of further claims to Tindouf, Algeria promised to support, or at least not to oppose, Morocco's claim to the Western Sahara. Accordingly, on the day following the signing of the two agreements, Hassan announced to the OAU meeting that Algeria would no longer interest itself in the Sahara question. The private Moroccan-Algerian understanding, though eventually repudiated by Boumediene, was largely supported by Algeria's statements and actions until mid-1975.

Ould Daddah later stated that at the June 1972 OAU summit, Morocco and Mauritania reached an understanding on a bilateral solution for the Sahara question involving two zones of influence, one in the south for Mauritania and the other in the north for Morocco. Hassan and Ould Daddah informed Boumediene of their accord and exchanged secret letters in his presence. Boumediene, in turn, expressed his satisfaction to Hassan and Ould Daddah about their understanding.[6] To formalize this understanding, Ould Daddah visited Rabat the following month, and a joint Moroccan-Mauritanian communiqué was issued concerning a political agreement on the Western Sahara.

The final regional summit during this period was held in Agadir, where the three heads of state met in July 1973 to coordinate policy further. In the communiqué issued after this meeting, the three leaders declared their "unshakable attachment to the principle of self-determination." This vague statement broke no new ground, which suggests that differences among the three parties were beginning to develop. Divergences were revealed, for example, in statements made by Hassan at a press conference a year later in September 1974. The king said at that time that he had convoked the Agadir summit in 1973 because Mauritania, which had spoken only of decolonizing and liberating the Sahara at Nouadhibou in 1970, had begun making territorial claims.

As Morocco, Algeria, and Mauritania began to collaborate in the early 1970s to exert diplomatic pressure on Spain, the government of Gen. Francisco Franco resorted to a series of delaying tactics designed to show the world that an evolution toward self-rule was taking place in the Sahara. Earlier, in an attempt to appease the United Nations, the Spanish had staged a referendum in 1966 in which eight hundred tribal chiefs declared their support of Spain. In March 1972, while affirming the territory's right to self-determination, Madrid stated that the Sahrawis had not asked for a referendum to decide their future. As evidence of progress toward self-rule, the Spanish pointed to the Jemaa, the Saharan general assembly they had created in 1967. In February 1973, the Jemaa sent Madrid a petition requesting "progressive participation" in the territory's internal affairs to "ready the Saharans for the future." In response the Spanish government in September 1973 published a program of partial self-government for the Saharan province as a "necessary preparation" for self-determination. The Madrid authorities made no mention, however, of how long the preparatory phase would last.

Some outsiders watched Spain's halting moves toward Saharan self-rule with a good deal of cynicism. In Mauritania, for example, the view developed that Spain was engaged in creating a puppet state whose phosphate wealth would remain under Madrid's control and was trying to build up the territory's population to give credibility to an independent Saharan state. As evidence, the Mauritanians adduced Madrid's attempt, through gifts and a variety of privileges, to attract tribes from southern Morocco, southwest Algeria, and northern Mauritania into the Western Sahara. The lures included the Jemaa, whose members were given salaries, and a nomad guard, whose pay and rifles proved sufficient to attract many Sahrawi men and, consequently, their families.[7]

By the middle of 1974, the Western Sahara issue began to move rapidly toward an armed conflict. For the preceding decade, however, the issue had been confined to diplomatic maneuvering and posturing among both the "concerned parties" — Spain, Morocco, and Mauritania — and the "interested party" — Algeria. After 1966, Madrid publicly supported Saharan self-determination; privately the Spanish stalled to ensure that an independent Saharan state would be to their liking. Morocco and Mauritania publicly supported liberation and self-determination while privately moving toward a bilateral solution of the question. Algeria posed as the champion of self-determination while privately blessing a Moroccan-Mauritanian solution. As one observer summarized the situation from 1966 to 1973, while Spain, Morocco, and Mauritania displayed a public adherence to self-determination, in private all three governments shared a deep mistrust of a genuine expression of Saharan popular will.[8]

Preparing for Confrontation, July 1974–October 1975

The pace of the Western Sahara's decolonization accelerated markedly in the summer of 1974 when Spain began to move toward a referendum in the territory and Morocco responded with a campaign to "recover its despoiled Saharan provinces." The last six months of 1974 marked a critical period in Moroccan-Mauritanian relations as the two countries moved from competition to an important coordination of strategy on the Sahara issue. The following nine months until the fall of 1975 proved to be a crucial period for Moroccan-Algerian relations – and consequently for the development of the Western Saharan conflict – as Algeria moved from tacit support of to active opposition to Morocco's campaign to take over the Sahara.

On July 2 and 3, 1974, Spain informed Morocco, Mauritania, and Algeria of the forthcoming publication of a statute that envisioned self-determination for its Saharan province. In the interim, Spain planned to grant internal autonomy to the Western Sahara as a first step toward this goal. The unilateral implications of the Spanish announcement were not welcomed in Rabat. Morocco could point, at a minimum, to Resolution 3162 passed by the UNGA on December 14, 1973, which requested that Spain consult with Morocco, Mauritania, "and any other interested party" (namely, Algeria) regarding the organization of a referendum in the Sahara to be held under U.N. auspices. On July 8, King Hassan, in a nationally televised speech, emphasized the problems in dealing with Spain over the Sahara and announced that 1975 would be the "year of destiny" for Morocco's recovery of the Western Sahara. The king ended this saber-rattling speech on a hard line, with a national call "to make this year one of internal and external mobilization, for the recovery of our territories."

On August 21, 1974, Spain belatedly announced its intention to comply with the 1966 UNGA resolution on a referendum and, in the first half of 1975, to hold a plebiscite under U.N. supervision to determine the future status of the Sahara. Whereas the Spanish had been unmoved by several

U.N. resolutions or diplomatic pressures by the northwest African states, they were almost certainly moved to action by the revolution in neighboring Portugal and the rapid Portuguese withdrawal from both Angola and Mozambique. Spain probably still hoped up to this time that the Sahrawis would vote for independence and that the weak Saharan state that emerged would rely upon Spain for economic support and military protection. In particular, Madrid envisioned that its investment in the facilities at Bu Craa and El Ayoun port might provide a guaranteed source of phosphate for Spanish agriculture, thereby ending Spain's dependence on Morocco for phosphate.

During 1974, the revolution in Portugal and Portugal's rapid withdrawal from Africa were also a major factor in the Moroccan decision to mobilize a Saharan campaign. In Rabat's view, the lesson of Portugal would not be lost on the Spanish, who could be expected to see the heavy liability of trying to hang on to one of the last remaining colonial territories in Africa. Over the years, Spain had maintained consistently good relations with Africa and the Arab world. Thus, King Hassan had reason to believe that Spain would now be willing to negotiate the surrender of the Western Sahara. In the past, Spain reluctantly had given up, one by one, the northern zone of Morocco, the southern province of Tarfaya, and the Atlantic coastal enclave of Ifni. With patient negotiations backed by diplomatic pressure, the Moroccan government expected Spain to give up the Sahara.

The Moroccan strategy to obtain the Western Sahara through negotiations with Spain was clearly threatened, first, by Madrid's announcement in July 1974 of Saharan internal autonomy and, second, by the prospect revealed in August of a referendum to be held in the first half of 1975. Negotiations would take time, and the immediate aim of Moroccan policy was to undermine, or at least forestall, the idea of a referendum. Accordingly, King Hassan demanded four conditions as a prerequisite for any form of voting in the Sahara: consultation with Morocco; U.N. supervision of the vote; prior withdrawal of Spanish troops and administrators; and repatriation of twenty thousand Sahrawi refugees who had fled to southern Morocco.[9] Then, on August 20, 1974, Hassan announced that "if the principle of independence is raised, Morocco will categorically refuse the referendum."[10]

Until the end of the 1960s, Moroccan leaders believed that the Sahrawi population, if given the opportunity to express its will freely, would opt to join Morocco. By 1974, however, Moroccans had serious doubts on this matter — engendered perhaps by signs of organized Saharan nationalist sentiment. Because the outcome of a referendum could no longer be predicted with certainty, the Moroccan government now viewed a genuine plebiscite as risky at best and quite possibly disastrous. Since Morocco had supported seven U.N. resolutions since 1966 calling for Saharan self-determination, the kingdom was placed in an ambiguous diplomatic situation.

Despite this ambiguity, in July 1974 King Hassan launched a diplomatic campaign to gain international support for Morocco against Spain. Prime Minister Ahmed Osman, Foreign Minister Ahmed Laraki, and leaders of the opposition parties all served as royal envoys to a large number of European, Arab, African, and Asian capitals where they explained the case for Morocco's historical and legal claims to the Sahara. The king's personal envoys argued against a referendum on the grounds that there was little chance that a free expression of opinion would take place; that a connection with the colonial power (Spain) might be perpetuated; or that independence might result, against Morocco's claims to the territory.[11]

The Moroccan diplomatic campaign, carried on from July to September 1974, achieved only limited success. Most countries outside northwest Africa had little knowledge of or interest in the Western Sahara issue. Several European nations were unwilling to jeopardize their relations with Spain. Some Third World countries were reluctant to oppose Algeria, which was then presiding over the Non-Aligned Movement and whose positions conformed to the relevant U.N. and OAU resolutions.[12] The eastern Arab world, where there was considerable sympathy for Morocco's opposition to Spanish colonialism, had already planned to make a concerted push on behalf of the Palestinians at the United Nations in the fall of 1974 and did not welcome the Sahara issue because it threatened to divert attention from the Palestinian question. In the end, only Egypt, the Sudan, the Gulf emirates, and Senegal formally declared themselves in support of Morocco.[13]

Given his commitment to recover the Western Sahara and the limited response to Moroccan diplomatic missions, Hassan seemingly had painted himself into a corner by the end of the summer. The king, bowing to the dictates of realism, cleverly extricated himself from the situation on September 17, 1974, by proposing a joint Spanish-Moroccan settlement of the Sahara question either through mediation by the United Nations and the International Court of Justice (ICJ) or by means of a referendum under international supervision. Hassan proposed the following conditions for a referendum: the Spanish Army and administration must first be withdrawn; then the Sahrawi population would choose between continued Spanish domination or annexation by Morocco, with no option for independence. Spain quickly rejected the Moroccan proposal.

In the efforts to put diplomatic pressure on Spain, it was especially important for Morocco to have the support of Algeria and Mauritania. Yet despite the efforts and summits from 1970 to 1973 to encourage regional cooperation over the Sahara's future, when Morocco actively asserted its claim to the territory and rejected the option of an independent Saharan state in mid-1974, it lost—at least for the moment—the support of its Maghreb neighbors. Algeria remained detached: while it made no territorial claims of its own, neither did it provide any support for Morocco. Relations between Morocco and Mauritania soured following King Hassan's diplomatic campaign to enlist international support and Spain's announcement of a referendum. Morocco labeled Mauritania a "troublemaker" for maintaining its claims to the Sahara, and during August 1974, Mauritania mounted its own diplomatic campaign to enlist support for its claims on the disputed territory.

At some point during the fall of 1974, Morocco and Mauritania reached an agreement, undisclosed at the time, to partition the Western Sahara after the Spanish withdrew. Although the precise timing of the secret agreement is unclear, it was probably concluded when King Hassan and President Ould Daddah attended the Arab summit meeting in Rabat in October 1974.[14] Ould Daddah later revealed that President Boumediene made an explicit declaration in support of a Moroccan-Mauritanian solution to the Sahara problem on October 29 at a private meeting of Arab heads of state and government at the Rabat summit. In this statement Boumediene declared: "I confirm that Algeria does not have any claim over the Sahara, that its only concern remains the understanding between Morocco and Mauritania. They have reached agreement on the part of the Sahara that should return to each of them. I was present when this agreement was reached; I approve it wholeheartedly and without reservation."[15] Ould Daddah also stated that at a meeting between himself and Hassan at Fez in December 1974, the two heads of state outlined the limits of the Mauritanian and Moroccan zones of influence in the Sahara and agreed on bases of economic cooperation in the territory.[16] Whatever the precise timing of the agreement, the evidence is clear: in August 1974, Morocco and Mauritania were pursuing competing strategies and pushing rival claims; four months later in December, the two countries were forming the Agency for Moroccan-Mauritanian Cooperation and carefully coordinating their strategies at the United Nations—the beginning of a cooperation that continued until 1979.

A good deal of adjustment was required before the Kingdom of Morocco and the Islamic Republic of Mauritania were able to pursue a closely coordinated strategy for the decolonization of the Western Sahara. Mauritania had maintained close working relations with Algeria since the mid-1960s. The two states shared a common socialist orientation, Algeria provided Mauritania with much needed financial and technical assistance, and Nouakchott followed the lead of Algiers on foreign policy issues. The close cooperation between Hassan and Ould Daddah over the Sahara issue, beginning in the fall of 1974, thus involved a fundamental realignment of Mauritania's foreign policy—away from Algeria, its natural ideological ally, and toward the conservative Moroccan monarchy and the West in general. What factors prompted Ould Daddah to pursue such a basic shift in policy? Part of the explanation may derive from the appearance in May 1973 of the Polisario Front. Mauritanian opposition figures, like Ahmed-Baba Miské, were prime movers in the front, and Ould Daddah may have feared the emergence of an independent Saharan state led by his political rivals. There was some concern among Mauritanian leaders that the ultimate Polisario objective might be the Greater Mauritania first enunciated as the goal of the Moors by Ould Daddah in 1957. In that event, the Polisario's liberation of Spanish Sahara would be only the first step in a progression encompassing the annexation (or reunification) of southern provinces of Morocco, bits of Algeria and Mali, and eventually all of Mauritania down to the edge of the Senegal River basin. Second, given Morocco's determination to annex the Sahara and Mauritania's inability to oppose Hassan's forces, Ould Daddah probably preferred to get at least part of the Sahara, rather than see Morocco take over the entire territory. Finally, Soviet involvement in Angola in 1974 may have alarmed Nouakchott about Moscow's intentions in Africa and encouraged Mauritanian leaders to seek closer relations with the West.

During the fall of 1974, Morocco pressed its case before the U.N. Fourth Committee, which adopted a resolution to approach the ICJ for an advisory opinion on the legal status of the Western Sahara at the time of its colonization by Spain in 1884. King Hassan, convinced of the soundness of Morocco's legal position, had proposed to Spain in September that the two countries submit this question to the World Court for adjudication—that is, request the binding arbitration of the ICJ. This option was not possible, however, because Spain refused to consent (under international law no state, without its consent, can be compelled to submit to ICJ adjudication).[17]

Morocco and Mauritania jointly submitted the Fourth Committee resolution to the UNGA on December 9, 1974. Under this resolution, adopted on December 13 as UNGA Resolution 3292, the General Assembly requested from the ICJ an advisory opinion on two questions: (1) Was the Western Sahara a territory belonging to no one (*terra nullius*) at the time of its colonization by Spain? And (2) if it was not, what "legal ties" existed between the territory and the Kingdom of Morocco and the "Mauritanian entity"? The resolution urged Spain to postpone the referendum it planned to hold in the first half of 1975. At Spain's request, the U.N. Committee of 24 was asked to send a visiting mission to the Western Sahara.[18] Most U.N. member-states were only too happy to see the Sahara question diverted to the ICJ. From the Moroccan standpoint, King Hassan, by referring the

Sahara question to the ICJ, effectively delayed the territory's decolonization, thus providing time to strengthen his country's position.

The first half of 1975 witnessed a hiatus in the Sahara dispute, with the involved parties occupied with preparation of their presentations before the ICJ. In February, to increase the pressure on Madrid to engage in serious negotiations with Rabat for a transfer of authority in the Sahara, Hassan renewed his demand for the return of the five Spanish enclaves on the northern coast of Morocco—Ceuta (Sebta) and Melilla, the fortress rocks of Alhucemas and Velez de la Gomera, and the Chaffarine (Zaffarine) Islands.[19] Spain was more irritated than pressured by the renewal of this demand, whose effect was to increase anti-Moroccan sentiment among the Spanish public. Within the Western Sahara itself, guerrilla activities against Spanish troops and military garrisons increased as several competing liberation groups tried to establish themselves as recognized forces. In consequence of Resolution 3292, a three-person U.N. mission visited the majority of cities and towns in the Sahara in May. The Polisario Front displayed the strength of its popular support to the mission by the fact that it was the only Saharan group able to organize mass demonstrations.

The hiatus was broken on May 23, 1975, when the Spanish government declared its intention "to transfer the sovereignty in the Territory of Sahara in the shortest time possible." Spain hoped that its withdrawal would not take place until after the ICJ opinion and an appropriate U.N. decision. Madrid's statement, however, left the door open for a quick unilateral exit from the Sahara in the event of a long legal and diplomatic delay that seriously compromised Spanish interests in the territory. The May 23 statement noted that Spain was prepared to take the "legitimate interests" of other states in the area into account in transferring sovereignty—which amounted to a public signal of Madrid's greater willingness to negotiate. The statement was the first public admission by Spain that it now placed the greatest emphasis on getting out of the Sahara quickly and that it did not rule out a unilateral withdrawal if the situation within the territory deteriorated badly.

Several factors had prompted Spain's decision to announce its departure, including the escalating pressures of guerrilla activity, the mutiny of local troops, and disapproval in the international community.[20] This sudden shift in Madrid's policy came in the wake of a series of setbacks and disappointments for the Spanish during the spring of 1975 in their efforts to prepare the Sahara for independence and to control public order. A major factor was the emergence of the militant and anti-Spanish Polisario Front as the dominant political and insurgent force in the territory. A second was the failure of Spain's own pro-Spanish independence group—the PUNS, launched in March 1975 at El Ayoun—to attract wide support among the Sahrawi population. Finally, the Spanish were disappointed by the demonstrated lack of strong identification with Spain among much of the civil population in the territory and even among the Saharan armed forces and police.

The effect of Spain's announcement of a possible rapid transfer of sovereignty in the Sahara was to increase tension in northwest Africa. Morocco had reinforced its troop deployments in border areas near the Sahara in September 1974; now, eight months later, Rabat again sent military reinforcements to the south and Algeria followed suit on its side of the border. In addition, the Algerians began to bring back the troops and equipment dispatched to Egypt at the start of the October 1973 Arab-Israeli War — a move that diplomatic observers in Algiers linked to rising tensions over the Sahara question.[21] The frequency of hostile articles in the presses of the two countries mounted, and a certain war fever was noticeable in both Morocco and Algeria during June 1975. At the same time, Rabat continued to coordinate with Nouakchott. Hassan met with Ould Daddah in Rabat, and a joint communiqué issued on June 12 after their meeting announced an agreement to cooperate to frustrate Spain's "maneuvers" designed to impede the ICJ proceedings.

The governments of both Morocco and Algeria were anxious to pursue bilateral negotiations in order to head off an armed conflict. In late June, Moroccan Foreign Minister Ahmed Laraki went to Algiers for several days of intensive talks. The high tension eased following a four-day visit to Rabat in early July by Algerian Foreign Minister Abdelaziz Bouteflika. At the conclusion of this visit, Morocco and Algeria issued a joint communiqué that suggested that the two countries had reached a compromise settlement of the Sahara question. In this communiqué, issued on July 4, 1975, Algeria repeated that it had no claim on Saharan territory. Both Rabat and Algiers expressed their determination to move ahead with joint economic projects previously agreed upon but not yet implemented. Most important, Algeria recorded "with a great satisfaction the understanding reached" by Morocco and Mauritania over the Western Sahara[22] — an apparent green light by the Boumediene regime to a takeover and partition of the territory by Rabat and Nouakchott.

There was considerable speculation at the time that the July 4 joint communiqué resulted from, and was reinforced by, important private agreements and understandings reached between Rabat and Algiers. The Moroccan-Mauritanian "understanding" endorsed by Algiers presumably referred to the secret agreement reached in October 1974 by Hassan and Ould Daddah to partition the Western Sahara between their two countries. In addition, there may have been an understanding that in return for Algerian acceptance of Moroccan-Mauritanian partition of the Sahara, Morocco would ratify the 1972 border agreement with Algeria. Finally, there may have been a firm agreement to go ahead with the joint exploitation of the

Gara Jebilet iron ore deposits in southwest Algeria—the second of the two Moroccan-Algerian agreements signed in Rabat in June 1972.

To the outside world, the July 4 joint communiqué suggested that Morocco and Algeria had reached a diplomatic breakthrough and had achieved a rapprochement over the Western Sahara and perhaps other contentious bilateral issues as well. This impression derived not only from the public commitments contained in the communiqué itself; it also was fed by the extensive publicity given the joint communiqué in Rabat and Algiers, the warm language used in subsequent public messages exchanged between Hassan and Boumediene, and the public displays of warm feelings by high officials in the days following July 4.

The implications of any Moroccan-Algerian rapprochement over the Western Sahara were of particular importance to Spain. Between the May 23 Spanish announcement on the transfer of sovereignty in the Sahara and the July 4 joint communiqué, Spain enjoyed considerable maneuverability among the Maghreb states interested in the future of its Saharan territory. If Morocco, Algeria, and Mauritania had now reached agreement on the Sahara issue, Spain had lost most of its leverage. In June, Madrid had invited the three states to attend four-party talks beginning July 9, but the invitation went unanswered. The Spanish recourse was to request U.N. Secretary-General Kurt Waldheim to sponsor four-party talks—a forum that was not likely to attract Morocco and Mauritania.

Despite any understandings that may have accompanied the joint communiqué of July 4, 1975, Algeria did not shift its position in the following months to support Morocco. In its presentation before the ICJ in mid-July, Algeria strongly reiterated its support of self-determination for the Sahrawi population and cited the need for a referendum organized and held under U.N. auspices. While asserting to the World Court that it was merely "an interested party" because of its shared border with the Spanish territory, Algeria nevertheless affirmed that intervention in support of national liberation struggles was lawful. These arguments clashed sharply with the position of Morocco, which presented itself to the court as the "immemorial possessor" of the Western Sahara. Morocco based its position on claims of sovereignty in the Western Sahara at the time of Spanish colonization and argued that since respect for territorial integrity took precedence over self-determination in international law, the Sahara ought to revert to Morocco without a referendum. Two weeks after its ICJ presentation, Algeria lobbied for recognition of the Polisario Front at the OAU summit meeting in Kampala, Uganda.

By mid-August, it was clear to Moroccan officials that Algeria had reneged on the July 4 communiqué. Algerians argued that the communiqué was vague and that it had been misunderstood by the Moroccans. One possible explanation for Algeria's seemingly inconsistent behavior is the argument that Bouteflika exceeded his government's instructions when he agreed to sign the joint communiqué and that Boumediene never approved the various understandings negotiated by his foreign minister. The circumstances and the timing of the joint communiqué, however, do not support this explanation. Bouteflika was in constant telephone contact with Boumediene during the drafting of the communiqué. It was reportedly Boumediene who had the reference to Moroccan-Mauritanian "agreement" (*accord*) over the Western Sahara in the draft communiqué changed to "understanding" (*entente*) in the final version. And the Algerians insisted during the drafting that the announcement of the communiqué be delayed until the evening of July 4 — after Bouteflika had returned to Algiers and Boumediene had had a chance to approve the final version.

The Moroccan disappointment with Algeria was evident in King Hassan's major policy speech on the Sahara problem on August 20. In this speech Hassan vowed that Morocco would recover the Western Sahara by the end of the year, through peaceful negotiations if possible but by force of arms if necessary. Morocco would not move decisively, however, until after the ICJ decision and subsequent U.N. resolution on the Sahara, both expected within two or three months. In a veiled reference to the Algerians, the king railed against the supposed friends of Morocco who reneged on their commitments. The speech was equally hostile toward the Spanish, who were accused of setting up a puppet government in the territory. Hassan declared that for Morocco, the Sahara was the equivalent of the Palestinian cause and Moroccans could expect the united support of the Arab world. Finally, the king announced that Morocco's relations with Third World countries would have to be re-evaluated if these states did not support the kingdom on the Sahara issue.

By the end of the summer of 1975, tensions were again high, not only between Morocco and Algeria but also between Morocco and Spain. Criticism of Algeria in the Moroccan press reached a high level. In addition to resentment against Algeria for having failed to shift its policy following the July 4 joint communiqué, Moroccan officials were further annoyed by what they perceived as collusion between Spain and Algeria to set up a puppet government in El Ayoun — a government that, in an independent Saharan state, would be responsive to Algerian political interests and Spanish economic interests. For its part, Algeria declared its unequivocal support for the principle of self-determination and increased material and diplomatic support for the Polisario Front.

As the parties to the Sahara dispute awaited the ICJ advisory opinion, it was clear that Algeria had become committed to opposing a Moroccan-Mauritanian takeover of the Western Sahara. One can only speculate why

Algerian leaders pulled back from the October 1974 and July 1975 endorsements of the Moroccan-Mauritanian solution. Some weight should be given to the importance that the Boumediene regime attached to the principle of self-determination — that is, to Algeria's ideological consistency. Another factor may have been Boumediene's unwillingness to accept the implications of Mauritania's close alliance with Morocco. Just two years earlier, a progressive Ould Daddah had denounced his agreements with France, and Mauritania had been very open to Algerian influence. Now, with Ould Daddah working in tandem with Hassan, Mauritania became a receptacle, not a barrier, to conservative Moroccan influence — a development that worked against a regional balance of power favorable to Algeria. Finally, Algerian leaders may have had second thoughts about their support of Rabat and Nouakchott and concluded that they had given up a strategic position unnecessarily.[23]

In retrospect, Algeria's change or reconsideration of its position was a critical factor in the evolution of the Western Sahara conflict. If Algeria had opted, at a minimum, to remain passive and neutral in the Sahara dispute during 1975 and 1976, limiting its support of the Polisario Front to humanitarian assistance to Sahrawi refugees, there is little question that the Sahara issue would have soon receded from international attention and that today there would be few remaining signs of an armed conflict.

The Tripartite Administration, October 1975–February 1976

On October 14, 1975, the report of the U.N. Visiting Mission, which had gone to the Western Sahara in the late spring, was published. The mission reported that within the Sahara the indigenous population "was categorically for independence and against the territorial claims of Morocco and Mauritania."[24] Among the political movements in the territory, it identified the Polisario Front as the most significant expression of Sahrawi opinion. In its conclusion the report called unanimously for a U.N. plebiscite in the Sahara on the question of independence.

On October 16, just two days after the publication of the mission's report, the ICJ rendered its long-awaited advisory opinion. The sixteen judges were of the unanimous opinion that the Western Sahara was not a territory without a master (*terra nullius*) at the time of its colonization by Spain. By votes of fourteen to two and fifteen to one, the judges found (1) legal ties of allegiance between the Moroccan sultan and some tribes in the Western Sahara, and (2) rights, including some land rights, which constituted legal ties between the Mauritanian entity and the Western Sahara. The court concluded, however, that these various legal ties did not constitute territorial sovereignty, and it reaffirmed the rights of the Sahrawi population to self-determination, as called for by the various UNGA resolutions from 1966 to 1973.[25] As one legal analyst summarized the thrust of the court's opinion: "The ICJ had ruled that Morocco and Mauritania have no valid claim to the Sahara based on historic title, but that, even if they did, contemporary international law accords priority to the Sahrawis' right of self-determination."[26]

In some diplomatic circles, there was a feeling that the ICJ advisory opinion was essentially a political decision to support the unimpeachable right of self-determination. In this view, if the legal investigation had been pursued to its logical conclusion, there is little doubt that it would have resulted in a judgment in favor of Moroccan sovereignty. One journalist, citing the exceptional complexity of the issue and the solid arguments of the various parties, termed the opinion the most ambiguous in the court's history.[27] Another source described the "lengthy and enigmatic opinion" as "a masterpiece of prudence and compromise, designed to give some satisfaction to each of the contestants but a decisive endorsement to none of them."[28] Other analysts read the opinion as an unequivocal rejection of Morocco's and Mauritania's historic claims.[29]

The Moroccan government interpreted the ICJ advisory opinion as a clear and strong endorsement of the kingdom's position. Moroccans seized upon the court's finding of legal ties to the Sahara, equated them with territorial sovereignty, and concluded that the United Nations' legal advisory organ had recognized Morocco's claim to the Spanish colony. The parts of the opinion that did not support Morocco were either ignored or discounted as misunderstandings of Moroccan legal traditions. This nationalistic and highly partisan reading of the ICJ opinion was articulated by Moroccan Foreign Minister M'hamed Boucetta in a 1980 interview:

> According to the constitutional Islamic laws at the time of 1860 to 1890, [relations of allegiance were] the essential relationship between the people of one region and the central power, at that time the sultan. All aspects of sovereignty were exercised at that time—it was the central power that nominated the administrators and the governors and the central power who levied taxation, and it was in the name of the central power that justice was carried out. The same money and stamps were used.[30]

The Moroccan government was in no way deterred by either the report of the U.N. Visiting Mission or the ICJ advisory opinion. On October 16, 1975, the same day the court's opinion was released, King Hassan addressed the Moroccan nation on television and proclaimed that the kingdom's historical claim to the Sahara had been vindicated. Hassan termed the World Court's opinion a final verdict and said that the time for decisive action had come. In a moment of high drama, the king announced that he would lead a massive peaceful march of 350,000 civilians, armed only with their Korans, to recover Morocco's Saharan territory. Hassan called on volunteers to begin to present themselves at government recruiting centers the following day. The ensuing preparations for the highly publicized Green March brought the confrontation over the Sahara to its highest point of tension.[31]

Prior to King Hassan's dramatic announcement, knowledge of the Green March had been kept from the outside world and even from all but a handful of Moroccans. The advance preparations for the march's unprecedented logistic efforts went on in complete secrecy. Detailed planning was limited to Hassan and four of his closest advisers.[32] The march was planned to last twelve days – sufficient time for the hundred-mile round-trip trek from the Moroccan-Saharan border to the outskirts of El Ayoun and then back to Tarfaya, just inside Moroccan territory. Since the marchers would find nothing to sustain them in the northern Sahara, all supplies – trucks, tents, blankets, food, and medicine – had to be provided.

The Moroccan Army was responsible for the organization, direction, and logistical supply of the Green March. Volunteers for the march were assembled in delegations drawn from all of Morocco's 28 provinces and two prefectures, accompanied by local secular and religious leaders. Provincial volunteer quotas were assigned, and as a security measure, some consideration was given to the political loyalty of the population of each province.[33]

The recruitment of volunteers for the march was intended to benefit from the considerable degree of unemployment in Morocco. By drawing from the mass of unemployed individuals, a large number of marchers could be recruited and assembled quickly with a minimum disruption of the country's productive capacity. For the unemployed, participation in the march offered the benefits of food, blankets, and a very small monetary subsidy.[34] As it turned out, the king's call for volunteers tapped an enormous wellspring of nationalist sentiment throughout Morocco. While the unemployed flocked to volunteer, so also a large number of Moroccans from all walks of life came out of factories and other jobs to sign up for the march. Within three days of Hassan's October 16 speech, the government announced that 524,000 volunteers had signed up at recruiting offices throughout the country – a total that permitted the rejection of individuals whose health or age made their participation questionable.

Within a week of announcing the Green March, King Hassan received firm support from the leaders of all of Morocco's political parties. Across the political spectrum, every party agreed to send a symbolic delegation to participate in the march, thus ensuring a show of national unity over the Sahara issue. In addition, Hassan received pledges of support from a number of outside sources, especially in the eastern Arab world. Egypt agreed to provide media coverage and offered military support if necessary.

Jordan, Gabon, and the Sudan promised to send symbolic delegations to join the march. The Palestine Liberation Organization (PLO) offered military aid. Saudi Arabia, Cameroon, the United Arab Emirates, Uganda, Qatar, Iraq, and Kuwait issued statements of support. Libya threatened war if the Sahara was not liberated — although the threat was directed against Spain and did not specifically support Morocco.

Though a bold and highly original idea, the Green March was also a risky undertaking. The march was likely to produce a confrontation with the Polisario Front (whose leaders announced they would mass people at the border to block the marchers' entry) or with Spain — or both — with Algeria in the wings. At a minimum, such a massive movement of civilians was fraught with the possibility of dangerous complications: problems in controlling unruly and highly emotional crowds at border assembly points; breakdowns in the supplying of food and water; and casualties from marchers who walked into Spanish minefields.

Whatever risks the Green March entailed, it offered King Hassan advantages over either doing nothing or undertaking a military intervention in the Sahara. If the king did nothing, he ran a definite risk that the Moroccan Army would move to recover the Sahara without him. If, on the other hand, he opted for military intervention, world public opinion would have condemned a Moroccan invasion, and the great powers would have intervened immediately with intense diplomatic pressure to stop a unilateral military move. In addition, the Moroccan Army could not expect to fare well against the much stronger Spanish forces. In the event of a full-scale invasion, some twelve thousand Moroccan troops, with very limited air support, would have found themselves badly outclassed by the sixteen thousand Spanish troops in the Sahara, plus an additional twenty thousand Spanish troops nearby in the Canary Islands — all with good air support and with considerable air power in reserve in Spain. And, in the end, a severe military defeat could have cost Hassan his throne.

King Hassan's principal objectives in organizing the Green March were diplomatic. The march would underscore Morocco's historical claim to the Saharan territory, and it would provide a psychological shock to the Spanish.

As a consequence of the preparations for the Green March, the weeks following the king's October 16 speech witnessed a flurry of diplomatic activity. Morocco used the organization of a large civilian march as a pressure tactic to induce Spain to negotiate a transfer of the Western Sahara on terms acceptable to Rabat (and Nouakchott). Generalissimo Francisco Franco, the fascist dictator who had ruled Spain with an iron hand for 36 years since the end of the 1936–1939 Spanish Civil War, fell seriously ill during this period, thus giving more leverage to the pro-Moroccan lobby in Madrid.

Algeria interpreted the report of the U.N. Visiting Mission and the ICJ advisory opinion as a clear endorsement of Saharan self-determination by means of a referendum under U.N. auspices. The Boumediene regime viewed with great misgivings Moroccan preparations for a massive civilian march into the Sahara. On November 2, the Algerian representative to the United Nations stated to the Security Council that if the massive Moroccan march crossed into Saharan territory, it would have dire consequences for peace and future relations in the area. He warned in solemn terms: "If the Security Council and the international community were not in a position to assume their responsibilities, Algeria would assume its own responsibilities. Algeria was not prepared. . . to recognize or to endorse any situation of *fait accompli* which could result from any kind of unilateral actions."[35]

At the end of October, in the midst of intense negotiations at the ministerial level between Morocco and Mauritania on one side and Spain on the other, Algeria sent its own representative to Madrid. Algiers was fearful that Spain, if offered economic incentives, would sell out its Saharan colony to Rabat and Nouakchott. The Boumediene regime had leverage of its own to bring to bear in the negotiations in the form of natural gas supplies. Madrid had made an economic cooperation agreement with Algiers in 1972, formally signed in 1974, that committed Spain to purchase 4.5 billion cubic meters of Algerian natural gas annually over the next twenty years. Algeria became virtually the sole supplier of natural gas to Spain and accounted for a third of all Spanish trade with Africa.[36] Algerian threats to cut supplies of natural gas to Spain were ultimately unsuccessful — perhaps, as one observer suggests, because Saudi Arabia countered Algeria's leverage by offering to fill any of Spain's needs in oil and gas.[37]

During the last two weeks of October and the first week of November 1975, the U.N. Security Council, meeting at Spain's request, adopted four largely innocuous resolutions in an ineffectual effort to head off the Green March. The first resolution asked Secretary-General Waldheim to consult with the involved parties and appealed to those parties to exercise restraint and moderation. Acting on this vague Security Council mandate, the secretary-general made a three-day trip in late October to Spain and northwest Africa to hold discussions with the heads of state of the involved countries in order to assist in the search for an acceptable solution to the Sahara problem. During his trip, Waldheim reportedly proposed a temporary U.N. administration of the Western Sahara for six months — that is, until a U.N.-controlled referendum could be organized. This proposal, which was thought to reflect the preference of a majority of the General Assembly, was accepted by Algeria, Spain, and Mauritania, but was rejected by Morocco.[38]

The second Security Council resolution, following Waldheim's short trip, merely called on the involved parties to avoid unilateral action and asked the secretary-general to continue and intensify his efforts. To continue the consultations, Waldheim dispatched as his special envoy French Ambassador André Lewin, who visited the capitals of the involved countries from November 4 to 6. The other two resolutions, adopted soon after the march had begun, called on King Hassan to end the march and to withdraw from Saharan territory. In all these "toothless" resolutions, it was reportedly the United States and France that successfully resisted more forceful actions by the Security Council.[39]

As preparations for the Green March progressed with the train and truck transport of large numbers of volunteers to the Tarfaya area, the prospect of a peaceful invasion of the Sahara by 350,000 Moroccans placed Spain in an awkward position. By the fall of 1975, the Spanish had given up hope of hanging on to their heavy phosphate investment and wanted only to get out of the Sahara gracefully. The official Spanish position called for a transfer of sovereignty to an assembly elected by the Sahrawis. Spain did not wish to appear to be leaving its colony in a manner counter to the wishes of the international community as expressed in the 1973 UNGA resolution calling for a referendum leading to self-determination. At the same time, Madrid did not want to get in the middle of an Arab dispute and was open to a solution agreeable to all three interested Arab states—Morocco, Mauritania, and Algeria. Above all, the Spanish Army was determined not to get involved in a colonial war in the Sahara, especially over a territory that the government had already announced it was prepared to give up. Nevertheless, the honor of the Spanish Army was involved, and Spain would not allow itself to be pushed ignominiously out of the Sahara by Moroccan forces. Thus, Madrid responded to King Hassan's October 16 speech by stating that its units in the Sahara would not fire upon peaceful marchers but that force would be used to repel any armed invasion.

Within the Spanish government and military, there were serious differences of opinion on the modalities of Saharan decolonization and the problems posed by the Green March. One faction, led by Foreign Minister Pedro Cortina Mauri, stressed the need to honor Spain's diplomatic commitment to the international community and favored a referendum in the Sahara. This faction's position was in line with General Franco's policy of leading the Sahrawis first to autonomy and then to self-determination, which probably would have led to independence. A second faction, composed mainly of army officers serving in the Sahara, shared this position, but for different reasons. These officers wanted to discharge their mission—the maintenance of public order in preparation for the holding of a referendum—in an honorable manner and to avoid casualties among their troops. They were opposed to ceding the territory. A third faction was composed of conservatives, or "ultras," and was headed by José Solis Ruiz, minister and secretary-general of the Falangist movement. This group favored an understanding with Morocco and opposed an independent Saharan state, which it feared would work against Spain's national interest. In particular, such a state, dominated by the Polisario Front, would aid the Movement for the Self-Determination and Independence of the Canary Archipelago (MPAIAC), a small group headquartered in Algiers that periodically attacked Spanish control of the Canary Islands.[40]

Morocco's attempts to negotiate a transfer of the Sahara with Spain were played out against the backdrop of General Franco's terminal illness and death. In the confusion created by Franco's incapacity, much of the Spanish government's decision making ground to a halt. In this situation of government paralysis, the initiative in Madrid passed to a small group of conservatives backed by the army and headed by President of the Government Carlos Arias Navarro. This pro-Moroccan lobby was composed especially of people from Franco's immediate entourage.[41] In the third week of October, after Franco's serious illness had occurred, Arias sent Solis Ruiz as a special envoy to confer with King Hassan in Marrakesh. Solis's mission, followed shortly by a visit of Moroccan Foreign Minister Ahmed Laraki to Madrid, marked the beginning of an intensive Moroccan-Spanish dialogue.

By the end of October 1975, preparations for the Green March had reached such an advanced state and national support within Morocco was running so high that the mammoth undertaking could not be called off easily. At the same time, since Rabat's negotiations with Madrid had entered a promising and possibly critical state, it was important for Hassan to avoid actions that would antagonize the Spanish government. On November 2, Prince Juan Carlos, who had become Spain's acting head of state, flew to El Ayoun where he pledged to preserve the prestige and honor of the Spanish Army and protect the rights of the Sahrawis. In this delicate and very tense situation, the immediate requirement of the Moroccan-Spanish negotiations was to find a compromise formula that would allow the march to take place, yet would restrain the marchers so that they stopped well short of El Ayoun and preferably before there was a confrontation with the Spanish Army.

The Green March crossed into the Western Sahara on November 6. In addition to representatives of all of Morocco's political parties, the march included delegations from Saudi Arabia, Bahrain, Jordan, Kuwait, Oman, and Qatar. By the time the marchers entered the Sahara, the Spanish troops deployed along the border had withdrawn and established a "dissuasion line," protected by twenty thousand mines, about twelve kilometers from the frontier. The mass of Moroccan marchers stopped short of this line, thus sparing the Spanish Army the dilemma of choosing between further retreat or firing on unarmed civilians. On November 9, King Hassan received word that a turning point in the negotiations had occurred: the Spanish had finally agreed to exclude the Algerians from the negotiations, and a Moroccan-Mauritanian agreement with Spain was now within reach.[42] With this information in hand, Hassan immediately instructed the 350,000 marchers to return to Morocco.

In retrospect, the Green March appears a bizarre event. Once preparations for the massive operation began, the march developed a momentum of its own. The complicated and enormous logistical arrangements required to transport and sustain the marchers functioned with impressive efficiency and a minimum of breakdowns. The march was accomplished without a major disruption of Morocco's productive capacity. The large number of civilian trucks requisitioned for the operation returned from the march soon enough to collect the fall citrus and wheat harvests, before a long delay in the negotiations with Spain might well have done Morocco considerable economic damage.[43] In the end, the march went far enough into the Western Sahara to allow King Hassan to save face, yet it stopped in time to save the honor of the Spanish Army.[44] And measured against its major objective — to pressure Spain into serious negotiations about the fate of the Sahara — the Green March must be judged an unqualified success.

In a last-ditch effort to undermine the negotiations, from which Algeria had now been excluded, President Boumediene focused his considerable powers of persuasion on Mauritania. During the previous year, while closely coordinating his Sahara policy with Morocco, President Ould Daddah had kept his options open by putting forth an independent claim to the Western Sahara in the Mauritanian presentation before the ICJ: in the event of a U.N.-controlled referendum, there was always the possibility that the Sahrawis would opt to join or federate with their Mauritanian brethren. Boumediene summoned Ould Daddah to a hastily arranged meeting at Bechar in southwest Algeria on November 10. At this meeting Boumediene warned Ould Daddah of the possibly disastrous consequences of siding with "reactionary and feudal" Morocco against "revolutionary" Algeria on the Sahara issue and urged the Mauritanian leader to reconsider his options. According to Ould Daddah, Boumediene underlined the weakness and vulnerability of Mauritania and threatened to use whatever force necessary to prevent a Moroccan-Mauritanian takeover of the Sahara:

> Your country is weak, fragile, with long borders difficult to defend. We have decided, against all comers, to support the Sahrawis, in the name of revolu-

tionary solidarity. We are going to place at their disposal all that we possess. And, if it is necessary, we will permit the involvement of fifty thousand, even one hundred thousand, Algerian volunteers to occupy the Sahara. They will also be able to attack you inside your borders, destroy your economic installations, and even attack your capital.[45]

Ould Daddah, convinced that Mauritania's interests in the Sahara issue were with Morocco, resisted Boumediene's threats and continued his alliance with Rabat.

Negotiations resumed in earnest in Madrid on November 11, and on November 14, Spain, Morocco, and Mauritania issued a joint communiqué noting agreement on a set of principles for an interim administration in the Western Sahara. According to the terms of this accord (see Appendix A), Spain agreed to leave the Sahara by February 28, 1976, and to transfer administrative authority—though not sovereignty—to a joint Moroccan-Mauritanian administration. In the interim period, as Spain gradually withdrew its military forces and civilian personnel, the three countries would share administrative responsibilities. It also agreed that the views of the Sahrawi population, as expressed through the Jemaa, would be respected. Four days later, on November 18, the Spanish Cortes endorsed the Tripartite Agreement by approving a law that authorized the decolonization of the Sahara.

According to some observers, the Tripartite Agreement also contained secret terms. Spain allegedly received considerable economic concessions, including a major share of the Bu Craa phosphate operations and fishing rights off the Saharan and Moroccan coasts in return for transferring control of the Western Sahara to Morocco and Mauritania.[46] Some of these terms are contradictory, however, and, apart from the retention of a 35 percent interest in Fosbucraa, very little evidence has materialized to support the notion of large-scale economic concessions to Spain.

It is more likely that within the Spanish Council of Ministers, the key decision-making group in Madrid, a majority of conservatives favoring an agreement with Morocco were able—in the midst of a domestic political crisis—to prevail over Foreign Minister Cortina for reasons of state: the desire to avoid a colonial war in the Sahara and the conviction that Spain's national interests would be better served if the territory passed to Moroccan-Mauritanian control instead of becoming an independent state dominated by the Polisario Front. This analysis is at least partly supported by the results of a Spanish parliamentary inquiry held in March 1978. According to the testimony of the dozen officials most directly involved in the question of Saharan decolonization, the major reasons that led the Spanish government to abandon the Sahrawi population rather abruptly were pressure in favor of Morocco by France and the United States (both of which preferred not to see the emergence of a new state in the Sahara with a "progressive" orientation); advantages to Spain from a transfer of the Sahara to Morocco (cessation of Morocco's claim to the Spanish enclaves and prevention of Algerian access to the Atlantic, seen as threatening to the Canary Islands); fear of the repercussions (seen in the revolution in neighboring Portugal) of colonial conflicts on the domestic political situation; and the danger of compromising the consolidation of the fledgling monarchy by maintaining a Spanish presence in the Sahara in the uncertain conditions of November 1975.[47]

If the Tripartite Agreement allowed Spain and Morocco to avoid a conflict, this same accord spurred a conflict between Algeria (and the Polisario Front) on one side and Morocco and Mauritania on the other. Boumediene was reportedly furious when he learned of the Madrid agreement. He had counted on the Spanish to respect the requirements of the various UNGA resolutions on Saharan decolonization so often invoked by Spanish Foreign Minister Cortina, a consistent supporter of Algeria. At the same time, he doubted that Spain and Morocco would ever be able to reach an understanding on the Sahara—especially after Madrid had resisted for so many years Rabat's efforts to negotiate a solution. Algerian leaders considered the Tripartite Agreement an act of Spanish treachery. The combination of Algerian surprise and bitterness may be linked to the possible existence of a secret agreement on the fate of the Sahara reached by Spain, Algeria, and the Polisario Front either at the beginning of 1975 or in September or October of that year. The agreement allegedly called for Spain to grant independence to the Western Sahara through a shrewdly controlled process of self-determination; Spain's interests in the territory would be preserved, and Spanish forces would turn over their posts progressively to the Polisario Front.[48]

At the more basic level of regional geopolitics, the Tripartite Agreement of November 14, 1975, represented a major victory for Moroccan diplomacy and a clear setback for Algerian policy. The Madrid accord frustrated Algeria on several counts. There now would be no Saharan ministate that Algiers could dominate. Mauritania, viewed as a swing state in the northwest African balance of power, was closely tied to Morocco and thereby removed from Algerian influence. In a November 21 interview with the French Communist party journal *L'Humanité*, Boumediene articulated his sense of the Western Sahara's importance in the regional balance of power as viewed from Algiers: "The Sahara is part of Algeria's security zone. . . . We have succeeded in establishing a certain equilibrium in the region; we cannot play with it."[49] At the level of international prestige, Algeria had been able in Third World affairs, especially in the Committee of 77 and the U.N. Fourth Committee, to play a major role quite out of proportion to its human and material resources. A defeat of a clear Algerian objective was therefore liable to damage Algerian leadership claims throughout the Third World.

Rather than accept defeat on an issue of considerable regional importance, the Boumediene regime girded up for a long drawn out struggle to contest the Moroccan-Mauritanian takeover of the Western Sahara. Algeria declared the Tripartite Agreement null and void and mobilized diplomatic support within the United Nations to ensure the strict application of the principle of self-determination to the decolonization of the Sahara. Just as he had threatened in his meeting with Ould Daddah at Bechar, Boumediene threw his full support behind the Polisario's war of national liberation.

Although significant Algerian backing for the Polisario Front began in the summer of 1975, this support was intensified, amplified, and diversified following the Tripartite Agreement in November. This policy—which has continued until the present—stands in sharp contrast to Algeria's very modest support of the Polisario from the time of the front's creation in May 1973 until mid-1975. During the first two years of the front's existence, the Boumediene regime even confiscated arms sent to the Polisario by Libya on the backs of camels or in Land Rovers across Algeria. Algerian authorities were somewhat disillusioned from their experience with Eduardo Moha's Morehob group in 1973 (see Chapter Two) and, partly as a result, became cautious in their dealings with Saharan liberation movements. Thus, as late as July 1975, a Polisario spokesman described Algeria's support somewhat bitterly as "extremely discreet."[50]

On the domestic political front, the Boumediene regime launched a well-orchestrated campaign in early December 1975 to drum up popular enthusiasm for the Polisario's struggle. To mobilize a population that was lukewarm about the Sahara issue, the Algerian government staged a Sahara Solidarity Week, which featured numerous public rallies and the establishment of a special fund for the support of the Polisario Front. In addition, Algeria upgraded its own military preparedness by reinforcing the garrisons along the Moroccan border in the Bechar and Tindouf regions and negotiating an estimated $500 million arms agreement with the Soviet Union.

The United Nations' reaction to the Tripartite Agreement was ambiguous. On the one hand, the Fourth Committee condemned the Madrid accord on November 27. On the other hand, the General Assembly passed two somewhat conflicting resolutions on December 10. Resolution 3458A, approved by 88 votes to 0 with 41 abstentions, was pro-Algerian and called for Saharan self-determination through U.N. supervision. Resolution 3458B, in contrast, was approved by the much smaller margin of 56 to 42 with 34 abstentions and was sympathetic to Morocco and Mauritania; it took note of the Tripartite Agreement and dealt with Saharan self-determination by reference to consultations in the presence of a U.N. observer. This circumstance of two conflicting resolutions typified the United Nations' inability to make a solid contribution to the solution of the Saharan decolonization issue—a situation aptly described by a quip often heard during the December 1975 meetings of the General Assembly that "the Algerians had the votes, the Moroccans, the territory."[51]

Following the signing of the Tripartite Agreement in mid-November, Spain rapidly withdrew its troops and administrative personnel from the Western Sahara. The withdrawal of Spanish military forces was completed on January 12, 1976. To fill the vacuum, Morocco moved quickly on the heels of the departing Spanish to establish an administrative structure and a security force in the northern Sahara. Moroccan Army units positioned themselves along the Algerian-Saharan frontier. On November 25, 1975, Ahmed Bensouda, director of King Hassan's royal cabinet and Morocco's newly appointed deputy governor for the interim administration in the Sahara, arrived in El Ayoun to assume his duties. That same week, Smara, a spiritual center with a population of about eight thousand and a Polisario stronghold, was occupied. Two weeks later, on December 11, a Moroccan force of about four thousand occupied El Ayoun, the administrative capital and, with a population of about twenty-five thousand, the largest city in the Sahara. A variety of lesser officials sent from Rabat soon began to take up positions in the Saharan capital. Rabat established postal service, airline connections, and telephone links with the northern Sahara, and army units gradually occupied major military outposts in the area.

In the southern Sahara, Mauritania proceeded simultaneously to establish security and install an administration. With fewer resources and a relatively small number of trained troops and administrators, the Mauritanians required considerable assistance from their Moroccan ally in order to take over their zone of the Western Sahara. As of November 1975, the Mauritanian Army numbered only about one thousand, the air force two hundred, the navy one hundred, and the gendarmerie some seven hundred men. To bolster and build up Mauritania's small armed forces so that they could cope with challenges from Polisario Front guerrilla units, President Ould Daddah ordered a full military mobilization on December 10. The weakness of Mauritanian military forces was evidenced by their inability to dislodge the Polisario from the Saharan town of La Guera, six miles from the Mauritanian seaport of Nouadhibou, until Moroccan units joined in the battle.

During the two months following the announcement of the Tripartite Agreement, the Polisario Front's combatant strength increased rapidly from an estimated eight hundred to about three thousand. At least two thousand of the new Polisario soldiers came from three groups with previous military experience: the Saharan territorial police, the "nomadic troops," and the Sahrawis who had served in the regular Spanish Army in the Sahara. These men brought to the front not only their training, discipline, and knowledge of the terrain, but also their weapons,[52] and they have constituted the experienced core of the Polisario military forces since early 1976. At the same time, however, other Sahrawis from these same three groups opted not to join the ranks of the Polisario. Thus, about eight hundred of the twelve hundred territorial police reportedly rallied to the Moroccan administration in late December.[53]

Throughout the Sahara, Moroccan and Mauritanian army units encountered heavy resistance from Polisario Front guerrilla forces, fueled and supported by Algeria. In addition, Polisario operations extended into Mauritania, and in early December the front simultaneously attacked six different locations in Mauritania. Especially hard hit was Ain Ben Tili along the border with Sakiet al-Hamra.[54] The Polisario claimed in late December that its forces had carried the war into Moroccan territory, although there is no confirming evidence for this claim.

During the three-and-a-half months of the tripartite interim administration (November 14, 1975–February 26, 1976), the Polisario Front's ability to prevent the Moroccan-Mauritanian takeover of the Sahara was seriously compromised by two factors. The first was a tactical error. The Polisario forces initially attempted to hold towns and to engage Moroccan troops in fixed battles, but they ran up against the Moroccans' superior numbers and firepower. Chastened and bloodied by this experience, the front's units reverted to the classic guerrilla tactics of small, hit-and-run harassment operations. By effectively employing Land Rovers on the rocky terrain of the northern Sahara, Polisario guerrillas were able to mine roads and ambush Moroccan patrols. Second, the Polisario Front was preoccupied during the period of the interim administration with the relocation of tens of thousands of Sahrawi refugees. According to one Polisario official, the front had to devote two-thirds of its efforts to organizing and teaching during this period and had only the remaining third to spend on fighting.[55] The Polisario initially grouped the bulk of the refugees in camps at Oum Dreiga, Tifariti, and Guelta Zemmur, in Rio de Oro near the Mauritanian border. When these towns were occupied by the Moroccan Army in the first few months of 1976, the refugees were relocated in camps in the Tindouf region of southwest Algeria.

In the northern Sahara, King Hassan's soldiers and administrators were perceived more as invaders than liberators, and as invaders they encountered strong anti-Moroccan feeling among the Sahrawi population. Many Sahrawis in El Ayoun rejected offers to remain in their positions under a Moroccan administration. Rather than acquiesce in a Moroccan annexation, a substantial number of Sahrawis in Sakiet al-Hamra closed their businesses and went into the desert or joined the Polisario Front.

Anti-Moroccan feeling among the Sahrawis was exacerbated by the heavy-handed nature of the Moroccan takeover. To establish security in the northern Sahara, the Moroccan Army found it necessary to control the population; this required forcing the remaining nomads into settled urban centers that could be fortified. This policy of forced settlement reportedly led to such brutal tactics as poisoning wells and the slaughtering of camels, although the Spanish had already removed some of the camels to the Canary Islands.[56] The lack of thorough documentation makes it difficult to assess the precise extent of these harsh tactics, but there is little doubt that the Moroccan Army and Air Force used considerable force as they moved into the northern Sahara. This judgment is supported by evidence gathered by human rights organizations—the Minority Rights Group, Amnesty International, and the International Federation for the Rights of Man—suggesting widespread suppression of the civilian population, including the use of napalm against refugees.

In the southern Sahara, the Mauritanian takeover was accomplished with a good deal less coercion. For one thing, the ethnic affinities between the Sahrawis and the Moors, who both speak Hassaniyya Arabic, facilitated a relatively smooth transition from Spanish to Mauritanian administration. There was little anti-Mauritanian sentiment to be found among the population in Rio de Oro. Another factor derived from the weakness of the Mauritanian military. Perhaps because they lacked the firepower and numbers of the Moroccan Army, the Mauritanians employed relatively little force as they moved into their zone of the Sahara and thus did not alienate the local population.

During the period of the interim administration, many Sahrawis fled their homes in the uncertainty that surrounded the Spanish withdrawal and the Moroccan-Mauritanian takeover. In several towns in Sakiet al-Hamra, only the very young and the elderly remained. To remove the maximum number of people from the control of the incoming administrations, the Polisario Front encouraged and assisted the flight of a large number of Sahrawis out of the territory. In a time of great uncertainty, the Polisario was able to play upon traditional Sahrawi habits of nomadism and to create a psychosis of fear.[57] On the other hand, many Sahrawi merchants and shopkeepers in the urban centers, especially El Ayoun, were sympathetic to the Moroccan-Mauritanian takeover, perhaps because they anticipated the establishment of a secure order beneficial to commerce. The Tekna and Ulad Delim tribes have a tradition of political adaptability, and a good number of Sahrawis simply waited to see which way the political and military winds would blow.

The size of the Sahrawi exodus during late 1975 and early 1976 (see Chapter Two) has become a matter of partisan debate. There are certain similarities to the flight of Arab refugees from Palestine in 1948-1949. In both cases there is sharp disagreement over the number of refugees and the cause of their flight. Some Sahrawis, who supported the Polisario Front or did not want to live under the control of the new administrations, left voluntarily. Others left out of fear—to escape the intimidation and repression of the incoming armies, either real or greatly exaggerated by the Polisario. Still others left at the urging and encouragement of the Polisario Front. Although the actual number of refugees is not known, it is likely that within a few months between a third and a half of the Sahrawi population left the Western Sahara and was resettled by the Polisario Front in refugee camps in southwest Algeria.

In February 1976, U.N. Secretary-General Waldheim sent a special representative, Swedish Ambassador Olaf Rydbeck, on a two-week exploratory mission to Madrid and the Western Sahara. Rydbeck hoped to study the modalities of a referendum in the territory through which the Sahrawi population could exercise its right of self-determination, as called for by both texts of UNGA Resolution 3458. While Algeria favored Rydbeck's mission, Morocco viewed it with suspicion and wanted it limited to information gathering. On his return to New York, Rydbeck announced to journalists that his visit had convinced him that the military situation in the Sahara made a significant consultation of the Sahrawi population "very difficult, if not impossible."[58]

During the last few weeks of the tripartite administration, Algerian and Moroccan troops clashed twice at Amgala, an oasis settlement southeast of Smara in Sakiet al-Hamra, and in the first battle about a hundred Algerian soldiers were taken prisoner. Aside from these two clashes, Algeria refrained from military intervention in the Sahara. The first Amgala battle was an accidental exception as the Algerian Army tried to withdraw before the arrival of the incoming Moroccan forces. In place of direct military involvement, Algeria supported the Polisario Front's guerrilla warfare with money, weapons, and equipment and provided training and a vital territorial sanctuary in the Tindouf region. Thus, by backing Polisario harassment operations, Algeria, while avoiding direct involvement itself, tried to oppose the Moroccan-Mauritanian takeover of the Western Sahara.

The Attempted Partition, February 1976–August 1979

As the tripartite administration of the Western Sahara concluded at the end of February 1976, Morocco and Mauritania attempted to incorporate the former Spanish colony into their own territories. At the same time, Rabat and Nouakchott tried to satisfy the requirements of UNGA Resolution 3458B of December 10, 1975, which called for Saharan self-determination through consultations with the assistance of a U.N. representative. On February 26, 1976, two days before the deadline stipulated by the Tripartite Agreement, Spain ended its presence in the Sahara. That same day, Morocco convened an "extraordinary meeting" of the Jemaa. The 65 members of the 102-man assembly present at this meeting voted unanimously to ratify the Tripartite Agreement and to reintegrate the Western Sahara into Morocco and Mauritania.[59]

Neither Spain nor the United Nations recognized the vote of the Jemaa. Immediately after the ratification of the Tripartite Agreement, the last Spanish governor in the territory, Commander Don Rafael Valdes Iglesias, declared that Spain no longer exercised any authority in the Sahara and deliberately absented himself from any further actions by the Jemaa. Spanish Foreign Minister Cortina, in a note to U.N. Secretary-General Waldheim, made clear Madrid's view that its withdrawal involved the transfer of administrative authority only, which left the question of sovereignty unresolved. Although a signatory of the Tripartite Agreement (which called for respect of Sahrawi opinion as expressed by the Jemaa), Spain shifted its position in the months following its withdrawal and began to call for consultation of the Sahrawi population under the supervision of a U.N. representative. For a variety of reasons, Waldheim refused Morocco's request to send an observer to the Jemaa meeting. The secretary-general declined on the grounds that the consultation should have been under U.N. supervision. And, in Waldheim's judgment, since neither Spain nor the tripartite administration had taken the necessary measures to assure the exercise of the right of self-determination, the presence of a U.N. observer would not have fulfilled the requirements of UNGA Resolutions 3458A and 3458B.[60]

The Polisario Front rejected the vote of the Jemaa and raised serious questions about the assembly's composition and legitimacy. The Polisario stressed that 67 of the 102 members of this territorial assembly had met at Guelta Zemmur on November 28, 1975, and signed a declaration dissolving the Jemaa and reaffirming "their unconditional support to the Polisario Front as the sole legitimate representative of the Sahrawi people."[61] To bolster its position, the front produced 57 members of the Jemaa at a press conference in Algiers on December 6 and two weeks later claimed that 97 Jemaa members had come over to the side of the Polisario. Not to be outdone, Morocco claimed that on December 12, 85 members of the Jemaa met in regular session in El Ayoun, including 10 who had earlier signed the Guelta Zemmur declaration, and that on December 22, 72 members endorsed the Tripartite Agreement in writing. Rabat could point out that both Jemaa President Khatri Ould al-Joumani and Vice-President Ahmed Ould al-Bachir had sworn allegiance to King Hassan on November 3, 1975, and January 14, 1976, respectively. Morocco alleged that Jemaa members had been forced, against their will, to meet at Guelta Zemmur and then go to Algeria and that when given an opportunity, enough of them had returned to allow the reconvening of the assembly on February 26, 1976. There is little question that Jemaa members were faced with, and responded to, pressures and blandishments from both sides. Given the contradictory claims and figures, one is left to conclude that some forty of the Jemaa members who had declared their support of the Polisario Front at Guelta Zemmur later voted in El Ayoun to ratify the Tripartite Agreement and to reintegrate the Western Sahara into Morocco and Mauritania.[62]

Despite the lack of international recognition, Morocco and Mauritania took the position that the Sahrawi population had exercised its right of self-determination through the vote of the Jemaa, and King Hassan stated that the Saharan issue was now closed. In support of this position are a variety of precedents in the decolonization of African territories. The Jemaa of the Western Sahara, in its composition and the manner of its election and selection, was fairly typical of the assemblies and legislative councils that often enacted the independence of African countries, including Somalia, the Sudan, Libya, and the French African territories.[63] Beyond Africa the decolonization of West Irian was similar to that of the Western Sahara. In 1969, in a process recommended and then ratified by the UNGA, the former Dutch colonial territory became part of Indonesia through collective consultations held with the indigenous population.

The Polisario Front moved quickly on the heels of the Jemaa vote. The following day, February 27, 1976, the front announced the creation of an independent Saharan state. At a gathering attended by journalists and supporters (the Polisario claims to have met in Bir Lahlu in Sakiet al-Hamra, whereas Morocco claims that the meeting took place in Algerian territory), M'hamed Ould Ziou, president of the Provisional Saharan National Council, proclaimed the birth of the SDAR. According to the communiqué issued at the time by the council, the SDAR was created as "a free, independent, sovereign state ruled by an Arab national democratic system of progressive unionist orientation and of Islamic religion."[64] A week later, on March 4, at a press conference in Algiers, Polisario Front spokesman Ahmed-Baba Miské announced the formation of an eight-man SDAR government of little-known Polisario figures. Mohamed Ould Ahmed, who had been in charge of the front's foreign relations, was named prime minister, and Ibrahim Hakim, a former Mauritanian diplomat, became foreign minister. The defense minister in the government-in-exile was Brahim Ghali Ould Mustapha, who had served from May 1973 to August 1974 as the Polisario Front's first secretary-general.

The creation of the SDAR marked a qualitative escalation of the Sahara conflict. The declaration of Western Saharan independence gave the

Polisario Front a greater margin to maneuver internationally. Instead of a struggling liberation movement, the front now had a government-in-exile that could compete against Morocco and Mauritania for international recognition. The creation of a Saharan republic also emphasized Algeria's commitment to Saharan independence and further reduced the chances that the Boumediene regime would accept a face-saving solution to the conflict. It was — and is — considerably more difficult for Algiers to abandon a Saharan republic, as distinct from the Polisario Front.

At the same time, however, the Polisario lost a short-term diplomatic advantage. At the time of the SDAR's creation, the OAU Council of Ministers was meeting in Addis Ababa, Ethiopia. The front was rapidly gaining momentum at this meeting for recognition as the legitimate liberation movement in the Sahara.[65] The rationale for this push for recognition of the Polisario Front suddenly disappeared. To be recognized as a new state, the SDAR now needed to begin, in a new procedure, to gain the support of a two-thirds majority of OAU members, as opposed to only a simple majority required for the Polisario's recognition as a liberation movement. The OAU compromised on this divisive issue by voting that recognition of the Polisario Front's provisional government was the prerogative of individual countries. The creation of the SDAR thus came as a pleasant surprise to Moroccan and Mauritanian diplomats. On the other side, there is some evidence that the decision to create an independent Saharan state was strongly opposed by some Algerian and Polisario leaders.[66]

During the first several months of 1976, as positions hardened on both sides, Moroccan-Algerian relations declined to a state of nonmilitary but prolonged antagonism. In late 1975 and early 1976, the Boumediene regime expelled thirty to forty thousand Moroccans, most of whom had lived for a long time in the Oran region of western Algeria. In early March, Algeria recognized the SDAR. Rabat and Nouakchott responded immediately by breaking diplomatic relations with Algiers. The war of words between Morocco and Algeria, which had begun in earnest during the fall of 1975, settled into a dreary propaganda exercise as each country's press highlighted and attacked the hostile policies of the neighboring government — an exercise that has continued, with sporadic abatements, until the present.

In the spring of 1976, Rabat and Nouakchott worked out the details of a division of the Sahara. On April 14, in an attempt to establish formal sovereignty over the Western Sahara, Morocco and Mauritania signed an agreement to partition the disputed territory. As shown in Map 4, this agreement set the Moroccan-Mauritanian border in the Sahara along a straight line starting at the 24th parallel on the coast and running southeast to a point near the 23rd parallel on the eastern boundary. The partition took into account Saharan tribal areas and tried to avoid as much as possible dividing

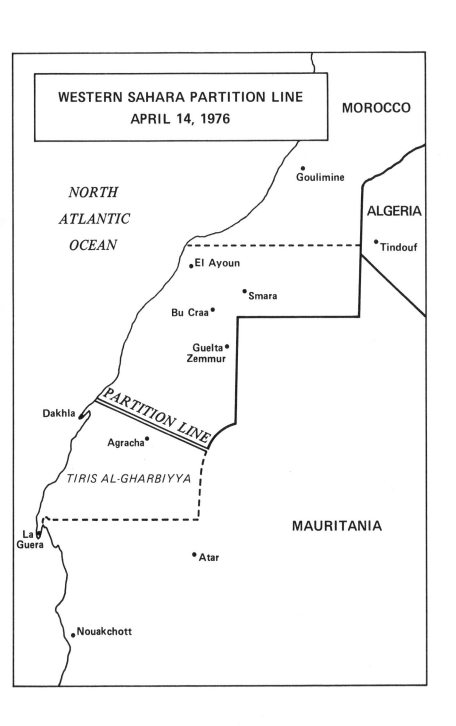

WESTERN SAHARA PARTITION LINE
APRIL 14, 1976

MOROCCO

NORTH
ATLANTIC
OCEAN

ALGERIA

Goulimine

Tindouf

El Ayoun

Smara

Bu Craa

Guelta
Zemmur

Dakhla

PARTITION LINE

Agracha

TIRIS AL-GHARBIYYA

La
Guera

MAURITANIA

Atar

Nouakchott

tribes. Thus, the area of the Ulad Delim was to the south of the new boundary while that of the Izarguien was entirely within the Moroccan portion to the north.[67]

According to the terms of the partition agreement, Morocco acquired the northern two-thirds of the Sahara, which contains El Ayoun, the capital and largest city, Smara, Boujdour, and the Bu Craa phosphate deposits. Mauritania acquired the southern third of the territory, which includes rich fishing grounds off the Atlantic coast, unexploited iron ore deposits at Agracha, and the port of Dakhla with a harbor of excellent potential. The two countries also signed an economic cooperation agreement that called for joint exploitation of all natural resources in the "recovered provinces," both underground and offshore. While this agreement allowed Nouakchott in principle to participate in the Bu Craa mining operation, there is no evidence that Mauritania in fact benefited economically from the phosphate wealth in the Moroccan zone. Morocco divided its portion of the Sahara into three provinces—El Ayoun, Smara, and Boujdour—while Mauritania incorporated the remainder as the province of Tiris al-Gharbiyya.

During the first few months of 1976, both Morocco and Mauritania extended their civilian administrative structures in the Sahara to fill the vacuum left by the departing Spanish and to consolidate control over the territory. In an effort to integrate the northern Sahara fully into the Moroccan motherland, Rabat sent personnel from several government ministries to work in the three newly acquired provinces. Moroccan civilian governors and lesser functionaries began serving in the provincial capitals of El Ayoun, Smara, and Boujdour, while pashas and caids were assigned to smaller cities and towns. The Ministry of Agriculture established three regional offices and staffed them with technical personnel to direct the distribution of machinery, seed, and fertilizer. By filling the administrative vacuum left by Spain's withdrawal, Morocco hoped to establish an indisputable presence in the northern Sahara and to demonstrate to the Sahrawis its capacity for governing and performing public services. Throughout 1976, Rabat underlined its control over the area by various public activities, including visits for foreign journalists to such key Saharan sites as Amgala, Mahbes, and Bir Lahlu.

The government personnel sent from Rabat formed part of a large-scale development program to bring the three Saharan provinces up to the level of the rest of Morocco. The program had two basic and related aims: sedentarization to promote control and security, and prosperity to win the hearts and minds of the Sahrawi population by providing amenities and services in the urban centers. Basic feasibility studies were done in the spring and summer of 1976, and that same summer the Moroccan government launched a bond drive to raise $230 million for development projects in the Saharan provinces over the next two years. The Saharan development program was drawn up formally, with the advice and assistance of Sahrawi tribal chiefs, in an Urgency Plan in May 1977 and approved a month later.[68]

By the end of 1978, the Moroccan government had spent about $300 million for various development projects in the northern Sahara, or $5,000–6,000 for every Sahrawi. The beneficiaries of this investment included a few thousand Sahrawis who, having fled Spanish and French territories from 1958 onward and resettled temporarily in southern Morocco, moved into the northern Sahara following the Moroccan takeover. The bulk of the money, $230 million, came from the Special Fund for the Development of the Saharan Provinces, with the remainder coming from regular government budgets. During 1978, Rabat allocated an additional $60–70 million for 25 development projects in the Sahara.

The variety and extensive nature of the development projects were clearly evident to visitors to the northern Sahara in the late 1970s and could be seen in the construction of schools, hospitals, and lodgings. In 1976–1977, three hundred lodgings were built in El Ayoun alone, and in late 1978 a thousand housing units were said to be under construction in that same city. The largest expenditures were on two major roads, one from Tan Tan through El Ayoun and the other from Tan Tan south to Smara. With an eye to future commercial expansion, heavy investments were made in the ports of Tarfaya, Boujdour, and especially El Ayoun. The Moroccans achieved impressive results in providing water for the urban centers. For most cities, including El Ayoun, Smara, and Guelta Zemmur, this involved the location, extraction, purification, and distribution of underground sources, while in Boujdour a desalination plant was constructed to provide water. In the field of education, fewer than seventeen hundred Sahrawi children were in school when the Moroccans moved into the northern Sahara in late 1975. Three years later, there were sixty-eight hundred Sahrawi children enrolled, and a full secondary cycle had begun.[69]

In the southern Sahara, Mauritania lacked the resources and the economic and administrative infrastructures to undertake a large-scale development program. On the other hand, the Mauritanians encountered relatively little opposition in absorbing their portion of the Sahara. Like Rabat, Nouakchott supplied administrative personnel to fill the vacuum left by the departing Spanish. Mauritanian administration of the southern Sahara was aided by Moroccan technical personnel who maintained and operated such facilities as electrical generators and airport control towers.

To underscore and consolidate popular support among the Sahrawi population for the Moroccan-Mauritanian takeover, both countries included their Saharan provinces in national elections. In August 1976, Sahrawis in the southern third of the territory voted in Mauritania's presidential and parliamentary elections, and eight Sahrawi representatives were elected to the National Assembly in Nouakchott. The Ould Daddah regime viewed these elections as an expression of approval by the Sahrawi population of Mauritanian annexation. Similarly, in November 1976, Sahrawis in the north voted in Morocco's nationwide local elections. In June 1977, nineteen thousand Sahrawis voted in the Moroccan parliamentary elections, and four Sahrawi deputies took their seats in the Moroccan parliament in Rabat. For King Hassan's regime, the large voter turnout in the Saharan provinces constituted a stamp of approval for the Moroccan takeover.

From 1976 to 1979, Algeria opposed the Moroccan-Mauritanian takeover of the Western Sahara by all possible means short of direct military confrontation. The sustained Algerian opposition took two major forms: support of Polisario Front military operations and efforts in international forums to keep alive the issue of Saharan self-determination. The diplomatic counterstrategy of Morocco and Mauritania consisted of lobbying efforts aimed at keeping the Sahara question off the agenda of international forums.

In July 1976, Morocco and Mauritania narrowly avoided a diplomatic setback at the OAU summit in Mauritius. At the ministerial meeting preceding the summit, Algeria succeeded in gaining the sympathy of most delegations for its Sahara position through hard-sell lobbying by a 66-member delegation, an energetic performance by Foreign Minister Bouteflika, and help from Libya. When a resolution backing the Polisario was passed by a 30–2 margin, Morocco threatened to withdraw from the OAU. Following an extensive lobbying effort by President Ould Daddah, however, a compromise solution was reached in which the OAU agreed in principle to hold an extraordinary summit to discuss the Western Sahara. This OAU compromise represented a diplomatic victory for Algeria, which had succeeded in reopening the Sahara issue. Furthermore, the meeting enhanced somewhat the Polisario Front's image on the international scene.

Jolted by the Algerian performance at the OAU summit, Morocco and Mauritania carefully planned and coordinated their tactics and then sent large and influential delegations to the Non-Aligned Conference (NAC) held the next month in Colombo, Sri Lanka. Their strategy at the NAC was to argue that regional organizations (like the OAU and the Arab League) were the most appropriate forums for the discussion of "bilateral" issues. The language on the Sahara issue that finally emerged in the NAC Political Declaration was a platitudinous compromise that simply noted with approval the action of the OAU summit in calling for an extraordinary summit to deal with the Sahara issue. This statement represented a Moroccan and Mauritanian diplomatic victory because it did not refer either to self-determination or the Sahrawi people. In contrast, the Algerians were forced to accept at the NAC far less on the Sahara question than they had won at the OAU summit a month earlier.

Like the NAC, the UNGA in December 1976 and again a year later preferred to accept the OAU compromise. Neither the NAC nor the United Nations was anxious to consider a divisive bilateral issue that had already been taken up by a regional organization (the OAU). The 1976 and 1977 UNGA resolutions were further successes for the Moroccan and Mauritanian diplomatic strategy of deferring consideration of the substance of the Sahara question. Preoccupied with other pressing issues (especially southern Africa), a majority of Third World states were content at the United Nations to reaffirm the course of action taken on the Sahara issue at the NAC. In addition, a lobbying effort during 1976 by high-level Moroccan and Mauritanian political emissaries had persuaded some Third World countries that the joint takeover of the Western Sahara was a fait accompli. These countries had no intention of becoming involved in efforts to revive the issue or of recognizing the SDAR.

The special summit meeting on the Sahara issue, which the 1976 OAU summit agreed to hold, was postponed repeatedly. In 1977, meetings scheduled for Addis Ababa, Ethiopia, in April and May and Lusaka, Zambia, in October had to be canceled. In declining to host the special summit, the Zambian government cited "security" problems. This explanation, in fact, reflected a lack of support or enthusiasm among OAU members for a public showdown on the divisive Saharan question.[70] The special summit was rescheduled, this time for Libreville, Gabon, but in March 1978 it was postponed again.

At its fifteenth summit, held in Khartoum, Sudan, in July 1978, the OAU tried a new approach. The summit commissioned Sudanese President Jaafar Numairi, the chairman of the OAU in 1978–1979, to form an ad hoc committee of "wisemen" to seek a solution to the Sahara conflict compatible with the right of self-determination. Composed of the heads of state of Mali, Guinea, Nigeria, the Ivory Coast, Tanzania, and chaired by Numairi, the Wisemen's Committee was charged with investigating the Western Sahara problem and reporting its findings to a special OAU committee in preparation for the extraordinary summit. The composition of the Wisemen's Committee was contested by both sides. King Hassan objected to the participation of Malian President Moussa Traore and Tanzanian President Julius Nyerere, especially after Tanzania recognized the SDAR in November 1978. On the other side, Algeria took strong exception to Sudanese President Numairi because of his pro-Moroccan sympathies. Another member, President Félix Houphouët-Boigny of the Ivory Coast, wary of the many pitfalls facing the committee, participated very little in its work and eventually dropped out altogether.

Threatened by paralysis, the essential work of the OAU Wisemen's Committee was carried out by a two-member subcommittee—the presidents of Mali and Nigeria—set up in December 1978. This subcommittee visited Mauritania, Algeria, and Morocco in May 1979, in coordination with a visit by the OAU secretary-general to Spain, and then presented its findings and recommendations in a report to the full committee in June. The report of the Wisemen's Committee called for an immediate and general cease-fire in the Sahara and recommended the exercise of the right of self-determination by the Sahrawi population through a free and general referendum. This report was presented to the OAU at its summit meeting in Monrovia, Liberia, in July 1979. During the initial voting, a resolution to adopt the Wisemen's report fell one vote short of the necessary two-thirds majority. Following a recess and reported arm-twisting by Algeria in the corridors, the resolution received the necessary 33 votes to pass. Amid considerable consternation several delegations, including those from Morocco and Senegal, walked out of the OAU summit. Morocco refused to recognize the findings of the Wisemen's Committee.

The report of the Wisemen's Committee and its adoption by the 1979 OAU summit constituted a significant erosion of diplomatic support among African states for Morocco's position that the Sahara issue was closed. This erosion of support had also been evident at the United Nations during the fall of 1978. At its 1978 session, the U.N. Fourth Committee again debated the Western Sahara question. Morocco lobbied unsuccessfully to remove the problem completely from the context of the United Nations, and in December the General Assembly passed two competing resolutions. The pro-Algerian resolution, passed by a wide margin, stressed the proper role of the United Nations; it made no mention of the OAU's role and for the first time mentioned the Polisario Front. The pro-Moroccan resolution, passed by a somewhat smaller margin, stressed the role of the OAU and made no mention of either the United Nations or the Polisario Front. The quality of Algerian diplomacy was evident in the 1978 U.N. session. By submitting a moderate resolution emphasizing the role of the United Nations and the right of self-determination, Algeria was able to win the votes of many delegations who were sympathetic to the Moroccan viewpoint.

Algeria's gradual success on the diplomatic front during the 1976–1979 period was matched on the military battlefield. On the military side of their two-pronged strategy, the Algerian government kept up a steady pressure against Morocco and Mauritania by providing arms, fuel, food and water, and a territorial sanctuary to support the guerrilla operations of the Polisario Front. The pattern of attacks during 1977 and 1978 demonstrated an increased Polisario capability to operate in large areas of Mauritania and southern Morocco, in addition to the Sahara itself. Bolstered by financial assistance and some weapons from Libya, the front gradually built up its combatant strength from about three thousand in early 1976 to eight to ten thousand by the end of 1978. Emboldened by a number of successful operations and an ability to move freely across the vast areas of desert hinterland, morale among the Polisario forces remained consistently high.

On the other side, Morocco adopted a defensive strategy aimed at providing security for urban centers and the Bu Craa phosphate deposits. Aside from occasional large-scale sweeping operations of marginal effectiveness, Moroccan forces concentrated on maintaining control of the principal population centers and the major oases. Wary of sustaining a high level of casualties in a drawn-out guerrilla war, the Moroccan Army, with twenty to thirty thousand troops in the northern Sahara, was reluctant to initiate aggressive search-and-destroy or clear-and-hold missions to secure the hinterlands. From 1977 to 1979, Morocco gradually withdrew its garrisons from, or was forced by Polisario pressure to abandon, several outlying towns, including Hausa and Ain Ben Tili, strategic points on major supply routes into the Sahara. Some towns—Mahbes, Tifariti, and Amgala—were overrun by Polisario forces, whereas other population centers—Hausa and Jdiria—were abandoned by the Moroccans.[71]

Polisario military tactics stressed mobility and the element of surprise. During 1976, the front operated in groups of five to eight Land Rovers, units small enough to conceal themselves in the hills during the day. At night, moving under the cover of darkness, Polisario guerrillas were able to employ a variety of light weapons—rifles, machine guns, land mines, mortars, antitank launchers, SA-7 shoulder-mounted missiles—and engage in hit-and-run operations to harass Moroccan forces and interdict supply columns. The front's units operated out of base camps in southwest Algeria, northwest Mauritania, and within the Sahara in the Guelta Zemmur and Oum Dreiga regions, where concealment was facilitated by an abundance of caves and hideouts. In the initial phase, the Polisario lacked effective radio communications and other logistical elements and was not adequately organized for coordinated military operations.

In 1977 and 1978, however, Polisario raiding parties involved large motorized columns of up to one hundred fifty vehicles that could move hundreds of miles with little risk of detection or, if detected, of effective interception. The guerrillas began to employ heavier, Soviet-made weapons, including 122-millimeter rockets, cannons, and Kalashnikov assault rifles, and their operations assumed much more impressive dimensions. In the spring of 1977, for example, the front was able to attack the Mauritanian mining town of Zouirat from two directions, one column from Tindouf and the other from northern Mali, and to mass in that attack firepower equal to that of a Moroccan regiment. By mid-1978, guerrilla forces had destroyed five sections (5.5 kilometers) of the conveyor belt that carried phosphates from Bu Craa to El Ayoun port, damaged electrical machinery in two control towers, and sabotaged seventeen power pylons.[72] In this period, Polisario units established forward base camps in southern Morocco. In the first few months of 1978, they used these camps to intensify their attacks in southern Morocco, including a strike as far north as Tata, a town about one hundred fifty miles north of the Western Sahara.

A basic element of the Polisario Front's strategy was to attack a variety of Mauritanian targets and thereby weaken the resolve of the Ould Daddah government to continue its occupation of the southern Sahara. With few sources of national power, a large territory of nearly four hundred thousand square miles (twice the size of France), and more than twenty-five hundred miles of virtually undefended borders with Mali and Algeria, Mauritania was highly vulnerable to guerrilla attacks and was clearly the weak link in the joint takeover of the Western Sahara. Following a series of initial Polisario attacks in December 1975 and Ould Daddah's call for a general mobilization, the Mauritanians rapidly increased their armed forces from only twenty-five hundred (which included gendarmerie and national guard units) to about ten thousand at the end of 1976. By mid-1978, the Mauritanian Army numbered about fifteen thousand, plus paramilitary units with another two thousand men.

In June 1976, Polisario forces numbering five to six hundred men with over a hundred vehicles traveled nearly a thousand miles from base camps near Tindouf in southwest Algeria to launch a bold and major attack on the Mauritanian capital of Nouakchott. There are some indications that the objective of the attack was to overthrow the Ould Daddah regime.[73] Only four Land Rovers were able to approach Nouakchott and shell the city with artillery. Mauritanian forces intercepted the bulk of the Polisario column at Akjoujt one hundred fifty miles northeast of Nouakchott and scored a decisive victory. Included among more than two hundred Polisario guerrillas killed was Mustapha Sayyid El Ouali, the front's secretary-general, principal founder, and inspirational leader.

In 1977, in an effort to knock Mauritania out of the war, the Polisario intensified its attacks. These attacks centered on targets within Mauritania itself, especially economic targets, and only rarely did the front strike at sites in the southern Sahara. In a highly publicized attack on May 1, the Polisario struck for the first time against Zouirat, the site of Mauritania's iron-mining operation, which provides 80 percent of the country's foreign exchange earnings. A French doctor and his wife were killed during this attack, and six other French citizens were taken prisoner. In July and August, guerrilla forces struck again at Nouakchott and Zouirat. Following the latter attack, Morocco sent five battalions to reinforce the beleaguered Mauritanian Army. During the late summer and the fall of 1977, Polisario units attacked Chinguetti, Aoussert, Zouirat, and Nouadhibou. When two French railway technicians were taken prisoner in late October, Paris felt compelled to intervene militarily to prop up the Mauritanian government and to discourage the further capture of French citizens. In December, French Jaguar aircraft based near Dakar in neighboring Senegal attacked and inflicted heavy losses on Polisario columns that were returning from raids against the Zouirat-Nouadhibou rail line.[74]

Polisario attacks against Mauritania took a heavy toll on that country's limited and underdeveloped resources. There is no question that the military buildup resulting from the Saharan conflict placed a heavy burden on the weak Mauritanian economy and diverted funds from badly needed development projects. The country's defense budget increased 50 percent from about $24 million in 1975 to $36 million in 1976. Between 1975 and 1977, the government's budget expenditures increased by 64 percent, and in 1978 defense spending accounted for 60 percent of the budget. At the same time, Mauritanians were required to contribute to a special defense tax that took three days' wages a month for people earning salaries and 2 percent of the gross income of companies—a burden made heavier by an inflation rate of 33 percent.

In addition, Mauritania received important financial assistance from wealthy oil-producing states in the Middle East. Funds to purchase arms were provided in large part by Saudi Arabia, Kuwait, and Abu Dhabi, conservative Arab states that were quite prepared to help Mauritania contain the Algerian revolution. The most important source of foreign assistance was Saudi Arabia, which provided an estimated $400 million from 1976 to 1978—about twice Mauritania's annual budget. Mauritania also benefited greatly from various forms of military and technical assistance provided by Morocco beginning in late 1975. In 1977–1978, there were six to eight thousand Moroccan troops stationed in various parts of Mauritania plus a three-thousand-man force in the southern Sahara. This military assistance and coordination was formalized in May 1977 by a joint defense agreement.

By late 1977, Mauritania was on the verge of bankruptcy. At a time when defense expenditures were rising rapidly to support the greatly enlarged armed forces, revenues from iron ore exports, the country's major source of foreign exchange, were declining. In 1977, because of reduced demand caused by the world recession and curtailed mining operations caused by Polisario attacks, these exports fell to their lowest level in ten years. They declined even further during the first half of 1978. By the end of 1977,

Mauritania's foreign debt had reached $467 million—an astonishing 92 percent of the country's modest gross domestic product of about $500 million. These economic problems were compounded in 1977–1978 by a resurgence of drought conditions, which had a devastating effect on the country's crops and herds. In these dire financial straits, Mauritania was able to avoid bankruptcy only through a series of grants and loans from Saudi Arabia, France, Morocco, and Libya.[75]

Mauritania's sagging economic fortunes and the seemingly unwinnable desert war in the Western Sahara were key factors that led a group of junior officers in mid-1978 to overthrow the eighteen-year civilian rule of Mokhtar Ould Daddah. A twenty-man junta, the Military Committee for National Recovery (CMRN), successfully staged a coup on July 10 without bloodshed. Whatever its precise origins, the coup was definitely not animated by radical or left-wing sentiments. The CMRN proclaimed that the armed forces had taken power "to save the country and the nation from ruin and dismemberment, to safeguard national unity and defend the existence of the State." The orientation of the CMRN was centrist, moderate, pro-French, and pro-Moroccan. There is, however, some evidence to suggest that the junta acted on July 10 to pre-empt a pro-Moroccan coup by more senior officers.[76] The CMRN quickly announced its intent to work out "a timetable with Morocco to set in motion a process leading to peace."

The July coup in Nouakchott surprised the foreign parties most concerned about the fate of Mauritania. Morocco suspected pro-Algerian forces were at work; Algeria did not know what to think. The Polisario Front reacted with great joy and immediately declared a unilateral cease-fire, which the Mauritanians were only too happy to accept. The new regime in Nouakchott, headed by Lt. Col. Mustapha Ould Salek, was desperate to get out of the Saharan war, and both sides scrupulously observed the cease-fire. Of particular concern to the Mauritanians, a *modus vivendi* was worked out along the vital 420-mile railway that brings iron ore from the mines at Zouirat in the interior to the port of Nouadhibou.

The Polisario strategy following the July 1978 coup was quite clear. By observing a cease-fire with Mauritania, the front gave the CMRN time to reconsider its options. The Polisario hoped to demonstrate to the new regime in Nouakchott the advantages of seeking an accommodation over the Western Sahara—or at least in the southern portion claimed by Mauritania. The front was convinced that there were elements within the Mauritanian Army and the general population who had some sympathy for its liberation struggle. At the same time, the half million Mauritanian blacks who inhabit the Senegal River basin had only a limited interest in the Arab war in the north; yet it was the blacks who were asked to bear the brunt of the fighting. By holding out an olive branch, the Polisario could bolster the position of the accommodationists within the CMRN.

The new Mauritanian leader, Ould Salek, soon renewed his country's links with Morocco. In August 1978, Rabat and Nouakchott declared their joint opposition to a new, independent state in the Sahara, though neither ruled out the possibility of a federated state with limited autonomy.[77] Mauritania's interest in an accommodation with the Polisario was countered by Morocco's determination to oppose a change of the status quo in the Sahara. A few weeks after the coup when President Houphouët-Boigny of the Ivory Coast suggested a semi-independent Saharan state in Tiris al-Gharbiyya to be federated with Mauritania, Ould Salek said on August 17 that he was "not against" a referendum in that area. In a strong speech three days later, King Hassan, on the other hand, left no doubt about his feelings. By declaring that he could not tolerate "a foreign frontier between Morocco and Mauritania," Hassan issued a clear warning about the implications of a bilateral Mauritanian-Polisario settlement.

The effect of the July 1978 coup in Nouakchott was to remove the Mauritanian Army from active participation in the war. With the Mauritanian forces now on the sidelines, the Polisario was able to focus all its military efforts against the fifty thousand Moroccan troops deployed in southern Morocco and the northern half of the Western Sahara. The front's leaders could count on the unswerving personal commitment of Algerian President Boumediene to their struggle.

Polisario officials were understandably concerned when Boumediene became seriously ill in the fall of 1978. In mid-November, the Algerian leader fell into a deep coma. Six weeks later, despite exhaustive care by an international team of medical specialists, Boumediene died on December 27 from Waldenstroem's disease, a rare bladder ailment. In his honor and perhaps to link their own cause more closely to militants among the new Algerian leaders, the Polisario launched the Houari Boumediene Offensive on January 1, 1979. As part of the stepped-up military campaign, battalion-size Polisario units began operating in both southern Morocco and the Western Sahara. A highlight of this series of strikes against Moroccan forces was a major attack on January 29 against Tan Tan, a provincial capital near the Atlantic coast in southern Morocco, one hundred fifty miles from the Algerian border, that is strategically located on the only major north-south road that runs from Agadir to El Ayoun. During February 1979, the second month of the offensive, the Polisario claimed to have launched more than forty operations, including a dozen artillery attacks against the sizable garrison at Lebouirat in southern Morocco.[78]

Mauritanian leaders came under increasing pressure in 1979 to find an honorable way out of the Saharan conflict. While desperate to get out of the war, the CMRN was constrained from acting unilaterally by its long-term interest in cooperation with Morocco. Talks between Mauritanian and Polisario leaders, both public and private, encouraged and assisted by Algeria and Libya, began in October 1978 and continued sporadically for nearly a year. At the end of 1978, SDAR Foreign Minister Ibrahim Hakim complained that Mauritania "wants to get out of the war without making peace." While the Polisario was beginning to become impatient with Mauritania's fence straddling, Hakim declined to set a time limit for the ceasefire.[79] In April 1979, Polisario leaders set a precondition for further talks with Nouakchott: the evacuation of Mauritanian troops from Tiris al-Gharbiyya.

In the meantime, however, a series of rapid internal political upheavals that involved a succession of three military cabinets in less than a year began in Nouakchott. In March 1979, Ould Salek, frustrated by his inability to resolve Mauritania's enormous problems, revised the 1978 constitutional charter in order to give himself full powers and dismissed ministers sympathetic to the Polisario Front and Algeria. The next month in a "palace revolution," Lt. Col. Ahmed Ould Bouceif, backed by a group of pro-Western officers who had not participated in the July 1978 coup, seized power and reduced Ould Salek to a figurehead president. The CMRN was shuffled and transformed into the Military Committee of National Welfare (CMSN). Ould Bouceif tried to distance the new regime from the coup of July 1978 and to strengthen Mauritania's alliance with Morocco. In late May, Ould Bouceif was killed when his plane crashed while returning form Senegal. As the new prime minister to replace Ould Bouceif, the CMSN designated Lt. Col. Mohamed Khouna Ould Haidalla, the 39-year-old defense minister and chief of staff, who consolidated his power seven months later in another palace revolution in January 1980.[80]

By the spring of 1979, it was clear that time was running out for the state of no war, no peace that Mauritania had enjoyed since mid-1978. In early May, Prime Minister Ould Bouceif declared that Mauritania was ready to seek peace in the Western Sahara conflict "on the basis of internationally recognized principles, as we adhere to the principle of self-determination."[81] Rabat did not try to prevent Nouakchott from pursuing negotiations with the Polisario Front. For the Mauritanian government, self-determination did not necessarily mean either an independent Saharan state or a referendum; there were other ways of assessing the popular will. Despite a willingness to negotiate, a Mauritanian delegation failed to appear in Tripoli on May 26 for a negotiating session with the Polisario arranged by the Libyan government. The Mauritanians complained that the Libyans had abused their confidence the month before by altering a simple *procès-verbal* and transforming it into a protocol, which the Polisario subsequently labeled a "peace accord."[82]

Several very sticky questions were at the heart of the Mauritanian government's indecisiveness. What were the maximum concessions that Nouakchott could make in negotiations with the Polisario? Could Mauritania carry out a settlement with the front that was unacceptable to Morocco? If the war resumed, what kind of performance could be expected from the Mauritanian Army? And finally, would the Polisario Front be willing to observe the cease-fire if negotiations bogged down?

The answers to at least some of these questions came in short order during the summer of 1979. In mid-July, the Polisario ended the cease-fire and captured Tichla, a town in the southern part of Tiris al-Gharbiyya located close to both the Mauritanian border and the Zouirat-Nouadhibou railway. On August 5, unwilling to face the continuing prospect of an unwinnable desert war that had brought Mauritania to the verge of political disintegration and economic collapse, the CMSN signed a peace treaty in Algiers with the Polisario Front. According to the terms of this treaty (see Appendix B), Mauritania renounced all territorial and other claims over the Western Sahara and agreed to withdraw from the "unjust war" in the territory. In return, the Polisario renounced all claims regarding Mauritania and signed a final peace agreement with Nouakchott. In a secret part of the treaty released later, Mauritania recognized the Polisario Front as "the sole legitimate representative of the people of the Western Sahara" and agreed to withdraw from Tiris al-Gharbiyya and hand it over directly to the Polisario within seven months.

In the course of two-and-a-half years of ruinous war, Mauritania had been brought to its knees. A year later the resumption of military pressure by the Polisario led the CMSN to sign an agreement renouncing all claims to the Sahara. Mauritania proved to be highly vulnerable to sustained guerrilla attacks, just as Boumediene had warned in his meeting with Ould Daddah at Bechar in November 1975. It was ironical that by the time this part of the Sahara drama played itself out, Ould Daddah had been forcefully removed from power in a coup and Boumediene had died prematurely of a rare disease.

Morocco and the Polisario Front, August 1979–1982

The peace treaty between Mauritania and the Polisario Front ushered in the latest phase in the evolution of the Western Sahara conflict. From the mid-1960s to 1975, Morocco, Mauritania, and Algeria opposed Spain's continued presence in the Sahara by diplomatic pressure, while the Polisario Front pressured Spain militarily from 1973 to 1975. Between November

1975 and August 1979, Morocco and Mauritania (the latter until July 1978) struggled both militarily and diplomatically against the Polisario Front, backed by Algeria and Libya, for control of the Western Sahara. With Mauritania forced out of the war, Morocco has been left since August 1979 to face the Polisario and its backers alone.

The removal of Mauritania from the war weakened Morocco's overall position in the Sahara conflict, though perhaps not to the extent anticipated by Algeria and the Polisario Front. Nouakchott moved from a close alliance with Rabat in their joint takeover and partition of the Western Sahara to a position of "positive neutrality" in the conflict. Within ten days of the peace treaty, Mauritania and Algeria restored diplomatic relations. Mauritania's defection from the conflict weakened Morocco's military position by facilitating the access of Polisario forces to the Sahara; it weakened Rabat's political position by undermining the diplomatic support of a number of African and Arab states for Morocco's takeover of the Sahara. On the other hand, the peace treaty ended the need for the Moroccan Army to help defend large areas of Mauritanian territory, but it in no way lessened Morocco's resolve to retain possession of the Sahara.

The news of the August 5 peace treaty caused considerable consternation in Rabat. Morocco pronounced the treaty null and void and denounced "the unconditional capitulation" of Nouakchott. King Hassan described the agreement as "a piece of paper signed at the end of a picnic." The Moroccan press termed Mauritania a "traitor," while Foreign Minister M'hamed Boucetta accused Nouakchott of having "violated solemn undertakings." Hassan called on Mauritania to abide by its international commitments, failing which Morocco would assume "its vital and obligatory responsibility to defend its continuity."[83]

Amid strong urgings by the press and political parties, a public hue and cry arose in Morocco for the kingdom to exercise its "right of pre-emption" in Tiris al-Gharbiyya. As Mauritanian soldiers and administrators withdrew from the southern Sahara, Morocco, with a fifteen-hundred-man garrison in the capital city of Dakhla, was well positioned to assert its authority. On August 11, the Moroccan flag was raised over the town hall in Dakhla. Large demonstrations of allegiance to King Hassan were organized in Dakhla, and on August 14, a group of tribal leaders from the southern Sahara flew to Rabat and swore allegiance to the Moroccan crown. That same day, Morocco annexed the former Mauritanian portion of the Western Sahara, incorporating the area into the kingdom as a new province, Oued Eddahab ("river of gold"), the Arabic name for Rio de Oro.

In a press conference on August 19, 1979, King Hassan outlined the possibilities of improving Moroccan-Algerian relations and tried to deflect the Polisario Front's efforts toward Mauritania. The king declared that the annexation of the southern Sahara had satisfied all of Morocco's territorial claims; as soon as political tensions between Morocco and Algeria eased, the Moroccan parliament could ratify the 1972 accord recognizing the border between the two countries. While speaking of Algeria in conciliatory tones, Hassan singled out Libya, backed by the Soviet Union, as the country most eager to see a Moroccan-Algerian war; such a conflict would leave the two countries so enfeebled that Libya could dominate North Africa. At the same time, the king dismissed the Polisario Front as a Mauritanian dissident movement and suggested that it either overthrow the government in Nouakchott or go home and help rebuild Mauritania. Hassan specified that Morocco would not defend Mauritania against an attack by the Polisario, for that would be a "family affair."[84]

In the following months, the Moroccan government took steps to integrate the southern Sahara fully into the kingdom. On March 3, 1980, in celebration of the nineteenth anniversary of his accession to the Moroccan throne, King Hassan proclaimed in a nationally televised speech that the Western Sahara was an "integral part" of Morocco and its annexation "an irreversible historical fact." The next day, to underscore this position, the king made a dramatic visit to Dakhla, where he received the traditional annual Moroccan renewal of vows of allegiance from Ministry of Interior officials, provincial functionaries, and local tribal chiefs. The occasion marked Hassan's first visit to any of the "recovered" Saharan provinces, and by going to Dakhla the king visibly committed his prestige to Moroccan sovereignty over all of the Western Sahara. In May 1980, all four Saharan provinces voted, along with the rest of Morocco, in two national referenda dealing with government reorganization.

The new Algerian regime led by President Chadli Benjedid, who had been elected in an orderly succession process in January–February 1979, showed no ostensible signs of lessening the strong support for the Polisario Front given by the late President Boumediene. Algiers welcomed the peace treaty between Mauritania and the Polisario and stressed that the treaty rendered null and void the Madrid Tripartite Agreement of November 1975. In the period since August 1979, Algeria has worked to solidify the international consensus in favor of Saharan self-determination and to increase Morocco's diplomatic isolation on the Western Sahara issue.

At the NAC held in Havana in September 1979, discussion of the Western Sahara issue centered on the OAU's efforts to resolve the problem. The NAC's Final Declaration noted that the recommendations of the OAU Wisemen's Committee had not been acted on yet and said that the Special OAU Committee created at the 1979 summit in Monrovia should guarantee that the Sahrawi population could exercise its right to self-determination and independence as soon as possible. The NAC welcomed the peace treaty between Mauritania and the Polisario, but it "deplored" Morocco's armed occupation of the southern Sahara.[85] The only consolation Morocco could find in the NAC's declaration was that the language was softened from "condemned" to "deplored."

In December 1979, at a meeting in Monrovia, the OAU Wisemen's Committee recommended that a peacekeeping force monitor a cease-fire in the Western Sahara in preparation for a referendum. In addition, the Wisemen called for Morocco's withdrawal from the former Mauritanian sector of the Sahara. As was the case at the NAC in Havana, Morocco found itself fighting a rearguard action. In this instance, the Moroccans were able to lobby for a change in wording from the original (French-language) draft, which called for Morocco's withdrawal from all of the Western Sahara, to the final (English) text, which called for a Moroccan withdrawal only from Tiris al-Gharbiyya.

By the time of the OAU summit in Freetown, Sierra Leone, in early July 1980, 23 African states had recognized the SDAR. During the summit, three additional states, including Libya, signed a letter to the OAU secretary-general supporting the admission of the SDAR into the organization. The Polisario Front now had a majority of 26 out of the 50 OAU members backing the admission of its "government." A heated debate on this question ensued, featuring acrimonious exchanges between the delegations from Morocco and Mozambique.[86] Morocco argued that the SDAR was neither independent nor sovereign, two attributes of a state required by the OAU charter. Rabat insisted that this question of the charter's interpretation required a two-thirds majority vote. To head off a divisive confrontation, Senegalese President Léopold Senghor urged an approach involving the Wisemen's Committee and an extraordinary OAU summit.[87]

Faced with the threat of Morocco and at least four other members to walk out of the OAU if the SDAR were admitted, the summit postponed a decision on the question of SDAR membership.[88] Nigeria then drafted a compromise resolution, which Senghor persuaded Morocco to accept. The resolution, adopted by consensus, extended the mandate of the Wisemen's Committee, to be chaired by Sierra Leone President Siaka Stevens, the head of the OAU during 1980–1981; it noted Morocco's new willingness to talk to "all interested parties" in the Sahara dispute; and it called for the Wisemen's Committee to meet in Freetown within three months.[89] The Moroccans qualified their acceptance of the compromise resolution by stating that they would cooperate with the Wisemen's Committee only under an impartial chairman. Citing Sierra Leone's recognition of the SDAR only a week before the OAU summit, the Moroccans made it clear that they did not consider President Siaka Stevens impartial. While Morocco was forced to make a significant concession in agreeing to talk to all interested parties, it also gained some time to define who those parties were.

The Wisemen's Committee duly met in Freetown in September 1980. During this three-day meeting, known as Freetown II, the committee heard separate statements from a total of fourteen "interested parties," ten of which represented pro-Moroccan groups from the Western Sahara. Rabat tried to stress the importance of the Aosario, the pro-Moroccan Saharan movement that the Moroccan government had created in 1977 to counter-balance the influence of the Polisario Front. Although Algerian President Benjedid and several other African chiefs of state attended Freetown II, King Hassan failed to appear (he had said prior to the meeting that he would come if procedural issues gave way to substantive discussions). Despite their agreement two months earlier at the OAU summit that they would meet with all interested parties, the Moroccans refused to attend joint sessions with the Polisario Front, and they prefaced the sessions they did attend with sharp criticism of the Wisemen's "lack of neutrality." At the same time, Morocco maintained its position that the mandate of the Wise-men's Committee was to open discussions between the "main parties" — that is, Rabat and Algiers — a position consistently rejected by Algeria.

Although Freetown II was the first gathering to be attended by all parties to the Sahara conflict, the meeting ended in apparent failure. No true nego-tiations were held at Freetown II, and the six-part peace plan, announced just before the Wisemen's Committee dissolved itself, contained no signifi-cant new elements. The plan's two main recommendations were a cease-fire within three months, to be enforced by U.N. peacekeeping forces, and a referendum to be organized by the OAU with U.N. assistance. The Poli-sario Front agreed to the referendum but then issued a war communiqué that denounced a cease-fire so long as Rabat failed to "come back to reason." On the other side, Moroccan Foreign Minister Boucetta repeated his country's opposition to a referendum and, while agreeing to the cease-fire in principle, warned that Morocco would open fire if it continued to be attacked. The peace plan proposed by the Wisemen's Committee at the con-clusion of Freetown II was referred to the OAU for consideration at its 1981 summit meeting.

The United Nations' consideration of the Western Sahara question in 1979 and 1980 closely followed, and generally deferred to, the OAU's handling of the issue. In November 1979, the UNGA adopted by a large majority a resolution that noted with satisfaction the OAU resolution from the Monrovia summit the previous July. The U.N. resolution welcomed the peace agreement between Mauritania and the Polisario Front, while it "deeply deplored" Morocco's continued occupation of the Western Sahara and "the extension of this occupation to the territory recently evacuated by Mauritania." Finally, the 1979 UNGA resolution recommended that the Polisario Front, "the representative of the people of Western Sahara," should participate in any search for a solution of the question.[90]

At the following year's session of the United Nations during the fall of 1980, Morocco lobbied in the Fourth Committee for the adoption of a resolution that referred the Western Sahara issue back to the OAU. The African group at the United Nations found it impossible to negotiate a text that was acceptable to both Morocco and Algeria; as a result two draft resolutions emerged. When faced with two similar resolutions in 1978, the Fourth Committee adopted both of them. By the time of the 1980 session, however, many African states questioned Morocco's commitment to the OAU process; some of them saw in the Moroccan draft resolution Rabat's familiar tactic of shifting the Sahara problem back to the OAU and then ignoring OAU decisions and mediation attempts. To gain support for its resolution, Morocco included in its final statement in the Fourth Committee a pledge that it would "continue to cooperate diligently with the ad hoc [OAU Wisemen's] committee to implement its mandate of Freetown, particularly as it relates to the free choice of the population."[91] This concession proved to be too little, too late, and on October 31, 1980, the Moroccan draft resolution fell one vote short of adoption in the Fourth Committee (40–41 with 58 abstentions).

One day earlier, the Fourth Committee adopted the Algerian draft resolution on the Western Sahara question. On November 17, 1980, the UNGA adopted the Algerian text as U.N. Resolution 3519 by the large margin of 88–8 with 43 abstentions. Among those supporting the resolution was Mauritania. The text of this resolution painted the Western Sahara issue as one of colonial occupation by Morocco. The 1980 text reaffirmed the main points of the previous year's resolution, including the right of the Sahrawi population to self-determination "and independence." The resolution deeply deplored the failure to implement the November 1979 resolution, and it urged Morocco and the Polisario Front to enter into direct negotiations. (This time the Polisario was referred to as "representative," rather than "the representative," of the people of the Western Sahara.)[92] The language of the 1980 UNGA resolution strengthened Algeria's claim that the Polisario Front was a major party to the Western Sahara conflict and, by the same token, increased the diplomatic isolation of Morocco.

In the weeks following Mauritania's withdrawal from the war, the Polisario Front launched several large-scale attacks to challenge Moroccan control of key locations in the Western Sahara. In mid-August 1979, a large Polisario force attempted to approach Dakhla but was turned back by Moroccan units at Bir Enzaran, a major town some seventy-five miles inland from the Atlantic coast. In late August, Polisario units approaching from three directions attacked Lebouirat, a fortified outpost in southern Morocco that is an important access point to the northeastern Sahara. In a dawn raid, the Polisario wiped out this garrison of fifteen hundred Moroccan troops, took more than two hundred prisoners, and captured enough equipment to supply a regiment.[93]

In early October 1979, the Polisario launched a major assault against Smara, the second largest city in Sakiet al-Hamra and the spiritual center of the Western Sahara. In one of the largest battles of the war, the front employed columns from three directions to form a combined attacking force estimated at two to five thousand. The Moroccan garrison of fifty-four hundred at Smara, warned of the approaching columns, held off the attackers until the Moroccan Air Force's French-made Mirage F-1 jet fighters, which are equipped for nighttime attacks, could arrive. This was the first combat use of the newly acquired Mirage F-1 fighter-bombers and the first Moroccan air attack by night, the prime time for Polisario effectiveness in previous battles. Benefiting from the element of surprise, the Moroccan Air Force inflicted heavy losses on both the Polisario forces engaged at Smara and Polisario vehicles en route to reinforce those units.[94]

Later that same month, Polisario columns overran Morocco's outnumbered eight-hundred-man garrison at Mahbes, an important outpost in the northeast corner of Sakiet al-Hamra located on the only access road between Tindouf and Smara.

By the fall of 1979, Moroccan public opinion was clearly aroused by both the scale and boldness of Polisario attacks. There was growing evidence that the front possessed a large arsenal of sophisticated Soviet-built armaments, supplied primarily by Libya, that enabled it to operate more like a regular army than a guerrilla force. In battles with Polisario units, Moroccan garrisons increasingly found themselves outnumbered and at a disadvantage in firepower.

In an attempt to wrest the military initiative from the Polisario Front and satisfy aroused public opinion, the Moroccan high command began to employ bold new tactics in the rough terrain of southern Morocco and the northern Sahara. In a major departure from its basically defensive strategy, the Moroccan Army formed several large mobile armored task forces whose objectives were to limit the mobility of the elusive Polisario forces, disrupt their communications, and hamper access to their supplies. The first of these task forces set out from Tan Tan in late October 1979. Colonel-Major (later General) Ahmed Dlimi, King Hassan's chief of security, led an armored column of six thousand men and fifteen hundred vehicles in a sweep of several weeks across southern Morocco and the Western Sahara. The force was named Operation Uhud, after a victorious battle fought by the Prophet

Mohammed; subsequent task forces formed in the following months were named Badr, after another battle waged by Mohammed, and Zallaqa, after an eleventh-century Almoravid victory by Yusuf ibn Tashfin against King Alfonso VI of Castile. These armored columns swept through the rocky Sahara for several weeks in search of Polisario arms, ammunition, and fuel caches, many of which were hidden in the forbidding Wadi Draa.[95]

The task forces improved morale among the Moroccan military and uncovered some arms caches. There was little direct contact with Polisario units, however, as the guerrilla forces were able to keep a safe distance from these large search-and-destroy missions. In the face of Morocco's enhanced ability to repel large-scale attacks and call in strafing aircraft, the Polisario returned in 1980 to the guerrilla warfare tactics that had brought its initial victories. In January, it resumed its penetration into Morocco with an attack on Akka, about one hundred miles southeast of Agadir. During the first two weeks of March, Polisario units ambushed and fought sporadically with a large Moroccan force (Operation Iman ["faith"]) trying to resupply the military center at Zaag in the southeast corner of the country near the Algerian border. This series of battles erupted along the Jebel Ouarkziz, a mountainous area of southeast Morocco just below the Wadi Draa. The five-thousand-man Moroccan force was made up of elite units from Operation Uhud plus young, inexperienced recruits from the Zallaqa division, who panicked and fled when attacked. According to Western journalists who toured the battlefield, the Moroccans suffered heavy casualties.[96]

The losses suffered in March 1980 by Operation Iman in the Jebel Ouarkziz region represented a low point for the Moroccan military. The setback demonstrated that despite the formation of large mobile task forces, Moroccan units were still vulnerable to Polisario attacks. In the following months, the Moroccan high command put into effect significant changes in organization and deployment that dramatically improved the performance of Morocco's military. New equipment was moved from the north to the southern zone, which comprises both the Western Sahara and southern Morocco, and some units in the southern zone were rotated. The high command accentuated improvements begun in the fall of 1979: the more effective use of air power to support ground forces under attack and tactical and organizational changes within the ground forces themselves. Most important, military leaders made long overdue changes in command and control — structural reform involving basic changes in Morocco's highly centralized command structure that allowed rapid responses to guerrilla attacks and effective coordination between the army and air force.

During the spring and summer of 1980, the changes introduced by the Moroccan high command were evident in improved military performance. In April and May, the Moroccan Army cleared a wide corridor in a 27-mile area from Ngueb Pass in the Ouarkziz Mountains to the isolated garrison of Zaag, 50 miles from the Algerian border. In this cleanup operation, Moroccan forces inflicted heavy casualties on well-entrenched Polisario units.[97] The successful effort to relieve Zaag involved improved ground-to-air coordination and better planning and suggested that the Moroccan military had made significant progress in conducting combined arms operations. The following month, the Moroccans again used effective ground-to-air coordination to repel Polisario attacks against Guelta Zemmur and Akka.

Since the fall of 1979, the improvement of army–air force coordination and the use of Mirage F-1s have enabled the Moroccan military to inflict a heavier level of casualties on the Polisario. Military morale has improved, and Moroccan forces have been in a less defensive posture. By the summer of 1980, Morocco was able to reverse the impression that it was losing the war militarily and to project the impression of a stalemate at worst.

Militarily, the Polisario Front reacted sharply to the outcome of the meeting of the OAU Wisemen's Committee in September 1980, which it described as the "last chance for peace." Morocco's refusal to engage in direct negotiations at Freetown II reinforced the Polisario's position that Rabat was not seriously seeking a settlement. Following Freetown II, the Polisario rejected a cease-fire (proposed by the Wisemen's Committee) as long as Morocco remained in the Western Sahara and proceeded to step up its attacks in southern Morocco and the Sahara. In late September, for example, Polisario forces ambushed Moroccan troops engaged in a sweeping operation in the Abattih area in the deep south of Morocco, and in October the front attacked M'Hamid, located about fifty miles south of Zagora, which is well north of the Sahara. Morocco responded in mid-October to these attacks with a major Western Sahara offensive, which it called purely defensive. Two armored task forces, Arak and Zallaqa, totaling about thirteen thousand troops operated in the area between Abattih and Smara.

In late 1980, it was evident that Morocco had made a major revision in its military strategy. Although the armored columns proved effective in the limited areas in which they operated, Morocco simply did not have the resources necessary to raise and maintain the very large forces—possibly several hundred thousand troops—that would be needed for a major offensive to pacify quickly all one hundred thousand square miles of the Western Sahara. For the near future, the Moroccan high command opted for the more modest military objective of establishing full security within the strategic triangle formed by Tan Tan in the north, Smara in the south, and El Ayoun in the west, and including the phosphate mines at Bu Craa. To protect this vital zone, the Moroccans began in September 1980 to construct a defensive barrier—a "security belt"—on the outer edge of what they call the "useful triangle." Morocco's Great Wall consists of a ditch, about twenty-three feet wide, in front of an earthen mound, about seven feet high, protected by barbed wire and mines, with special radar equipment to detect guerrilla movements. This line of defense is further reinforced by observation points and fortified bases of operations installed at varying distances depending on the nature of the terrain.[98]

By serving as a trap for vehicles, the defensive barrier can block access into the triangle area. Morocco aims to isolate the Polisario from the civilian population, so that the guerrillas no longer would be, in Maoist terminology, like "fish in the sea." Though not impregnable, the barrier greatly inhibits fast escapes for Polisario units trying to operate within the protected zone. It also served as a protective buffer for the construction, a few miles to the west, of an all-weather paved road between Tan Tan and Smara, which reduced by half the transport supply time between the two cities.

By summer of 1982, the Moroccans had completed their Great Wall from Messeid south past Smara, around Bu Craa, and then west to the Atlantic coast near Boujdour. Another section of the wall was constructed in the southeast corner of Morocco, from the Ouarkziz Mountains south to within twenty-five miles of the Algerian border, around Zaag, and then north to rejoin the Jebel Ouarkziz. Using bulldozers protected by the mobile Zallaqa brigade, the Moroccans constructed over three hundred miles of barrier despite some delays caused by Polisario attacks. Including part of the Jebel Ouarkziz, where the Moroccans have blocked the passes, the Great Wall runs continuously for nearly four hundred miles from southeast Morocco to the Atlantic coast. Since the spring of 1981, the Moroccan Army has continued to build new fortifications at intervals along the sand wall.[99] Once full security is established within the strategic Tan Tan–Smara–El Ayoun triangle area, Moroccan forces will begin the arduous task of enlarging the secure zone. This lengthy and costly process will involve pushing outward from the Great Wall, east and south, to move against Polisario bases in the rest of the Western Sahara.

Since the construction of the anti-vehicular sand barrier, the Polisario Front has concentrated its military efforts on Moroccan targets outside the defensive perimeter. In late March 1981, a Polisario force numbering from fifteen hundred to two thousand attacked the two-thousand-man Moroccan garrison at Guelta Zemmur, about a hundred miles south of the wall. After thirteen days and heavy reinforcements, the Moroccans prevailed by force of numbers and inflicted an estimated three hundred casualties on the front. In mid-April, the Polisario launched its first attacks in southern Morocco in six months against Sidi-Amara and Hassi-Aribia, two Moroccan posts in the Wadi Draa sector about fifteen miles south of Tata. And in mid-August, a Polisario force attacked five miles south of Messeid, just outside the wall.[100]

In mid-October 1981, a heavily armed Polisario force of three thousand attacked Guelta Zemmur from two directions. During this battle — the biggest of the Saharan war — the front employed sophisticated Soviet-made surface-to-air missiles and shot down five Moroccan aircraft, thus neutralizing Morocco's ability to respond quickly with air power. The Polisario forces inflicted heavy casualties on the 2,600 Moroccan troops at Guelta Zemmur, soon overwhelmed the garrison, and captured 230 prisoners. Guelta Zemmur was retaken only after the intervention of elite Moroccan units from the Bu Craa sector. Rabat claimed that the Polisario had escalated the military conflict by introducing into battle Soviet-made SA-6 missiles and T-52 and T-54 tanks and argued that the sophistication of these weapons required the presence of non-African military personnel.[101] Although it is likely that at least some of the Moroccan aircraft were downed by SA-6 missile systems, there is no evidence to confirm the presence of tanks in the rugged terrain of the Guelta Zemmur area; instead, both the Polisario and Algeria acknowledged the use of Libyan-supplied Brazilian EE-9 Cascavel wheeled armored vehicles.

Morale in the Moroccan military declined following the defeat and heavy losses suffered at Guelta Zemmur. Difficulties in providing adequate logistical support to garrisons outside the Great Wall led to a decision by the Moroccan high command to evacuate and withdraw troops from both Guelta Zemmur and Bir Enzaran in November 1981. During the first few months of 1982, the Moroccan Army continued to strengthen its positions along the defensive perimeter. At the same time, the Moroccan Air Force flew frequent sorties against suspected Polisario positions outside the wall to limit the size of troop concentrations and disrupt the front's planning.

By the time of the eighteenth OAU summit meeting in Nairobi, Kenya, in late June 1981, Morocco found itself increasingly isolated on the diplomatic front. Within the Sahara, however, the construction of the Great Wall, by enhancing the security of the settled population, made Moroccan leaders more confident about the outcome of a referendum. In an attempt to improve its diplomatic position and to stave off admission of the SDAR to the OAU, King Hassan went to the Nairobi summit and publicly declared for the first time Morocco's willingness to hold a referendum in the Western Sahara in keeping with the recommendations of the OAU ad hoc Wisemen's Committee. In a carefully worded address to the OAU heads of state and government, Hassan offered to hold what he termed a "controlled referendum" in the Sahara that would take into account Morocco's historical rights to the territory. After heated debate on this issue, the OAU summit adopted by consensus a resolution that set up a seven-nation ad hoc implementation committee to make the necessary arrangements for a "general and regular referendum of self-determination" of the Western Sahara's population and invited the parties to the conflict to observe an immediate cease-fire. The resolution requested the Implementation Committee to meet with the interested parties by the end of August to work out the modalities of a cease-fire and the organization of a referendum. Lastly, the resolution requested a U.N. peacekeeping force to maintain peace and security during the organization and holding of the referendum and subsequent elections.[102]

The 1981 OAU resolution involved two compromises by Morocco. First, the Moroccan government had previously rejected the idea of a referendum on the grounds that it was unnecessary. In Rabat's view, the Sahrawi population had already exercised its right of self-determination by the Jemaa's February 1976 vote to become part of Morocco (and Mauritania) and by the Sahrawis' participation in several Moroccan elections and referendums. Second, Morocco accepted the term "self-determination" in connection with the referendum even though it had previously refused to accept it.

In accepting these compromises, Morocco was able to seize the diplomatic initiative on the Western Sahara issue. The 1981 OAU resolution did not mention the Polisario Front by name. In contrast, at the 1980 summit meeting, a majority of 26 African states supported the admission of the SDAR; a year later, this question was pushed off the OAU's active agenda. Thus, by demonstrating some flexibility, Morocco was able to postpone the question of OAU recognition of the SDAR. The 1981 OAU resolution became the framework for further discussion of the Sahara dispute. By continuing its military attacks, the Polisario Front henceforth risked international censure and loss of support within the OAU by appearing to be the obstacle to the organization's peace plan. At a minimum, the Moroccans gained time to secure further their defensive perimeter in the "useful triangle" of the northern Sahara.

Algeria supported the 1981 OAU resolution and applauded Morocco's willingness to accept a referendum in the Sahara as a step forward toward peace. At the same time, however, Algiers declared that Rabat first must withdraw its army and administration. In contrast to Algeria, the Polisario Front immediately rejected the resolution, which it denounced as a Moroccan ruse. The front accused King Hassan of asking the OAU to legitimize Morocco's military occupation of the SDAR.[103] The Polisario had always insisted that the "Sahrawi people have achieved self-determination through arms," and in February 1981, it had declared that the time had passed for a referendum. In mid-July, two weeks after the Nairobi summit and presumably under pressure from Algeria, the front issued a communiqué containing a series of hard-line conditions for the referendum. The communiqué called for direct negotiations with Morocco to work out the modalities of a cease-fire and a general, free, and regular referendum; the complete withdrawal of Moroccan forces from all the Western Sahara to a distance of 150 kilometers beyond Morocco's 1956 borders — that is, considerably north of the Wadi Draa; the complete withdrawal of the Moroccan administration; the return of all Sahrawis, including those residing in Algeria, to their native towns and villages; the establishment of a provisional international administration in the Western Sahara, made up of U.N. and OAU personnel, with the collaboration of the SDAR; operation of this administration for at least three months prior to the referendum; and the liberation of all Sahrawis held by Morocco. The mid-July communiqué went far beyond the OAU resolution adopted at Nairobi in June. Predictably, the Polisario conditions were unacceptable to Morocco.

In late August 1981, the OAU Implementation Committee met in Nairobi to work out the details of a cease-fire and referendum in the Western Sahara. At this meeting, known as Nairobi II, the committee received oral and written views from the various parties to the conflict (both King Hassan and President Benjedid attended). The parties appeared individually, and thus there was no negotiation between Morocco and the Polisario Front. At the conclusion of Nairobi II, the Implementation Committee issued a decision (see Appendix C) that specified the details of the referendum, which would offer the Sahrawi population the choice between independence or integration with Morocco. The decision called for U.N. collaboration in holding the referendum and an impartial interim administration to work with the existing (Moroccan) administration and to be assisted by an adequate OAU and/or U.N. peacekeeping force. The decision also urged the parties to the conflict to agree on a cease-fire through negotiations held under the Implementation Committee's auspices, and it called for the confinement of troops to their bases during the holding of the referendum.[104]

Morocco had reason to be pleased with the outcome of Nairobi II. The Implementation Committee's decision allowed the Moroccan Army and administration to remain in the Western Sahara during the organization and holding of a referendum; it based voter eligibility mainly on the 1974 Spanish census; and it neither mentioned the Polisario by name nor explicitly called for direct negotiations with the front. Algeria, in its long and legalistic presentation to the Implementation Committee at Nairobi II, stressed the need to apply internationally accepted standards and practices to organizing and holding a referendum of self-determination in the Sahara.[105] The Polisario reaction to Nairobi II was more categorical. The front refused to accept either a cease-fire or a referendum without the prior withdrawal of the Moroccan Army and administration from the Western Sahara.[106]

At the UNGA session in the fall of 1981, Morocco tried to keep the treatment of the Western Sahara issue within the context of the ongoing efforts of the OAU Implementation Committee. Algeria, however, insisted on pushing a stronger resolution. OAU Chairman Moi of Kenya appealed to both Morocco and Algeria to withdraw their resolutions from the Fourth Committee in favor of a consensus resolution that simply took account of the Nairobi I resolution and the Nairobi II decision. Morocco withdrew its resolution as a compromise gesture, but Algeria did not. Because of Morocco's willingness to compromise and the statement made by Kenya, thirteen African countries abstained and four others were deliberately absent for the vote on the Algerian resolution, which the Fourth Committee adopted with fifteen fewer votes in favor than in 1980. Immediately thereafter, the Fourth Committee adopted by consensus a draft decision submitted by Kenya, which satisfied the Moroccan position. On November 24, the UNGA adopted the Algerian resolution by a vote of 76 to 9 with 57 abstentions (including fourteen African states). This resolution (see Appendix D), beyond taking note of Nairobi I and II, named Morocco and the Polisario as "the two parties to the conflict" and urged these two parties to enter into direct negotiations to establish a cease-fire and organize a referendum.[107]

The OAU Implementation Committee met for a second time in Nairobi on February 8–9, 1982. Since the committee was unable to arrange direct negotiations between Morocco and the Polisario Front at this meeting, known as Nairobi III, it consulted individually with the several parties — Morocco, Algeria, Mauritania, and the Polisario. When the Algerian delegation argued that Morocco and the Polisario Front should be named as the two parties to the Sahara conflict, Nigeria, Sierra Leone, and Guinea reacted strongly, insisting Algeria was also a party to the conflict, and the effort to name the parties failed. Since the Implementation Committee found that the various parties were unwilling to go beyond Nairobi II on substantive issues, it tried to define further the modalities of a cease-fire and referendum. In its decision issued at the conclusion of Nairobi III, the committee stated that it would appoint a commissioner, with the consent of the parties, to head the interim administration. The decision called for close cooperation between the interim administration and the existing (Moroccan) administration, which would remain in place.[108]

The Polisario Front rejected the decision of Nairobi III and continued to insist on direct negotiations with Morocco. Both Rabat and Algiers were muted in their public reaction to the February meeting. Neither government was willing to go beyond the decision of Nairobi II. The next step in the Implementation Committee's work was for Chairman Moi to shuttle among the parties to the conflict and get their agreement to the Nairobi III decision. The Polisario responded to this step by announcing that it would not meet with Moi.

In late February 1982, the work of the Implementation Committee was sidetracked from another direction. At the annual meeting of the OAU Council of Ministers in Addis Ababa—usually devoted to administrative and budgetary affairs—OAU Secretary-General Edem Kodjo of Togo seated the SDAR delegation for the first time. Kodjo termed his action an "administrative decision" based on formal notification by a majority of OAU members of their recognition of the SDAR. This action, done in disregard of the ongoing efforts of the Implementation Committee, upset many delegations attending the meeting. Amid strong denunciations of Kodjo's action, Morocco led nineteen OAU members in walking out of the meeting to protest the seating of the SDAR.[109]

The surprise development at the OAU meeting in Addis Ababa threatened not only the work of the Implementation Committee but also the future of the OAU. Morocco, although reaffirming its commitment to cooperate with Chairman Moi and the committee, insisted that Kodjo's action be rescinded. As long as the SDAR was allowed to participate as a member of the OAU, Morocco and a number of other African states would boycott the organization.

The seriousness of the OAU's predicament became manifest in the summer of 1982, when 21 nations refused to attend the annual summit scheduled to be held in Tripoli August 5–8. The OAU charter requires two-thirds of the 50 member-states for a quorum. In the absence of the necessary 34 states, efforts to convene the summit were abandoned on August 7—the first failure to assemble a quorum since the establishment of the organization in 1963. In addition to states opposed to the admission of the SDAR, at least two countries boycotted the Tripoli summit to express their hostility to the African policy of Libya's Colonel Qadhafi and to prevent Qadhafi from becoming OAU chairman for a year.[110]

The successful boycott of the 1982 OAU summit was a clear victory for Moroccan diplomacy and a defeat for Libya, Algeria, and the Polisario Front. The admission of the SDAR was at least temporarily blocked, and efforts to resolve the Western Sahara conflict were focused again on the Implementation Committee and the 1981 Nairobi resolution calling for a cease-fire and a referendum. The hard-core supporters of the SDAR were left to lick their wounds—and perhaps to plan their own boycott of the 1983 OAU summit in Conakry, Guinea, whose President Sékou Touré is a member of the Implementation Committee and a firm supporter of Morocco. As for the OAU, the same organization that in 1981 had supported a referendum of self-determination in the Western Sahara was laboring in the fall of 1982 under the burden of an administrative action that prejudged the outcome of Saharan self-determination—and threatened in the process to drive out more than a third of the OAU membership.

4 | The Role of Third Parties

In addition to the parties directly involved in the evolution of the Western Sahara conflict, several other states have played roles of varying importance. The most important, though not the only, role of these third parties has been that of arms supplier to the parties directly involved. Moreover, third parties have provided important financial and diplomatic support to the principals in the conflict. This chapter analyzes the roles of the more important third parties—Spain, Libya, France, the United States, and the Soviet Union. Three other parties, covered in passing, have aided the disputants: Saudi Arabia has provided sizable financial assistance to Morocco and Mauritania, Egypt has supplied occasional arms to Morocco, and Cuba has provided medical personnel to the Polisario Front.

Spain

Spain has consistently reaffirmed the positions it adopted at the time it withdrew from the Sahara in February 1976. First, Madrid considers that its international responsibilities in the Western Sahara ended on February 26, 1976. Second, under the terms of the Madrid Tripartite Agreement of November 14, 1975, Spain transferred the administration, but not the sovereignty, of the Sahara and authority over its coastal waters to Morocco and Mauritania. Third, Spain does not consider that the Sahrawi population has expressed itself freely and therefore Saharan decolonization has not yet taken place. Finally, Spain maintains strict neutrality on the Western

Sahara issue. It has not recognized either the Polisario Front or the SDAR and, since 1977, has prohibited all arms supplies to the warring parties.[1]

With the February 1976 transfer of administrative authority to Morocco and Mauritania, the emerging leaders of post-Franco Spain hoped to wash their hands of the Sahara conflict. Within domestic Spanish politics, however, the Madrid Tripartite Agreement has become a contentious issue. The major opposition party, the Spanish Socialist Workers Party (PSOE), rejects the Tripartite Agreement, viewing it as null and void from the perspective of international law. The PSOE's stand on this issue closely resembles the official Algerian position. Spanish Socialist leader Felipe González has visited the Western Sahara, and the PSOE has condemned Madrid's abandonment of its former Saharan province to Morocco and Mauritania.[2]

On the international level, the parties directly involved in the Saharan conflict have subjected Spain to various pressures. Morocco, on the one hand, and Algeria and the Polisario Front, on the other, have tried to exploit Spain's vulnerability with respect to the Spanish enclaves on Morocco's northern (Mediterranean) coast, its fishing fleet in the Atlantic, and the Canary Islands. In an effort to maintain good relations with both Morocco and Algeria, Spain has made some tactical concessions, but it has not changed its basic positions on the Sahara issue.

From 1976 to 1978, Spanish policy on the Sahara issue favored Morocco. Spain supplied arms to Morocco until mid-1977, it signed a fishing agreement in 1977 that was advantageous to Rabat, and the Spanish and Moroccan governments supported each other in international forums.[3] During this same period, Spanish-Algerian relations were strained. In the months following the Tripartite Agreement, Algiers welcomed a number of Spanish opposition figures, some of them in exile, who denounced Madrid for betraying the Sahrawi people. In addition, the Boumediene regime gave one hour daily on Radio Algiers to Antonio Cubillo, leaders of MPAIAC, during which Cubillo broadcast the "Voice of the Free Canaries." In December 1977, in response to a strident article in the government-controlled Algerian daily *El Moudjahid* that called for the independence of the Canary Islands, Madrid recalled its ambassador in Algiers. The Algerian attack on Spain's control of the Canaries served to rally all Spanish political factions strongly behind the government. Realizing that it had made a tactical error, the Boumediene regime abruptly ended MPAIAC's broadcasts on Radio Algiers in January 1978.[4]

In 1978–1979, increased pressures by Algeria and the Polisario Front led Spain to adopt a more balanced posture on the Western Sahara issue. With material aid from Algeria, MPAIAC had carried out by 1978 a hundred bomb attacks in the Canary Islands, and one of its bomb threats was partially responsible for a midair collision of two commercial airliners that killed several hundred tourists. During 1978, five Spanish trawlers fishing off the coast of the Sahara were attacked by Polisario guerrillas operating from rubber boats. In April 1978, during one of these attacks, eight Spanish fishermen were taken prisoner, and the following August six Spanish fishermen were killed in another attack. Spain complained to Algeria about these attacks, but Algiers insisted that Madrid deal directly with the Polisario Front. To secure the release of the fishermen, Javier Rupérez, a representative of Spain's ruling Central Democratic Union (UCD), attended the Fourth Polisario Congress in September 1978 and signed a joint communiqué affirming that the front was the sole legitimate representative of the Sahrawi people.[5]

The release of the eight Spanish fishermen in October 1978 led to normalization of Spanish-Algerian relations. This development was strengthened by the visit in the spring of 1979 of Prime Minister Adolfo Suárez to Algiers. During this visit, Suárez, in his capacity as president of the ruling UCD, met with Polisario Secretary-General Mohamed Abdulaziz, which constituted UCD recognition of the front. While this meeting did not imply official Spanish government recognition of the Polisario, it nevertheless provided a counterpart to the policy of Spanish Foreign Minister Marcelino Oreja, who was firmly opposed to recognizing the front. The UCD recognition of the front did not stop the Polisario from capturing, in the fall of 1980, a total of 40 Spanish fishermen. This time the Spanish government not only refused to deal with the front but also initiated an active international campaign to denounce the "dealings of the Polisario."[6]

Spain stood to benefit economically from normalization of its relations with Algeria. In the wake of the Madrid accords, the Boumediene regime had discouraged new Algerian contracts with Spanish companies. Nevertheless, in 1979, Spain ranked fifth among suppliers of Algerian imports, and trade between the two countries was increasing, as was the dependency of Spanish industries on Algerian oil and gas supplies. In particular, Spain had a considerable long-term interest in the construction of a trans-Mediterranean pipeline to bring Algerian natural gas to the Iberian peninsula. At the same time, Spain hoped that improved relations with Algeria would dampen the Algerian government's interest in raising the issue of the independence of the Canaries in the OAU.[7]

Since 1978, the regional challenge to Spanish diplomacy has been to normalize relations with Algeria without, in the process, alienating Morocco. Spain has been grateful for the occasional Moroccan declarations of the Spanishness of the Canary Islands. At the same time, when Spanish-Moroccan relations become strained, Rabat does not hesitate to raise the issue of the Spanish enclaves of Ceuta and Melilla or to apply pressure over fishing rights. When relations are good, nothing is said about the enclaves.

In periods of tension, however, Rabat talks of the need to recover these last portions of Morocco's national patrimony still under foreign control.

In the fall of 1978, Spanish-Moroccan relations suffered as Madrid attempted to improve its ties with Algiers. In response to the attendance of the UCD representative at the Polisario Front's Fourth Congress, Moroccan Foreign Minister M'hamed Boucetta delivered a speech in Washington in which he revived his country's claims to Ceuta and Melilla. King Juan Carlos responded by postponing a planned visit to Rabat. Simultaneously, the UCD declared that Spain could not give in to Moroccan "blackmail" on the enclaves question.[8] In light of the Suárez visit to Algiers the following spring, the Moroccan government was anxious to improve its relations with Madrid. The visit of Juan Carlos to Morocco in June 1979, during which the Spanish king reaffirmed his support of the Tripartite Agreement, helped to ease the tension in Spanish-Moroccan relations.

In addition to the enclaves issue, the other major pressure point in Spanish-Moroccan relations has been fishing rights off the Moroccan and Saharan coasts. On February 15, 1978, by a vote of 175 to 142, the Spanish Cortes ratified the 1977 bilateral fishing agreement with Morocco and reaffirmed the Tripartite Agreement. During the visit of King Juan Carlos to Fez, Morocco agreed to accelerate its ratification of the fishing accord and, in the interim, to work out an agreement to avoid the seizure and inspection of Spanish fishing boats in Moroccan waters. In the spring of 1980, however, this issue reappeared dramatically. When King Hassan remarked on French television that Spain was largely responsible for the continuing bloodshed in the Sahara, the Spanish Foreign Ministry and press rejected Hassan's statement. A few days later, the Moroccan Navy detained 21 Spanish fishing vessels and escorted them to Casablanca. Their catches were impounded, and over two hundred Spanish fishermen were held temporarily.[9]

These tensions were resolved with the payment of modest fines by some of the detained Spanish fishing vessels. Behind the capture of the 21 fishing boats was Rabat's desire to base Spanish-Moroccan commercial relations on friendship and cooperation. The Moroccans sought a comprehensive agreement — one that included the overland shipment of their country's citrus produce through Spain — to be tied to a future fishing agreement.[10] Morocco never ratified the 1977 fishing agreement with Spain, and the two countries dealt with the fishing issue through a series of interim agreements. After difficult negotiations, including one interruption in January 1981 that prompted the Spanish to withdraw their fleet from Moroccan territorial waters, Spain and Morocco concluded yet another temporary fishing agreement. The agreement, signed on April 1, 1981, in Madrid and valid for one year, involved substantial concessions in favor of Rabat, including increased fishing royalties, Spanish aid to promote Morocco's fishing industry, and increased Moroccan exports to Spain.[11] A year later, this agreement was renewed temporarily until the end of 1982, pending the negotiation of a multiyear accord.

By the spring of 1982, Spain still had not agreed to the free transit of Moroccan citrus. In the absence of this concession, Morocco was not willing to sign a long-term fishing agreement. The value of the Spanish catch in Moroccan waters exceeded $500 million in 1981 and Spanish fishing boats operating from the Canary Islands are dependent, because of their limited range, on access to Moroccan fishing grounds. Thus, Spain has an economic incentive to maintain extensive commercial relations with Morocco on terms that are attractive to the Moroccans. Spanish-Moroccan relations have been fairly good since the spring of 1981, and there were signs of further improvement in 1982, including Madrid's willingness to sell nonlethal military equipment to Rabat.

Spain, however, continues to tread a delicate path in its Western Sahara policy. The Spanish government has allowed the Polisario to open an office in Madrid but has not recognized the front or the SDAR. Madrid is anxious to see an end to the Sahara conflict and is quite willing to participate in the search for a solution. In October 1978, for example, Spain requested at the United Nations that the Saharan conflict be resolved by negotiations as soon as possible and that the Sahrawis be allowed to exercise their right of self-determination. Among the parties to the conflict, the Polisario Front considers that Spain, because of cultural and linguistic ties, is the country best suited to reach an understanding with the Sahrawi people.[12] On the other hand, King Hassan has advised Spain not to play a mediating role in the Western Sahara dispute and has stated that an attempted mediation effort by Madrid would hinder close Spanish-Moroccan relations.[13] Madrid's continued support of the 1975 Tripartite Agreement is important to Morocco, while its position that Saharan self-determination has not taken place is welcomed by Algeria and the Polisario Front. Any change by Spain from these basic positions carries a high risk of strained relations with one or more of the parties to the conflict.

Libya

Unlike Spain, the revolutionary government in Libya has not attempted to steer a neutral course in its policies toward the Western Sahara conflict. The regime led by Col. Mu'ammar al-Qadhafi, which came to power in a September 1969 coup that overthrew the Libyan monarchy, has long been an important supporter of the Polisario Front. This support has necessitated an uneasy cooperation with Algeria. Curiously enough, Libya also provided financial assistance to Mauritania during that country's direct involvement in the Sahara conflict. The most consistent aspect of Libya's Saharan policy since 1976 has been hostility toward Morocco. In 1981, Qadhafi moderated this hostility, if only for tactical reasons.

To an unusual degree, Libya's foreign policy reflects the objectives of Mu'ammar al-Qadhafi, the dominant political figure and unchallenged leader of the Socialist People's Libyan Arab Jamahiriya. Qadhafi is a complex Arab politician and a man of contradictions. A Bedouin, he came to power without the softening influence of a transitional generation in contact with the modern world. Qadhafi's outlook has remained essentially tribal, tempered only by four years at a military academy. As a Bedouin, he was an outsider in Libyan society. As a national leader, he is an outsider in international politics, where he retains an essentially confrontational view of the world.

With fanatical zeal, considerable political skill, and large oil revenues, Qadhafi pursues the goal of Arab unity in a radicalized Arab world, both as an end in itself and as a necessary precondition for the destruction of the Israeli state. He was heavily influenced during his youth and early adulthood by the example of Egypt's pan-Arab leader, Gamal Abdel Nasser. As a good Nasserist and Third Worlder, Qadhafi has given high priority to extending Libya's influence in Africa, propagating the Islamic faith, and promoting revolutionary programs and regimes in Third World countries.

During the evolution of the Western Sahara dispute, some of Qadhafi's objectives have clashed, producing ambiguities and inconsistencies of policy. As a result, Libyan involvement in the Sahara dispute has resembled a curious, veiled game—a pattern typical of Libya's policy since the early stages of the conflict. In the early and mid 1970s, when the Western Sahara was still under Spanish domination, Libya was at the forefront of Arab states urging an armed struggle against the colonial occupation of an Arab territory; in 1975, for example, the Libyans criticized Morocco for its reluctance to engage Spanish forces in an armed confrontation. Following Spain's withdrawal in 1976, Qadhafi initially opposed the creation of a Saharan ministate, but because he considers Morocco's policy to be aggressive and its attitude to be colonialist, he now favors the Sahara's right to self-determination and even Saharan independence.

During the first two years of the Polisario's existence, from 1973 to 1975, Libya was the front's largest financial and material supporter. Qadhafi, somewhat hyperbolically, claims that Libya founded the Polisario and provided the arms that made it a viable force against the Spanish presence in the Sahara. Mauritania, though sympathetic to the struggle against Spanish colonialism, had limited means at its disposal, and Algeria's support was modest. When Morocco and Mauritania moved into the Sahara in late 1975, Algeria threw its full support behind the Polisario.

Since 1976, Libya has put its own financial, military, and diplomatic weight behind the front, complementing and sometimes exceeding Algeria's support. The Polisario has an office in Tripoli, and Qadhafi frequently meets its leaders. With considerable wealth and Soviet-supplied military equipment at its disposal,[14] the Qadhafi regime has provided financial aid, weapons, and training to some of the Polisario units, medical help, and schooling in Libya for some Sahrawi children. Although the precise amounts of this aid are not known, it is probable that Libya assumed a gradually increasing share of the Polisario's expenses from 1976 to mid-1981.[15] With the normalization of relations with Morocco in mid-1981, Libya suspended shipments of military supplies to the Polisario, although it continued to meet the payroll of Polisario leaders and perhaps provided stipends for the guerrilla forces. In light of Tripoli's considerable aid, it is quite possible that pro-Libyan factions have developed within the ranks of the Polisario; Mustapha Sayyid El Ouali, for example, the inspirational leader of the front from its founding in 1973 to his death in battle in 1976, was known for his pro-Libyan sympathies. Beyond occasional allegations in the press, however, little is known publicly about factional divisions within the Polisario movement.

Libyan support for the Polisario Front has been a mixed blessing for Algeria. Tripoli has been an enthusiastic and generous ally of Algiers in the Sahara conflict, but while its support has lessened Algeria's financial burden, Libyan aid to the Polisario has also increased the front's freedom to maneuver. By mid-1979, for example, Chadli Benjedid, then recently elected Algeria's president, was known to be upset by mounting Libyan aid to the Polisario. This aid helped the front to operate with considerable independence of Algeria and to strike repeatedly at uncontested areas of southern Morocco.[16] It is in Algeria's interest to maintain a restraining influence over the Polisario, lest the front provoke an unwanted war between Algeria and Morocco.

The specter of Libya's gaining dominant influence over the Polisario must be a source of concern to any Algerian government. If at some future point Algeria should opt for a compromise settlement with Morocco, Libya could encourage the Polisario to continue its war of liberation without Algerian support. In this situation Libya's willingness to overcome imposing difficulties of logistics and furnish the Polisario with food, fuel, and military supplies would depend largely on the prevailing political alignment in the Arab world. A lack of unity among progressive Arab states would deter Libya from pursuing a policy strongly opposed by Algeria.

The government of Chadli Benjedid, like that of Boumediene before it, views the Qadhafi regime with considerable misgivings. Algeria is often alarmed by Qadhafi's interventionist politics and is wary of his potential for destabilizing actions. Benjedid reportedly warned Qadhafi in 1981 that Algeria would not tolerate any Libyan destabilization of Tunisia, Mali, Niger, or Upper Volta. The Algerians had very mixed feelings about the Libyan intervention in Chad in 1980–1981, and Benjedid publicly disapproved of Qadhafi's plan for a merger with Chad and his intention to keep Libyan troops there. Algeria is uneasy about what the Libyan intervention in Chad means for other fragile African states like Niger and Mali. Moreover, Libya's seizure of the Aouzou strip of northern Chad raises troublesome questions about Algeria's own borderlands with Libya, which Libya also claims.[17]

In the case of Mauritania, Libya's policy has been curiously supportive. Since the early 1970s, Qadhafi has been favorably disposed toward Mauritania as an Islamic republic. During a 1972 visit, Qadhafi pledged financial support to restore Mauritanian mosques and promote the use of Arabic in the educational system; the following year, he provided monetary aid for a variety of Mauritanian development projects, including the construction of a road from Atar to the Islamic holy city of Chinguetti and a power plant and water-distribution system for Nouakchott. From 1976 until Mauritania's withdrawal from the Sahara conflict in 1979, Libya financed several Mauritanian cultural and economic development projects.[18]

As the Saharan conflict escalated militarily in 1977–1978, contradictions emerged in Libya's attempt to maintain close relations with Mauritania and the Polisario Front, two parties at war with each other. Qadhafi did not approve the Polisario's use of arms, supplied by Tripoli, to attack Libya's ally, Mauritania. He was particularly offended by the front's raids against Chinguetti, the site of a major Islamic sanctuary and a town in which Libya had financed important installations. Concern for the plight of Mauritania as an Islamic state led Qadhafi to receive President Ould Daddah warmly in Tripoli in the spring of 1978 and to promise him financial assistance for the development of key sectors of the Mauritanian economy.[19]

Mauritania's involvement in the Sahara conflict may help explain why Libya did not publicize its support for the Polisario during the earlier stages of the war and why since mid-1978, when the Polisario began to direct all its efforts against Morocco, the Libyans have been more open about their backing of the front's struggle. Libya increased its involvement in the Western Sahara issue after the July 1978 coup in Nouakchott led to a Mauritanian-Polisario cease-fire. In the following months, Qadhafi received Mauritanian envoys, hosted secret Mauritanian-Polisario talks, and again offered financial aid to Mauritania.[20] At the same time, another factor that may account for Libya's increasingly public support of the Polisario was France's highly visible involvement in several parts of Africa in late 1977 and throughout 1978, especially French military actions against the Libyan-backed Frolinat rebels in Chad.

Libyan policy toward Morocco has been considerably less complicated. On a personal level, Qadhafi has a visceral dislike of Hassan, whom he regards as a pretentious monarch and an anachronism in the late twentieth century. On the ideological level, Libyan leaders oppose the regime in Morocco as a feudal, pro-Western monarchy in an age of revolutionary Arab socialism. Radio Tripoli broadcast congratulations, for example, at the time of the July 1971 coup attempt, when it appeared momentarily that King Hassan had been overthrown. On specific issues Qadhafi was incensed by Hassan's support of Egyptian President Anwar Sadat's peace initiative with Israel. Within the context of the Western Sahara conflict, Libya's recognition of the SDAR in April 1980 led Morocco to break diplomatic relations. Libyan opposition to Morocco has taken the form of military support for the Polisario Front and diplomatic support for the SDAR. On the military level, Libya wanted its weapons to be used exclusively against Morocco, while diplomatically, within the OAU, Libyan lobbying has included offers of financial largesse to several poor African states to gain their support for the SDAR.

In June 1981, Libya took steps to improve relations with Morocco and showed a certain willingness to moderate its position on the Western Sahara conflict. The Libyan moves came in the wake of a large diplomatic offensive launched by King Hassan in May 1981, in which he sent emissaries to 90 countries to explain the situation in northwest Africa in light of the "Libyan threat."[21] More important, Libya wanted to ease its isolation, caused, in part, by the intervention in Chad. Israel's bombing attack against an Iraqi nuclear reactor in June heightened this sense of isolation and led Qadhafi to fear a military attack on Libya by an alliance of Israel, Egypt, and the United States. Simultaneously, Libya was anxious to improve its chances of hosting the 1982 OAU summit.

Qadhafi sent two envoys to King Hassan in June, and in response Hassan sent his trusted adviser Ahmed Reda Guedira. Libya wanted to resume diplomatic relations, but found unacceptable Morocco's condition of ending support for the Polisario. Nevertheless, at the OAU ministerial and summit meetings in Nairobi in late June, Libya greatly moderated its diplomatic backing of the front. Tripoli remained silent on the Western Sahara issue and did not support SDAR membership in the OAU. In return Morocco did not condemn Libyan involvement in Chad. This mutual restraint suggested that Tripoli and Rabat had worked out some sort of tactical compromise. In late July, Tripoli and Rabat announced a normalization of relations. Because of the deep mutual distrust and personal antipathy between

Qadhafi and King Hassan, however, prospects for a true rapprochement between Libya and Morocco are not very good.

The 1981 tactical compromise suggests that Libya's stand on the Western Sahara issue is subservient to broader strategic objectives of the Qadhafi regime. While supporting the Polisario's war of liberation first against Spain and later against Morocco, Libya's backing of the SDAR has been ambiguous. It hesitated until April 1980 before recognizing the SDAR, and even then its action owed more to the pressure of events than to any desire to grant formal recognition. Qadhafi seriously questions the economic viability of an independent Saharan state. Politically, Libyan policy is "unionist": Qadhafi is opposed to further "Balkanization of the Arab nation"[22] – the antithesis of his goal of Arab unity.

Libya views the Western Sahara as potentially only one element in a larger political entity and would prefer to see the territory federated with another country, preferably Mauritania, an Arab and Islamic state. From 1977 to 1979, Qadhafi urged Mauritania to unite with the Polisario by giving Tiris al-Gharbiyya to the front. In April 1981, following an attempted coup in Nouakchott in March by disaffected, expatriate army officers allegedly backed by Morocco, Qadhafi called for a Mauritanian–Western Saharan merger, with full unity rather than a federation, and encouraged the SDAR to join the Steadfastness Front of Arab states opposed to the Camp David accords. At this time, he also advocated without success the creation of an "anti-imperialist pact" among Algeria, Libya, Mauritania, and the SDAR, in order to isolate Morocco. This support of a merger and an anti-imperialist pact is consistent with Qadhafi's commitment to Arab unity.

Appeals to larger political entities also reinforce Qadhafi's desire to unite all the Saharan tribes from Chad to Mauritania under his leadership. There are probably a large number of Saharan tribesmen, hard pressed by the repeated Sahel droughts, who would welcome a Libyan-inspired United States of the Sahara if such a country promised them an improved livelihood.[23] Thus far, this Greater Saharan idea remains a vague vision rather than a concrete plan. Nevertheless, Qadhafi has promoted regional coordination to encourage this concept, as evidenced by his support for the March 1980 Saharan Summit Conference held in Bamako, Mali, which was attended by the chiefs of state of Algeria, Libya, Mauritania, Mali, and Chad. Libya's intervention in Chad, its sponsorship of the dissident Liberation Front of North Mali, and its support for various antigovernment groups in Niger point in the direction of a Libyan-dominated pan-Saharan confederation. A larger Saharan entity is, however, not part of the Polisario Front's long-term strategy. A Greater Sahara is even less acceptable to Algeria and represents an implicit challenge to its desires to be the dominant power in North Africa.

France

Like Spain, France has maintained a policy of juridical neutrality on the substance of the Western Sahara issue. It has not recognized Moroccan or Mauritanian sovereignty in the Sahara, nor has it recognized the Polisario Front or the SDAR. Unlike Madrid, however, Paris has been the leading arms supplier to Morocco, a role that has complicated its relations with Algeria. France has been less vulnerable than Spain to pressures by Algeria or the Polisario to limit its support for Morocco. Finally, France's involvement in the Sahara conflict has been complicated further by its self-appointed role as guardian of Mauritania's independence and territorial integrity.

France has been the dominant external power in northwest Africa since the beginning of the twentieth century. As the former colonial ruler in Algeria, Mauritania, and Morocco, France has a more substantial involvement with those countries than does any other outside power. Only with the Western Sahara itself and the Polisario Front are French ties of secondary importance. France retains important political, economic, and cultural relations with both Morocco and Mauritania. Following Algeria's bitter and bloody revolutionary war of national liberation (1954–1962) against French colonial domination, Franco-Algerian political relations have often been strained, although economic and cultural relations have been of considerable significance. A salient feature of French involvement in the Western Sahara dispute has been the attempt to manage support for Morocco and Mauritania in ways that do not jeopardize France's relations with Algeria. While there was little effort under Valéry Giscard d'Estaing to strike a genuine balance among the conflicting parties, the French have moved to a more neutral position since the 1981 election of François Mitterrand.

Since Morocco in 1956 and Algeria in 1962 achieved independence from France, the aims and objectives of French policy in these two countries have been to further French political, economic, and cultural interests in the absence of direct political control. In the cultural sphere, French policy aims at maintaining the privileged position that French language and culture occupy in the former North African possessions. Although the size of the resident French communities in Morocco and Algeria has decreased dramatically since independence, continuing French economic interests in the two countries are nevertheless considerable. The economies of both countries are closely linked to that of France. Although Algeria's trade with France fell from about 70 percent of its total trade in 1965 to 28 percent in 1974, over half of Morocco's trade is still with France. Together, Algeria and Morocco import more than $3 billion worth of French products annu-

Table 3

FRENCH TRADE WITH ALGERIA AND MOROCCO, 1975–1981
(millions of U.S. dollars)

| | Imports from France | | | | | | |
	1975	*1976*	*1977*	*1978*	*1979*	*1980*	*1981*
Algeria	1,769	1,529	1,910	1,652	1,962	2,642	2,574
Morocco	747	865	1,025	1,021	1,426	1,196	1,300
	Exports to France						
	1975	*1976*	*1977*	*1978*	*1979*	*1980*	*1981*
Algeria	699	721	847	739	1,126	1,730	2,604
Morocco	387	416	466	560	673	778	691

SOURCE: Embassy of France, Washington, D.C.

ally, and as Table 3 shows, the trend has been toward an increasing volume of trade with a consistent surplus in France's favor. French investment in Morocco is an estimated $500–600 million. In Algeria, in the wake of nationalization after 1965, current French investment is on a more modest scale.

To protect and promote these economic interests, France maintains good relations with its former North African possessions partly through grants of economic and technical assistance. France agreed to provide Morocco with nearly $40 million in development credits in February 1974. French financial aid to Morocco was $48 million in 1976 and $49 million in 1977. French assistance to Morocco also takes the form of import quotas and customs reductions, the acceptance of Moroccan laborers in France, and advantages to Morocco under the Common Market association agreement.

Since the outbreak of the Western Saharan conflict in 1975, French relations with Morocco have been excellent while ties with Algeria have been somewhat strained. During the presidency of Valéry Giscard d'Estaing (1974–1981), the French government found itself in agreement on many foreign policy issues with the moderate, pro-Western monarchy in Morocco. In addition Franco-Moroccan relations benefited from the personal friendship between President Giscard d'Estaing and King Hassan.

All long-standing contentious bilateral issues between France and Morocco were settled during Giscard's May 1975 visit to Rabat. France agreed to provide Morocco with $168 million in development credits in July 1975 and, in March 1976, agreed to provide $200 million in government loans and commercial credit. Hassan underscored Morocco's intimate links with France by his highly publicized visit to Paris in November 1976 and a seventeen-day stay in France in the spring of 1980. A new series of Franco-Moroccan economic cooperation agreements was signed during Prime Minister Raymond Barre's visit to Morocco in January 1981. These agreements center on France's leading role in the development of Morocco's industry and energy sources. Specifically, France agreed to take the lead in financing $1.5 billion for Morocco's nuclear power program and $3 billion for twelve phosphoric acid plants over five years as part of a $6 billion expansion of the Moroccan phosphate industry.

In the context of the Western Sahara conflict, the major feature of Franco-Moroccan cooperation has been France's role as the principal supplier of weapons to Morocco's armed forces. The Moroccan military has been primarily French-equipped since independence, and arms deliveries since 1975 have been a natural outgrowth of a long-term military supply relationship. Recent French arms supplies to Morocco have been on a large scale and span the entire spectrum from light arms to heavy weaponry to a Crotale antiaircraft missile system. These armaments include 60 Mirage F-1CH jet interceptor aircraft, 24 Fouga strike planes, 24 Alpha jet tactical support aircraft, 40 Puma troop-carrying helicopters, and 400 VAB armored personnel carriers.[24] The total value of French arms sales to Morocco between 1974 and 1981 is probably in the range of $1.5–2.0 billion, not including weapons supplied through military credits. French military support also has included France's willingness to accept large Moroccan arrearages.

In contrast to its excellent relations with Morocco, France's relations with Algeria during the Western Sahara conflict have been strained. In addition to Algerian displeasure over French support for Morocco in the Sahara dispute, strains in bilateral relations have resulted from a large Algerian trade deficit with France, which averaged nearly $1 billion a year from 1975 to 1980. In 1976, Algerian government offices in France were bombed, and other incidents affected Algerian workers and their families in France. Since Algerians make up the largest immigrant group in France, the possibility of friction is ever present.

Franco-Algerian relations were strained further following a Polisario attack in May 1977 against the Mauritanian mining complex at Zouirat. Two French civilians were killed during the attack, and six French employees of the Mauritanian iron-mining company SNIM were taken prisoner. The French government, outraged by the taking of civilian hostages, complained to Algeria and asked the Boumediene regime to use its considerable influence with the Polisario to secure a rapid release of the prisoners. In response Algiers used its good offices to arrange discussions between the Polisario and the French government. During these meetings, the Polisario tried to make tactical use of the six prisoners to press the French government to use its influence on Mauritania to open a dialogue with the front.[25]

In October 1977, the Polisario took two French railway technicians as prisoners. The French government decided soon thereafter to intervene militarily to discourage the further capture of French citizens and to protect Mauritania against "threats of destabilization."[26] High-flying reconnaissance aircraft systematically monitored the vast Mauritanian desert. In December, France launched Operation Lamantin ("sea cow"). Jaguar aircraft operating from the French air base at Ouakam near Dakar in neighboring Senegal attacked and inflicted heavy losses on Polisario columns returning from raids against the Zouirat-Nouadhibou rail line.[27] The Polisario released the eight French prisoners/hostages in late December. The front continued to strike at Mauritanian targets, and France launched periodic Jaguar attacks against Polisario vehicles until mid-1978, when the July coup in Nouakchott ushered in a cease-fire on the Mauritanian front.

The Algerian government strongly condemned France's military intervention in 1977–1978. Algiers spoke of the threat of French imperialism and accused France of playing the role of "gendarme of Africa."[28] In Algerian eyes the intervention of the French Air Force in the Sahara conflict on the side of Mauritania confirmed the existence of a Paris-Rabat-Nouakchott axis.[29] In retaliation, the Algerian government resolved to reduce purchases of French products and the number of new contracts. In November 1977, the Algerian minister of commerce ordered industrialists to stop importing French goods, and in January 1978, the minister of energy and petrochemicals instructed the national companies under his jurisdiction to stop buying from France.[30] In 1978 and 1979, Paris and Algiers took steps to resolve their bilateral problems, and Franco-Algerian relations began to improve.

In 1975, the French government encouraged the negotiations and Spanish concessions that produced the Madrid Tripartite Agreement. According to Spanish officials involved in the agreement, France (along with the United States) pressured Spain in favor of Morocco because Paris preferred a Moroccan-controlled Sahara to a progressive new state.[31] President Giscard d'Estaing publicly expressed his opposition to the creation of "microstates," even though he decided in favor of independence for Djibouti and the Comoros, with populations of 273,000 and 344,000 respectively.[32] By 1980, after four years of destabilizing conflict in northwest Africa, the French government moved to a position of cautious neutrality. Although French diplomacy stated that "the Polisario does not exist,"[33] Paris tried in 1980 to give Algiers an impression of balance in its posture on the Western Sahara issue. The modest policy shift was more in tone than in substance — a difference in what the French government said or did not say, rather than a reduction of arms supplies to Morocco. At the parliamentary level, France's professed neutrality in the Western Sahara dispute was enhanced in January 1981 by a visit of five French deputies, representing the country's four major parties, to the Saharan refugee camps in the Tindouf region and to Polisario-controlled areas in the Western Sahara and southern Morocco.[34]

France vigorously encouraged King Hassan to be forthcoming at the OAU summit in Nairobi in June 1981, and it subsequently gave its unequivocal support for a referendum in the Western Sahara. Looking toward a settlement of the Sahara dispute, all the parties to the conflict, including the Polisario Front, would welcome an active French mediating role because of France's deep involvement in, and understanding of, North Africa. For its part, France would be opposed to any solution based on confederation because it wants to see Mauritania exist as a buffer state between Arab North Africa and black sub-Saharan Africa. There is an additional desire to protect French cultural and economic interests in Mauritania, which are vulnerable to Moroccan or Algerian/Polisario influence. There is some evidence, for example, that France pressured Morocco to dissuade it from intervening in Mauritania following the July 1978 coup against the Ould Daddah government.[35] And in October 1979, when Morocco delayed withdrawing its troops from Bir Moghrein following the Mauritanian-Polisario peace treaty, France responded to Nouakchott's invitation to send a small military unit to Nouadhibou to protect Mauritania and to guarantee its sovereignty and territorial integrity.

The election of François Mitterrand as president in May 1981 and a Socialist majority in parliament in June brought France its first leftist government in 23 years. Moroccans place great stock in their country's special relationship with France, and the change of government in Paris caused considerable concern that the new French leaders would establish privileged relations with socialist Algeria, Morocco's regional rival.

Since coming to power, the Mitterrand government has moved to a position of greater neutrality in French policy toward the Western Sahara issue. The French Socialist Party has ties to the Polisario, and its program calls for recognition of the front. Algerians have welcomed a more balanced French policy between Morocco and Algeria, proclaimed by Mitterrand during a November 1981 visit to Algiers. Nevertheless, President Mitterrand has close and long-standing ties with Morocco, and French Minister of Commerce Michel Jobert was born there. During its first year in power, the Socialist government nationalized important French arms manufacturers, including the Dassault aviation company, which produces the Mirage. But given the employment factor, it is uncertain, even if the influence of the powerful French arms lobby diminishes, that arms sales to Morocco will be affected—at least not before the current bilateral military arms agreement expires in 1985.

It is most likely, in view of France's heavy involvement in the economic and commercial sectors of Morocco, that the Socialist government will move carefully and avoid any major shift in its Sahara policy. The French government cannot afford the luxury of implementing Socialist doctrines in all of its foreign relations, and it is fully aware that any contact with the Polisario Front would seriously affect France's close relations with Morocco. Thus, in August 1981, when the Quai d'Orsay officially received Polisario representatives for the first time, the Mitterrand government quickly denied that this reception represented any change in French policy. And although the Polisario was allowed to open an office in Paris in February 1982, the French government showed no intention of granting the front formal recognition.

United States

Like Spain and France, the United States has maintained an official policy of neutrality on the substance of the Western Sahara issue. It has not recognized Moroccan or Mauritanian sovereignty in the Sahara, nor has it recognized the Polisario Front or the SDAR. Like Paris, Washington has been an important arms supplier to Morocco, though on a smaller scale. Since U.S. support for Morocco has been less significant than that of France, it has not been such a major factor in U.S.-Algerian relations. Finally, unlike French policy, the United States' involvement in the Sahara conflict is not affected to any appreciable degree by the Mauritanian factor.

In sharp contrast with both Spain and France, the United States was never a colonial power in northwest Africa. The initial U.S. contact of any significance with the area came in the 1942–1943 North African campaign of World War II. During the first twenty years after the war, the United States made little headway in cutting into France's dominant influence in the region. In the late 1960s, however, during an exceptional rupture in relations between Paris and Rabat, the United States was able to develop more significant political ties with Morocco. And during the 1970s, U.S.-Algerian commercial relations grew to impressive proportions. In contrast, the United States has not developed important political, economic, military, or cultural relations with Mauritania.

The United States enjoys close political relations with the moderate, pro-Western government of Morocco. Because of Morocco's strategic position commanding the southern access to the Mediterranean, Washington has a vested interest in a friendly government in Rabat. Washington and Rabat share much the same assessment of the destabilizing potential in Africa of the Soviet Union, Cuba, and Libya. King Hassan helped arrange and initially supported President Sadat's peace efforts with Israel before falling in line with the general Arab condemnation of the 1979 Egyptian-Israeli Peace Treaty. Hassan dispatched Moroccan troops in both 1977 and 1978 to help repel invasions of Zaire's mineral-rich Shaba province by Angolan-based rebels. Until 1978, the United States maintained a naval training facility at Kenitra, and two navy communications installations northeast of Rabat that served as important relay stations for facilities in the eastern Mediterranean region. In addition, Moroccan ports are generally open to visits by ships of the U.S. Sixth Fleet stationed in the Mediterranean. In contrast, commercial relations between the two countries are modest. The United States accounts for only 4–6 percent of Morocco's foreign trade. Moroccan imports have long centered on French products, and this trade preference is reinforced by U.S. self-sufficiency in both phosphates and food products, Morocco's major exports.

The United States' relations with Algeria, on the other hand, are just the reverse of those with Morocco. Washington and Algiers often disagree on foreign policy questions, especially north-south issues, where Algeria has been an architect of the New International Economic Order. Political relations, therefore, are correct but not close. These relations have improved since the more moderate regime of Chadli Benjedid took office in early 1979 and have benefited from Algeria's displeasure with the Soviet intervention in Afghanistan and the effective Algerian mediating role in ending the hostage crisis between the United States and Iran.[36] In contrast, large-scale commercial relations have developed during the past decade. In 1977, the United States replaced France as Algeria's principal trading partner and absorbed nearly half of Algerian exports, including 56 percent of Algerian crude oil and 28 percent of its liquefied natural gas. The oil imports, over 400,000 barrels per day, were valued at nearly $6 billion in 1980. And in 1981, the United States purchased about 50 percent of Algeria's high-quality oil, which represented 5 percent of total U.S. crude oil imports. Algerian natural gas also has made important inroads in the U.S. market, although deliveries under a major contract were halted in April 1980 because of a price disagreement.[37] Completing this commercial relationship, since the mid-1970s U.S. firms have signed contracts worth $6–8 billion with Algerian state-owned companies to provide technology and construction for Algeria's extensive development efforts.

The principles of U.S. policy toward the Western Sahara conflict have been clear. The United States supports efforts among the parties to negotiate a settlement of the conflict. Washington acknowledges Morocco's administrative control in the Sahara but not Rabat's claim to sovereignty. It supports the principle of self-determination in the Western Sahara but does not consider that Saharan self-determination has taken place. Further, it maintains that independence is not the only appropriate outcome of an act of self-determination. The United States has no interests in the Western Sahara itself and takes no position on the substance of the issue. The U.S. government has no preferred specific substantive solution of its own for the Western Sahara conflict and could live with any outcome to the dispute. Finally, though supporting negotiations and compromise by all parties, the United States does not want to play a mediating role because, in its view, other governments are better placed to perform this function.

The principles of this policy have been easier to enunciate than to implement. Though having no public preference for a settlement, it is clear that U.S. regional interests would not be served by the emergence of a weak Saharan ministate. Such a state is likely to be dominated by Algeria and would vote against the United States and its allies on most issues in the United Nations. Even worse for the United States' regional interests, a Saharan ministate possibly would be open to Libyan and Soviet influence, in which case the Western Sahara could become a base for interventionist activities in West Africa. In addition, the United States has no interest in a costly and festering war that could undermine the stability of the Moroccan monarchy or, alternatively, escalate to a full-scale Moroccan-Algerian war. Finally, Washington and Rabat have had serious policy disagreements over the proper use of U.S.-supplied weapons. This issue became a major factor in U.S.-Moroccan relations and requires more detailed examination.

Table 4

U.S. Arms Transfers to Morocco, 1974–1981
(millions of U.S. dollars)

Fiscal Year	Foreign Military Sales Agreements	Deliveries	Credits	Commercial Arms Exports
1974	8	4	3	0.038
1975	281	2	14	1.0
1976	105	16	30	4.1
1977	37	34	30	21.6
1978	7	87	43	12.0
1979	4	134	45	8.9
1980	321	65	25	17.4
1981	48	136	33	3.1
Total	811	478	223	68.1

SOURCE: U.S., Department of Defense, *Congressional Presentation: Security Assistance Program, FY 1983* (Washington, D.C., 1982), pp. 520–21, 526–27, 538–39, 550–51.

The United States' military supply relationship with Morocco began in 1960. The bulk of U.S. arms supplied to Morocco during the 1970s formed part of a modernization program for Morocco's general forces and were unrelated to the Western Sahara conflict. A U.S. military mission, headed by Brig. Gen. Edward Partain, went to Morocco in early 1974 to assess the needs of the kingdom's armed forces. The Partain mission proposed the equipping of two armored brigades to strengthen Morocco's defensive capabilities on its eastern frontier, where the Algerians have a considerable numerical superiority in armor and aircraft. The two brigades were to be completely formed by 1978–1980 entirely through military sales, with the total package costing about $500 million.[38] As Table 4 shows, the principal agreements for this military package were signed in 1975 and 1976, while the bulk of the deliveries were not made until 1978–1980. Military credits to Morocco have ranged from $14 million to $45 million a year from 1975 to 1982, far too modest to finance the arms purchases. The gap has been filled by generous financial aid from Saudi Arabia and, to a lesser extent, Kuwait, Qatar, and the United Arab Emirates. Although the precise amounts of this financial support are not known, it is probable that Saudi aid to Morocco has averaged between $500 million and $1 billion a year since 1975.[39]

In September 1977, Morocco asked the United States to provide counter-insurgency aircraft and Cobra attack helicopters, which most likely would be used in the Western Sahara and Mauritania. Morocco's use of U.S.-supplied weapons is subject to limitations imposed by a 1960 security assistance agreement between the two countries as well as by the Arms Export Control Act. Without prior consent, U.S.-supplied weapons may be used only for internal security and legitimate self-defense. The stipulation of the 1960 agreement was intended to prevent the use of U.S. arms against Israel, while the Arms Export Control Act covers all foreign military sales. During congressional hearings on Saharan self-determination in October 1977, a State Department representative acknowledged reports of the occasional use of U.S.-supplied F-5 aircraft for reconnaissance purposes beyond Morocco's internationally recognized borders but concluded there was "no evidence of any substantial violations of the provisions governing Morocco's use of U.S.-origin equipment." He went on to say, however, that Morocco's extensive use of this equipment in the Sahara "would pose serious problems."[40]

In March 1978, during congressional hearings on foreign assistance, the State Department admitted that Morocco had been using between six and ten F-5 aircraft in the Western Sahara illegally since mid-1976 but contended that this use did not constitute "substantial violations" of U.S. law.[41] Nevertheless, that same month, the U.S. government informed Morocco that it had withdrawn consideration of its arms request. In November, the

Carter administration announced that it would limit arms sales to Morocco because of Rabat's continued refusal to honor the 1960 agreement. However, the administration stated that it would permit sales of "defensive" arms, and in February 1979, it approved the sale to Morocco of six Boeing CH-47C Chinook heavy-lift helicopters, produced under license in Italy, under the category of "defensive" arms. The helicopter sale was a onetime exception to the Carter administration's arms policy for Morocco and resulted from "special circumstances" caused by considerable personal pressure from King Hassan.[42]

The continuing difference in interpretation between Washington and Rabat over Morocco's boundaries did not affect the sale of military equipment unsuited for the guerrilla war against the Polisario Front. In April 1977, Morocco signed a three-year $220-million contract with Westinghouse to provide a system of air defense radar installations, a supporting communications system, and a control center.[43] The State Department had no objections to this sale because it was intended for the defense of Morocco proper and because the Polisario has no air force.

The refusal of the Carter administration to lift its arms sales restrictions caused bitterness and resentment in Rabat, where some Moroccans felt betrayed by the United States.[44] Washington's reluctance to provide arms for what Moroccans considered legitimate self-defense introduced an element of friction into the United States' harmonious relations with Morocco. In December 1977, for example, King Hassan postponed a scheduled visit to the United States, and in the spring of 1979, he asked for the withdrawal of the U.S. ambassador in Rabat, Richard Parker, an experienced and very able diplomat with considerable expertise on North Africa.

During this period, the U.S. government began to change its view of the Saharan war. In congressional hearings held in July 1979, the Carter administration stated that repeated and serious Polisario attacks inside Morocco since January 1979 had changed the legal nature of the war. Despite disagreement on the use of F-5s in the Sahara, the executive branch decided to supply F-5 spare parts and to consider other Moroccan arms requests on a case-by-case basis.[45]

In October 1979, the Carter administration reversed itself and approved the sale of a $235-million arms package to Morocco, including six OV-10 Bronco armed reconnaissance planes, twenty F-5E jet fighters, and 24 Hughes 500 MD helicopters, to be delivered in 1981–1982. Several factors influenced this decision. In the context of broad foreign policy considerations, the Carter administration felt the need to reassure friends of the United States that U.S. military supply relationships were stable and reliable. With specific reference to Morocco, that country was facing a threat to its internal security. In addition, Morocco was a trusted and supportive ally of the United States in a year when Washington was being criticized for not having done enough to help keep the Shah of Iran in power. Finally, Saudi Arabia, an obviously important ally of both the United States and Morocco, urged approval of the sale and offered to provide the financing. In the top-level meeting that preceded the presidential decision, National Security Adviser Zbigniew Brzezinski strongly supported the full arms package for Morocco because of the great importance of Saudi Arabia to the United States and the need to support the United States' friends.[46]

When presented to Congress in January 1980, the Moroccan arms package ran into opposition in both the House and the Senate. A leading opponent of the weapons sale was Stephen Solarz, chairman of the House Subcommittee on Africa, who had made a fact-finding trip to northwest Africa in August 1979. Solarz argued in a *Foreign Affairs* article and in congressional hearings that the arms sale was not in the United States' national interest; that it would reward King Hassan for his aggression and would hurt U.S. relations with such key African countries as Algeria and Nigeria; and, finally, that U.S. assistance in the suppression of a genuine national liberation movement (the Polisario Front) would be a fundamental contradiction of basic American principles.[47]

In defending the Moroccan arms package in congressional hearings, the Carter administration cited the need to help friends of the United States. It identified the avoidance of a Moroccan military defeat in the Sahara conflict as a major U.S. interest. The executive branch reaffirmed its support of the concept of self-determination, as well as its reservations about Morocco's claims of sovereignty over the Western Sahara. It also argued that the arms were intended to be used not only to defend against attack in southern Morocco but also to offset Soviet arms in the Polisario's arsenal so as to give the Moroccans the necessary confidence to negotiate. Assistant Secretary of State for Near Eastern and South Asian Affairs Harold Saunders testified that the weapons in question "will give Morocco a sense of support that can contribute toward negotiation of a solution which reflects the wishes of the inhabitants" of the Western Sahara "and which may in some ways be personally difficult for King Hassan."[48]

The concerned committees and subcommittees in both the House and Senate put in writing their understanding that arms deliveries to Morocco would be linked to progress in negotiations. The House Foreign Affairs Committee, for example, urged that any deliveries of counterinsurgency equipment to Morocco "should be related to Morocco's willingness to help achieve a cease fire, to negotiate the relevant Western Sahara issues, and to cooperate with international efforts to mediate the dispute."[49] This suggested that the weapons transfers would be completed only if King Hassan's government demonstrated good faith in efforts to reach a negotiated political solution in the Western Sahara. While this approach of conditional weapons sales may have assuaged congressional opponents of the Moroccan arms package, it has proven extremely difficult to implement without seriously straining U.S.-Moroccan relations. In late February 1980, the 30-day deadline for Congress to oppose the proposed sale passed, and the arms transfer went forward. That same month, the Moroccan government decided against purchasing the 24 helicopters, half of which were to carry TOW antitank missiles, the other 12 to be equipped as gunships, with rockets and machine guns.

The January 1980 congressional hearings signaled an evolution of U.S. policy on the Western Sahara conflict. The Carter administration concluded that Morocco and the Polisario Front were locked in a costly but unwinnable war of attrition, and it had no illusions that additional U.S. weapons would enable Morocco to achieve a military victory. With the intensified effort to reach a negotiated settlement, the government announced its intention to alter gradually its position of prohibiting State Department officials from visiting the Western Sahara or having contact with the Polisario.[50] The ice was broken on April 3, 1980, when the Polisario lobbyist at the United Nations met with the State Department's director of North African affairs at his Washington home. In September, the State Department put out feelers for another meeting with the Polisario, but the front responded that a meeting would be possible only in "liberated territories" of the Western Sahara. Nevertheless, in December, the State Department's country officer for Algeria and the deputy chief of mission of the U.S. embassy in Algiers visited the Tindouf region, where they had discussions with Polisario officials. These meetings did not imply any U.S. recognition of the claims or status of the Polisario Front; they were similar to U.S. diplomatic contacts with organizations like SWAPO, the Namibian national liberation movement, whose claim to special status and rights is not recognized by the United States.

The Moroccan government was no doubt pleased to see the conservative Reagan administration take office in Washington in January 1981. The new administration soon articulated its prevailing view that "America's allies and close associates should expect understanding and reliable support. It would not be in the spirit of this administration's policy if support for America's traditional and historic friends—to meet reasonable and legitimate needs—were to be withheld or made conditional other than under extraordinary circumstances." In particular, the new administration felt "very strongly that traditional old friends such as Morocco deserve special support and consideration."[51]

The Reagan administration moved immediately to support Morocco's pending arms request—108 M-60A3 main battle tanks and twelve transport vehicles worth $189 million. Morocco made this request in August 1980 after being informed by Washington that the M-60 production line was going to close down. The request was vigorously debated within the executive branch until November, when the Carter administration shelved the issue out of concern for offending Algeria, which had begun to play its crucial intermediary role in the hostage crisis with Iran.[52] Since the tanks are badly suited for fighting the highly mobile Polisario forces in rugged desert terrain that contains narrow wadis and steep, rocky slopes, the arms request encountered little opposition from Congress.

In March 1981, the Reagan administration removed the limitation placed on arms sales to Morocco by Congress a year earlier. In a little publicized move, the State Department disclosed in congressional testimony that henceforth the U.S. government would not make military sales "explicitly conditional on unilateral Moroccan attempts to show progress toward a peaceful negotiated settlement. This position. . .recognizes the reality that there are players other than Morocco in the Western Saharan conflict. . . with a capacity to influence the outcome."[53] To show its evenhandedness, the Reagan administration also agreed in 1981 to sell Algeria six Lockheed C-130 transport planes. Since the aircraft were valued at just under $100 million, the deal could be handled as a commercial sale, which does not require congressional approval.

In the wake of the Polisario's October 1981 victory at Guelta Zemmur, in which the front employed Soviet-made SA-6 missile systems for the first time, Morocco once again requested military equipment from the United States. Between October 1981 and February 1982, a stream of high-level U.S. officials visited Morocco, including Secretary of Defense Caspar Weinberger, Assistant Secretary of Defense Francis West, CIA Deputy Director Bobby Inman, State Department troubleshooter Gen. Vernon Walters, Secretary of Commerce Malcolm Baldrige, and Secretary of State Alexander Haig. During Francis West's visit in November, the United States agreed to provide Morocco with various measures to counter the SA-6 missiles, including training in evasive flying tactics and electronic countermeasures equipment that could be retrofitted on Morocco's U.S.-supplied F-5E aircraft.

During Secretary of State Haig's visit in February 1982, the United States and Morocco agreed to establish a joint military commission. Haig also expressed an interest in obtaining transit rights at former U.S. military air bases in Morocco for use by the Rapid Deployment Force then being planned for the Middle East. These transit rights would permit U.S. planes to land and refuel during periods of military emergency in the Middle East.[54] Washington's interest in transit rights was pursued during meetings of the joint U.S.-Moroccan military commission in Fez in April. Closer military cooperation between the United States and Morocco was accompanied by increased U.S. financial assistance. Thus, during its congressional presentations in March 1982 in support of foreign aid, the Reagan administration requested $100 million in military sales credits for Morocco for fiscal year 1983, up from $30 million the previous year. The following month, the Pentagon notified Congress of its intent to sell Morocco 321 Maverick air-to-ground missiles for $29 million.

The question of U.S. use of Moroccan air bases was a major subject of discussion during King Hassan's official state visit to Washington, May 18–20, 1982. Negotiations were completed the following week, and on May 27, the United States and Morocco concluded an agreement allowing U.S. military planes to use Moroccan air bases during emergencies in the Middle East and Africa. The main facilities made available to the United States were the military side of the international airport at Casablanca and the military airfield at Sidi Slimane, about sixty miles northeast of Rabat.[55] Morocco reportedly retained a veto over the transit of U.S. forces if they were to be used against an Arab country friendly to Morocco.

The United States has tried to avoid any direct involvement in the Western Sahara conflict, which it views as a regional issue that requires a regional solution. Prior to the Green March in November 1975, Washington urged King Hassan to refrain from any precipitous unilateral action. The United States voted for the 1975 UNGA resolution (3458B) that took note of the Madrid Tripartite Agreement because that accord represented a negotiated solution to the conflict by the parties most directly involved. It voted for subsequent UNGA resolutions that referred the Sahara issue to the OAU as the appropriate regional organization to deal with the dispute and in 1980 withheld its support for the Moroccan draft resolution in the U.N. Fourth Committee until Morocco made a public commitment to the OAU referendum process. Washington has tried to be responsive to Morocco's legitimate needs for national defense—that is, it has tried to support Morocco enough to defend itself and encourage negotiations but not enough to overrun the Western Sahara. At the same time, the United States has attempted to nurture a growing relationship with Algeria. These two aims, though not always compatible, lie at the heart of the United States' Sahara policy. Finally, the United States has no desire to be caught in the middle of a conflict not of its own making.

Soviet Union

Soviet policy toward the Western Sahara conflict resembles, in many ways, that of the United States. Like Washington, Moscow has maintained an official policy of neutrality on the substance of the Sahara issue. It has not recognized Moroccan or Mauritanian sovereignty in the Sahara, nor has it recognized the Polisario Front or the SDAR. Like the United States, the Soviet Union has important relations with both of the major powers in northwest Africa, only the ties are just the reverse of Washington's. Moscow has long had substantial political and military links with Algeria and in the 1970s developed major economic relations with Morocco. And, as in the case of U.S. involvement, the Mauritanian factor has not had any noticeable influence on the Soviet Union's involvement in the Sahara conflict.

Like the United States, the Soviet Union has never been a colonial power in northwest Africa. Following Algerian independence in 1962, Moscow built upon its public support for the National Liberation Front (FLN) during the 1954–1962 revolutionary struggle against French colonial domination and established close political ties and a military supply relationship with Algiers. The USSR developed more modest ties with the Moroccan monarchy, centering on cooperation in the economic and educational fields and some limited weapons supplies. Like Washington, Moscow has not developed any significant political, economic, military, or cultural relations with Mauritania, where the Soviets' main interest is access to the rich Atlantic fishing grounds. In 1978, in support of this interest, the USSR signed an agreement with Mauritania that provides for Soviet aid in building Mauritania's fishing fleet and fish-processing industry.[56]

The Soviet Union's relations with Algeria are of considerable importance both politically and militarily. Because of Algeria's revolutionary experience, its socialist ideology, and its leading and progressive role in Third World politics, Moscow and Algiers find themselves in agreement on most international issues. The USSR has been a major diplomatic supporter of Algerian positions on Third World issues and considers Algeria an important means of entree into North Africa. The Soviet Communist party expresses its public approval of the Algerian FLN as a vanguard party that is building socialism.[57]

Moscow has been a consistent and important supplier for Algeria's armed forces. Although the Benjedid regime has taken steps to diversify military suppliers, up to 90 percent of Algerian arms are of Soviet origin, including some of the latest and most costly equipment exported by the USSR. The Algerian Army is equipped with 650 T-54, T-55, T-62, and T-72 medium-size tanks and 830 BTR armored personnel carriers, and the Algerian Air Force's 295 combat aircraft include 60 MiG-17s, 90 MiG-21MFs, 20 MiG-23BMs, and 10 MiG-25Rs.[58]

Beginning with an estimated $500 million deal in late 1975, the Soviet Union has responded quickly during the Saharan conflict to Algerian requests for advanced weapons for a major military modernization program.

The highlight of this arms supply relationship was a five-year military sales agreement between the USSR and Algeria in mid-1980 worth an estimated $3 billion. As a result of several large arms deals since 1975, Algeria has become the fourth largest purchaser of Soviet weapons among Third World countries. Although precise details of Soviet arms sales to Algeria since 1975 are not available, their total value is probably $4-5 billion.[59] In addition to the hard currency earned from these weapons sales, the Soviet Union derives specific military and strategic benefits from its close relations with Algeria. Fiercely independent, Algeria has not permitted Soviet bases to be established on its territory, but it does allow Soviet vessels to make port calls. Furthermore, Soviet aircraft overfly Algeria and use its airfields for refueling stops, which was of vital importance during the extensive Soviet airlift to Angola in 1975-1976.

In the economic sphere, the USSR has provided assistance to a variety of Algerian development projects.[60] Under a 1976 framework accord, the Soviets agreed to build an alumina complex, including a 600-megawatt power plant and a rail spur; a heavy machinery and electrical complex; a dam and irrigation works; a second steel mill in western Algeria, to process iron ore from Gara Jebilet; and oil refineries. By 1979, the USSR had committed $290 million to the aluminum plant. That same year, there were 11,500 Soviet and East European economic technicians in Algeria.[61] President Chadli Benjedid's June 1981 trip to Moscow produced an announcement of several new Soviet aid projects for Algeria, including a 630-megawatt power plant, a cement works, and some twenty new professional training centers. In trade relations, however, the Soviet Union and Algeria have little to offer each other.

In contrast to its ties with Algeria, the USSR has developed significant economic and commercial relations with Morocco dating from an initial trade agreement, concluded in 1958, that has been regularly renewed and extended. Since the mid-1960s, Moscow has provided assistance to a variety of economic, scientific, and technical projects in Morocco. In 1978, Soviet economic ties with Morocco expanded dramatically with the signing of a multibillion dollar phosphate agreement in March and a $300 million fishing agreement in April. The phosphate accord involves $2 billion of untied currency loans by the Soviet Union for the construction of a phosphate industry complex in the Meskala area, inland from Essaouira. The agreement also calls for a 30-year barter arrangement involving guaranteed deliveries by Morocco of enriched (triple super) phosphate, gradually increasing in amount to 10 million tons a year, in exchange for large amounts of Soviet oil, timber, and chemical products; at 1978 prices the overall value of this trade exceeds $9 billion. This agreement, which King Hassan termed "the contract of the century," is the largest commercial deal the Soviet Union has ever concluded with a Third World country.[62] The fishing agreement provides Morocco with financing for a large-scale program to create a maritime fishing industry. When questioned about this agreement by Algiers, the Soviet Union insisted that the accord, although it mentioned "the Atlantic coast," did not apply to the territorial waters of the Western Sahara.[63]

Soviet political and diplomatic ties with Morocco, however, are not close. Rabat's moderate and pro-Western alignment in international issues does not find favor in Moscow, and King Hassan frequently denounces Soviet involvement in Africa and Afghanistan. On occasion, Hassan has said that Morocco also is fighting the Soviet Union because of the sophisticated Soviet weapons used by the Polisario Front.[64] Since he has not moved against Soviet interests in Morocco, however, this anti-Soviet rhetoric appears to be a tactical stance to gain French and U.S. support. There is no evidence that the Soviets have supplied arms directly to the Polisario, and unlike the United States, the Soviet Union does not place legal and specific end-use limitations on its weapons sales — in this case to Algeria and Libya. Nevertheless, the USSR must approve the transfer of Soviet-made arms to third parties, and it is probable that the Soviets grant at least tacit approval of arms transfers to the Polisario through Algeria and Libya.

The Soviets have patiently built up their diplomatic and cultural presence in Morocco. They are probably attracted, among other things, to potential access to Morocco's strategically placed ports and facilities. Although Moscow's long-term aims in Morocco are not easily identifiable, it is likely that the Soviets are positioning themselves to be ready to act effectively in the event that a progressive or revolutionary regime replaces the monarchy.

In view of the Soviet Union's record of active and strong support for national liberation movements, the striking feature of Moscow's involvement in the Western Sahara conflict has been its restraint. The Soviets make very few public statements about the Sahara issue and continue to declare their neutrality. The Polisario Front is the only major African liberation movement that the USSR has never recognized. No Polisario officials have ever gone to Moscow. The Soviet Union has not even established party-to-party contacts with the Polisario, much less accorded the front the status of a national liberation movement. Rather, Moscow publicly has portrayed the Saharan question as a matter of conflicting positions between Algeria and Morocco. In contrast to the USSR's strong and visible support for the Palestinian resistance movement — the PLO mission in Moscow was granted diplomatic recognition in 1981 — the Soviets have not identified themselves directly with the Polisario cause. Instead, they have been content to vote for pro-Algerian resolutions at the United Nations on the basis of support for the right of self-determination in the Western Sahara. On occasion, when meeting with supporters of the Polisario Front, the USSR has reaffirmed its public support for Saharan self-determination.[65]

The basic Soviet interest in the Saharan conflict has been to avoid entanglement in a quarrel between two states with which Moscow seeks to maintain good relations. By exercising restraint in the Sahara dispute, the Soviets seek to protect their interests in both Algeria and Morocco. Moscow's role of arms supplier to Algeria, which is of major importance to the Algerians, is tolerated by the Moroccans, who also received some Soviet weapons in the 1960s and mid-1970s. It is clear, however, that any open and direct Soviet involvement in the Sahara conflict would cause King Hassan to break relations immediately with the USSR. Morocco gave a warning in this regard in the fall of 1975, when the Soviets took an active pro-Algerian position in the U.N. debates on the Sahara question.[66] Rabat immediately severed relations with East Germany, a close ally of the Soviet Union, and then froze negotiations on the Meskala phosphate agreement, which was on the verge of completion.

With the exception of the seizure and detention of two Soviet trawlers fishing off the Western Sahara in December 1980, relations between Moscow and Rabat have remained close. After being dormant for a period, the Meskala agreement has gone forward, and the first aspects of its implementation have taken place. Morocco has renewed its citrus agreement with the USSR. For its part, Moscow is quite willing to sell weapons to Morocco. The Soviets have been careful not to do anything to embarrass the Moroccans in the Western Sahara issue. Morocco retains the option of canceling the Meskala agreement, and this accord will remain a pressure point in Soviet-Moroccan relations in the future. The USSR's desire to have an assured long-term source of fertilizer is linked to the expansion of Morocco's phosphoric acid facilities. Thus, the Soviets need the Meskala agreement more than the Moroccans do, which gives Rabat considerable leverage.

The Soviet Union has much to lose and little to gain in the Western Sahara conflict. For Soviet foreign-policy makers, the whole issue of eventual Western Sahara independence is relatively unimportant but potentially troublesome. Unlike Ethiopia or Angola, an independent Saharan state would not be fertile ground for communist ideology or Soviet penetration. On the other hand, if the dispute escalates to the level of a major Moroccan-Algerian conflict, the Soviets are likely to be caught in the agonizing dilemma of having to take sides and thus seriously alienate one of the conflicting parties. If faced with a necessary choice, the USSR is likely to side with Algeria, which would jeopardize the Soviet presence in Morocco. Given the risks involved, the Soviets will continue their policy of considerable restraint in the Sahara dispute and avoid open or direct involvement in the conflict.

5 | Toward a Resolution of the Conflict

The Western Sahara conflict has continued since 1975. The resultant blood-shed, population displacement, economic cost, and military tension have caused considerable strains in northwest Africa at both the national and regional levels and led, in 1978, to the overthrow of a civilian government in Mauritania and its replacement by a military regime. This concluding chapter examines the possibilities of resolving the costly Sahara dispute. Despite a variety of mediation attempts, the contending parties remain locked in irreconcilable positions. A new approach to a negotiated solution is required to overcome the existing deadlock. To be successful, the approach will need to be both flexible and sensitive to the regional dynamics of the conflict.

Failure of Previous Mediation Attempts

The failure to resolve the Western Sahara dispute has not resulted from a lack of mediators. A wide variety of outside parties has recognized the dangers inherent in a festering conflict and has attempted to promote a peaceful settlement. At various times since 1975, Saudi Arabia, Egypt, Tunisia, Iraq, Libya, Senegal, the Ivory Coast, Nigeria, Guinea, Togo, Kuwait, Gabon, France, Spain, the PLO, the Arab League, and the OAU have tried to encourage a reconciliation of the warring parties. Some of the mediating parties, like Saudi Arabia and the OAU, have made several attempts to resolve the conflict.

In early 1976, Egypt and Saudi Arabia tried to find a formula to end hostilities in northwest Africa. Both these important states from the eastern Arab world were spurred to action by the two armed clashes between Moroccan and Algerian forces at Amgala in the northern Sahara. Egyptian Vice-President Hosni Mubarak shuttled for a week between Fez and Algiers, and President Anwar Sadat spoke by telephone with King Hassan and President Boumediene. Mubarak proposed a cease-fire and a foreign ministers' meeting, to be followed by a Moroccan-Algerian-Mauritanian summit meeting. This Egyptian mediation effort collapsed when Algeria insisted on Morocco's evacuation of the Sahara as a precondition to a summit and Morocco did not agree to the proposed summit meeting.[1] Saudi Arabia urged both Rabat and Algiers to settle their differences, and in late 1976, Crown Prince Fahd and Foreign Minister Saud visited northwest Africa in an unsuccessful effort to mediate the dispute.

In addition to efforts by outside parties, the conflicting parties themselves have made halting efforts to discuss their differences. These meetings were intended to be secret, but one side or the other usually saw an advantage, after the fact, in announcing them publicly. In the summer of 1977, for example, King Hassan met with the Polisario at Ifrane in Morocco, but each side's conditions for a settlement were unacceptable to the other. In late 1977 and early 1978, high-level Moroccan and Algerian representatives discussed a political solution in Fez and Lausanne.[2] As a consequence of these contacts, there is some evidence that King Hassan and President Boumediene planned to meet in Brussels in the fall of 1978 to try to find a solution to the Western Sahara conflict. This very promising negotiation had to be canceled because of the serious illness of Boumediene, who fell into a deep coma in mid-November from which he never emerged.[3] In 1979, high-level Moroccan representatives reportedly met with Polisario officials in Bamako, Mali. In 1980, high officials from both Morocco and Algeria met in Geneva, and in 1981, King Hassan and President Benjedid had brief contacts on two different occasions in Taif, Saudi Arabia.

The details of these various mediation attempts and contacts between the conflicting parties are less important than their failure to produce a settlement. King Hassan's government remains committed to the recovery of the Sahara and its integration into the Moroccan state and refuses to deal directly with the Polisario Front. Algeria continues to support Saharan self-determination and insists that the dispute must be resolved through negotiations between Morocco and the Polisario. The front remains committed to the struggle to secure international recognition for the SDAR as an independent, sovereign state comprising the historical territory of the Western Sahara.

Underlying these mutually exclusive positions are a variety of factors that impel the opposing parties to continue the conflict and discourage significant compromises of basic aims. Only Mauritania, which bowed out of the conflict when it signed a peace treaty with the Polisario Front in August 1979, has found the burden of the struggle too heavy to bear. For the other three parties, the prospect of victory or the lack of an alternative strategy has outweighed the advantages of abandoning the struggle.

The Moroccan campaign to annex the Western Sahara is supported by a national consensus and broad public support. Since the activation of the campaign in 1974, Moroccan political parties of all shades — especially the nationalist Istiqlal party but also including the opposition Socialist Union of Popular Forces (USFP) — have been more militant than the palace, and in this sense King Hassan has been a follower and rallier, rather than a leader, of public opinion on the Sahara issue. Even among Moroccan revolutionary left-wing groups, which have a small following among Moroccan students and workers living abroad, mainly in France, only one organization — the Marxist-Leninist "Ilal Amam" group — supports the struggle of the Polisario Front.[4] Because of the unpopularity of this position among Moroccans, the Ilal Amam movement has found it necessary to use such ambiguous formulas as "The Sahara is Moroccan, but it is not for the corrupt regime."[5] Within Morocco, political parties have criticized the government's handling of the Sahara issue, but these criticisms have focused on tactics — excessive military restraint or diplomatic blunders — not basic policy goals.[6] In September 1981, for example, when the USFP withheld its support of the government's Sahara policy following Nairobi II, the party's main objective was to protest that it had not been consulted before the king agreed to commit the country to a potentially risky referendum in the Sahara.[7]

The economic and military burdens of the war have been considerable for Morocco but so far have not caused either the government or the public to reconsider the Sahara campaign. Since 1976, the Sahara war has cost from 25 to 40 percent of Morocco's national budget. The total costs of the war may be as high as a billion dollars a year. While the direct impact of these military and administrative expenses has been cushioned by generous Saudi aid, the economic repercussions of the war have nevertheless been felt throughout Moroccan society. War-related costs were one factor cited by King Hassan in 1978 when he shelved Morocco's Five-Year Development Plan (1978–1982) and replaced it with a three-year austerity transition plan. Economic strains were evident in June 1981 when government-controlled price increases of staple products led to bloody riots in Casablanca. The complaints of the demonstrators, however, were directed against the government's economic and educational policies, not the Sahara campaign.[8] In the larger economic context, Morocco's difficulties since 1975 have been caused more by several years of drought and poor harvests, depressed world prices for phosphate, and basic structural problems than by expenses related to the Sahara conflict. In short, Morocco has experienced problems typical of a non-oil-producing Third World country during an international economic recession.

On the military side, Moroccan casualties probably have ranged from a low of 25–50 a month to a high of 100–150, suggesting a total of 1,000–1,500 a year, beginning in 1976.[9] In light of the genuine national commitment to the Sahara issue, this level of casualties has not caused morale problems among the Moroccan military. Some problems of morale have arisen because of the heat, poor food, isolation, late pay, and difficult fighting conditions in combating an elusive guerrilla enemy. These factors were more of a problem from 1977 to 1979, when Moroccan forces were in a defensive position and were limited in their abilities to respond quickly and effectively to Polisario attacks. Since the spring of 1980, structural changes in the military and offensive operations have improved morale considerably, and the Moroccan military appears capable of sustaining the war for a very long period.

As the ultimate decision maker and source of authority in Morocco, King Hassan is the primary architect of his country's Saharan policy. There is little question that the King has exercised a restraining influence — not only on the Istiqlal party, which still espouses Morocco's irredentist claims to territories in western Algeria, but also on military commanders who want to attack Polisario sanctuaries across the border in the Tindouf region of southwest Algeria. As the political-religious leader of the Moroccan state — both secular ruler and spiritual leader (imam) — one source of Hassan's legitimacy is his role as defender of Morocco's territorial integrity. By restoring a portion of the national patrimony, the annexation of the Western Sahara has enhanced the king's legitimacy. At the same time, however, by tying his prestige so closely to the Sahara campaign, Hassan has severely restricted his negotiating options. The king has little room to maneuver on the Sahara issue. While the costs of retaining the Western Sahara are heavy, loss or abandonment of the territory could cost Hassan his throne if not his life.

On the other side, the Polisario Front is equally capable of sustaining the conflict — provided its sources of support from Algeria and Libya do not dry up. Since the Polisario has almost no economic resources of its own, it is not directly vulnerable in the conventional sense to the material costs of the war. Its casualties probably have averaged half or less of those of Morocco. Since 1976, the front has demonstrated an impressive ability to build up its military forces, to employ increasingly heavy and sophisticated weapons, and to adapt its tactics to deal with new weapons systems introduced by Morocco. Some analysts stress that the population base of up to one hundred thousand from which the Polisario draws will limit the front's ability to field an army to a maximum of fifteen to twenty thousand men and that as the front increasingly fights as a conventional army, it will risk exhausting its limited human resources.[10] The Polisario is able to replace its human losses, however, by recruiting new cadres in northern Mauritania and perhaps in western Algeria, northern Mali, and northern Niger.[11] It is likely that the front will not scale down its activities or make other tactical adjustments to reduce casualties until it begins to suffer more than a thousand killed or permanently out of action a year. Given its population base and ability to recruit in neighboring Saharan territories, the Polisario should be able to sustain losses of up to a thousand personnel a year for many years into the future.

The Polisario Front appears committed to a long struggle. As a movement that began with few material or political assets, the Polisario has very little to lose. In this sense it can well afford to be uncompromising in its demand for full independence of all of the Western Sahara. As a liberation movement challenging an established power, the Polisario does not have to win the Saharan conflict in the conventional sense of forcing Morocco to accept its terms. As a new force challenging the status quo, all the Polisario must do over the next several years is to avoid losing — that is, it must avoid either being eliminated by Morocco or reduced to a level where it is no longer taken seriously by the international community. By seizing the military offensive from Morocco in 1978–1979 and by achieving recognition for the SDAR by nearly fifty states, the Polisario Front has done considerably better than avoiding defeat.

Despite its impressive performance, however, the Polisario remains heavily dependent on political and especially material support by Algeria and Libya. In the highly unlikely circumstance that both those countries were to cut off support, the Polisario would soon be reduced to a low level of activity, although it would certainly not disappear. In the more likely case that Algeria phased its support down (or out), the Libyans might move in and try to fill the void. Even if the Polisario relocated its population in northern Mauritania or Mali, problems of distance and logistical support would necessarily mean a decline in material supplies. The importance of the Algerian territorial sanctuary should also be stressed. If that sanctuary were lost or abandoned, the Polisario would be highly vulnerable both to the economic pressures of the harsh desert environment and the military pressures of the Moroccan Army and Air Force.

In contrast to Morocco and the Polisario Front, Algeria has some flexibility in its Saharan policy. The Polisario struggle against Morocco is not an especially popular cause among the Algerian public, for whom the Western Sahara is a somewhat distant territory of questionable value. Few Algerians are ready to die for the principle of Saharan self-determination. The costs to

Algeria of the war are both direct and indirect. The direct costs include $36,000–50,000 a day for food and medicine to support the refugee population in camps in the Tindouf region,[12] plus undisclosed sums for gasoline and some of the military supplies for Polisario forces. These direct costs are modest and are easily borne by the Algerian government. Indirectly, however, the Sahara conflict contributes to regional tensions that oblige Algeria to spend large sums of money on building up its own military forces.

Whereas President Boumediene was personally and ideologically committed to the cause of Saharan self-determination, his more pragmatic successor, Chadli Benjedid, is probably somewhat less committed. While President Benjedid has reaffirmed Algeria's support of the Polisario, his personal prestige is not closely linked to the front's fortunes. Since 1979, Algerian leaders have been more concerned with domestic issues than was the Boumediene regime. Any sharp shift in policy on the Sahara issue would be difficult because it would run counter to Algeria's revolutionary past and its strong support for the principle of self-determination. Nevertheless, the Benjedid government, with its power consolidated, is reasonably well positioned to support a compromise settlement of the Sahara dispute.

The "Sade" Plan

The July 1978 coup in Nouakchott, which quickly led to a cease-fire between Mauritania and the Polisario Front, spurred efforts to promote a negotiated settlement of the Western Sahara conflict. The French government was particularly active in these efforts, although it did not associate itself publicly with any specific proposal. In the months following the coup in Mauritania, France attempted to spur negotiations by proposing several settlement scenarios. These scenarios were not put forward as final solutions but rather as working hypotheses for future discussions, without any obligation on the parties involved.

One of the more intriguing scenarios to emerge at this time was known as the "Sade" (Sahara Demain, or Tomorrow's Sahara) plan. This plan was potentially significant because it tried to take into account and reconcile the interests of each of the parties involved in the Sahara conflict and included an attempt to end the Moroccan-Algerian border dispute.[13]

As shown in Map 5, the Sade plan proposed the following division of the Western Sahara:

> 1. A new Saharan state would comprise a third of the area of Rio de Oro then occupied by Morocco; Tiris al-Gharbiyya; and two sections of Mauritanian territory (ceded by Mauritania), one west of Zouirat and the other south of Bir Moghrein.

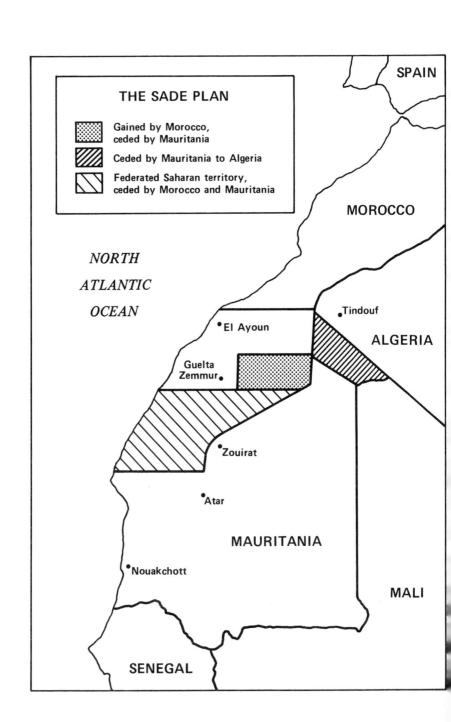

THE SADE PLAN

Gained by Morocco, ceded by Mauritania

Ceded by Mauritania to Algeria

Federated Saharan territory, ceded by Morocco and Mauritania

SPAIN

MOROCCO

NORTH
ATLANTIC
OCEAN

Tindouf

ALGERIA

El Ayoun

Guelta
Zemmur

Zouirat

Atar

MAURITANIA

Nouakchott

MALI

SENEGAL

2. This Saharan state would immediately enter into federation with Mauritania. Morocco would keep two-thirds of that part of the Sahara it occupied from 1975 to 1979, to which would be added the region of Bir Moghrein and Chegga (ceded by Mauritania).

3. Algeria would receive from Mauritania a section of land that would lengthen its southwestern corner and secure the frontier at Tindouf.

4. Mauritania thus would give up some territory to Morocco and Algeria as compensation for the creation of a federal state consisting of Mauritania within its new frontiers and the Saharan state.

The reactions of the various parties to the Sade plan are not known. According to at least one source, a "just and lasting" settlement corresponding in most of its aspects to the Sade plan was received favorably by Mauritania, Algeria, and Libya, but not by Morocco or the Polisario Front.[14] The Sade plan was perhaps of most interest to Mauritania. In exchange for giving up relatively uninhabited territories devoid of resources, Mauritania would gain a peaceful and federal relationship with a Saharan political entity. Morocco would give up some Saharan territory but would receive other territory from Mauritania. More important, it would find a peaceful exit from a costly war. For Algeria the territory ceded from Mauritania would ease concerns about encirclement by Morocco. At the same time, however, the Sade plan would involve a serious accommodation for Algeria in its support of the principle of self-determination. Finally, the Polisario Front could have been expected to reject the Sade plan totally because it fell so far short of the goal of an independent Saharan state comprising all of the Western Sahara.

A Saharan Zone

In retrospect, the timing was not favorable for a settlement in the second half of 1978. The Polisario's Mauritanian strategy had succeeded. By concentrating its military efforts against the weaker of its adversaries, the front had strained Mauritania's resources to the point where a military regime anxious to withdraw from the Sahara conflict seized power in Nouakchott. Flushed with this success, the Polisario was encouraged in the conviction that time was on its side. There was no incentive for the front to accept a compromise settlement that involved fundamental revisions of its basic goals. On the other side, the Moroccan government saw in the death of President Boumediene and his replacement by a more pragmatic leader the possibility of an accommodation with Algeria that would considerably weaken the Polisario. Thus, Morocco also felt that time was working in its favor and had little incentive to compromise its Saharan campaign.

Rather than giving either side a decisive advantage, developments since 1978 have produced a military stalemate. Continual bloodletting is likely, during the next several years, to erode the conviction held by both Morocco and the Polisario Front that time is working in their favor. It is extremely difficult to make precise forecasts. Nevertheless, it is unlikely that the Sahara conflict will continue indefinitely, at least not in the present costly form of a war of attrition. At some future point, when the timing is more favorable, there will be a need to give serious consideration to the outlines of a compromise settlement.

One possible approach to a settlement could involve a "Saharan Zone," proposed here by the author and presented in Maps 6–8. This zone would leave the Sakiet al-Hamra northern panhandle under Moroccan sovereignty. The Saharan Zone would comprise Rio de Oro plus a portion of northern Mauritania extending eastward to the Algerian border. Two other small border changes would offer partial compensation to Mauritania: (1) the southeast corner of the Western Sahara would become Mauritanian territory, to ensure that the new rail track carrying iron ore from Zouirat to Nouadhibou would be entirely within Mauritania; and (2) the southern border of the Western Sahara would be extended in a straight line westward to the Atlantic Ocean, so that the western half of the narrow Capo Blanco peninsula, where Nouadhibou is located, would become part of Mauritania. The Enlarged and Diminished Saharan Zones represent territorial variations of the basic approach, the first more favorable to the Polisario Front and the second more favorable to Morocco.

The final status of the Saharan Zone would be determined by a referendum in which the Sahrawi population would express its preference. Participation in the referendum would be limited to Sahrawis who inhabited the Western Sahara in 1974 plus, perhaps, the 20,000–35,000 Sahrawis who left the territory in the wake of the 1957–1958 uprising. In order to be acceptable to Algeria and the Polisario Front, the referendum would have to be a genuine exercise of self-determination. The range of choices in such a referendum is wide, but three major options suggest themselves: an independent Saharan state, a confederal association with Morocco, and a confederal association with Mauritania. Within the latter two options lie a variety of possibilities ranging from a high degree of autonomy to a high level of integration. If a majority of the Sahrawi population opted for a confederal association with either Morocco or Mauritania, a second referendum could be held to offer choices to define the nature of the confederal relationship. In both cases, to gain international acceptance the referenda should be administered by an impartial body, preferably the United Nations.

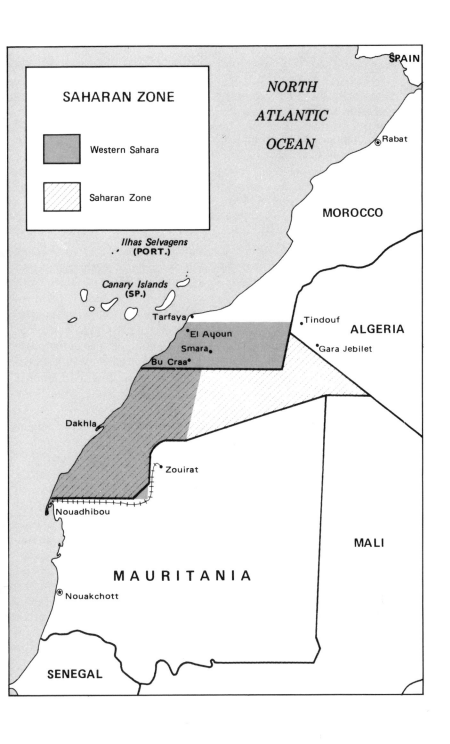

SAHARAN ZONE

Western Sahara

Saharan Zone

SPAIN

NORTH

ATLANTIC

OCEAN

⊛ Rabat

MOROCCO

Ilhas Selvagens
(PORT.)

Canary Islands
(SP.)

Tarfaya

•Tindouf

ALGERIA

•El Ayoun

Smara.

•Gara Jebilet

Bu Craa•

Dakhla

•Zouirat

Nouadhibou

MALI

MAURITANIA

⊛ Nouakchott

SENEGAL

The specific features of a Saharan Zone, as well as its precise boundaries, would be the subject of negotiations among the parties to the conflict. The negotiations would stand a better chance of succeeding if they were conducted in private. Negotiations would necessarily precede a referendum since voter eligibility and the modalities of the referendum are issues that, themselves, would be subject to potentially difficult negotiations.

A number of regional linkages could ensure that a Saharan Zone settlement of the Western Sahara conflict would be part of a larger settlement of long-standing regional disputes. These linkages could include joint exploitation (in effect, profit sharing) of Bu Craa phosphates between Morocco and the Saharan Zone; joint exploitation of mineral resources in Rio de Oro (for example, iron ore at Agracha) between Mauritania and the Saharan Zone; joint exploitation of iron ore deposits at Gara Jebilet between Algeria and Morocco; and ratification by Morocco of its 1972 border agreement with Algeria.

An underlying assumption of this approach is that a compromise agreement between Morocco and Algeria would be a necessary precondition of any permanent settlement of the Western Sahara conflict. The Sahara conflict is part of broader disputes between the two countries. Without a broader regional settlement, a resolution of the Western Sahara conflict would be difficult to achieve or, if somehow achieved, would not be likely to last.

A principal attraction of the Saharan Zone is that it meets major demands of all three key parties to the conflict. There could be enough in this approach to make it appealing to each party so that by giving up a little each could gain a lot. By making a few compromises, the antagonists could move away from the present zero-sum configuration of regional politics in northwest Africa toward a situation of mutually agreeable and beneficial trade-offs.

Morocco would give up its claim to Rio de Oro, agree to share the mineral wealth in Sakiet al-Hamra, and effectively renounce future irredentist claims to parts of Algerian territory. In return, Morocco would find an honorable way out of a costly war and would resolve its long-standing border and security problems with Algeria. Control of Sakiet al-Hamra would ensure that the exploitation of Saharan phosphates did not threaten Morocco's impressive position in the international phosphate market.

Algeria would give up the short-term gain of a low-cost war that drains Moroccan resources and would agree to share the mineral wealth at Gara Jebilet, which has yet to be exploited. In return, Algeria would resolve its long-standing border and security problems with Morocco, thereby avoiding, or at least curtailing, an expensive arms race that could last for many years. By supporting a settlement that is essentially consistent with the right

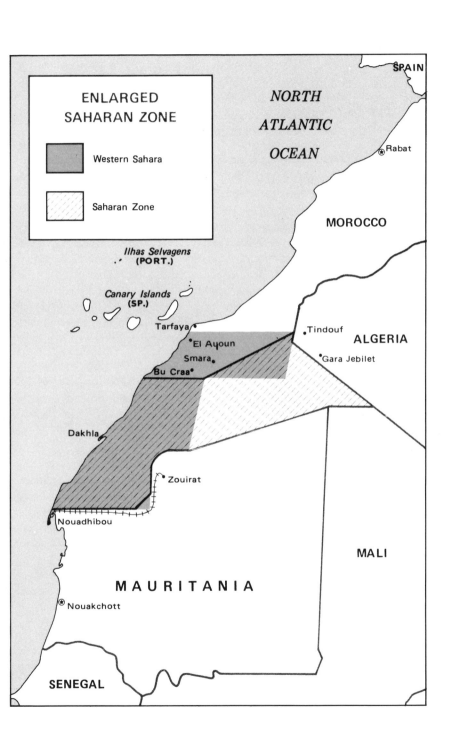

ENLARGED
SAHARAN ZONE

Western Sahara

Saharan Zone

NORTH
ATLANTIC
OCEAN

SPAIN

⊛ Rabat

MOROCCO

Ilhas Selvagens
(PORT.)

Canary Islands
(SP.)

Tarfaya

•El Ayoun
Smara•
Bu Craa•

•Tindouf

ALGERIA

•Gara Jebilet

Dakhla

Zouirat

Nouadhibou

MALI

MAURITANIA

⊛ Nouakchott

SENEGAL

to self-determination, Algeria would not be compromising its principles and thus need not risk a loss of international prestige. Algiers would receive the additional benefit of depriving Libya of the opportunity to manipulate the Polisario, a situation that is of increasing concern to Algeria.

The Polisario Front would give up its struggle for an independent Saharan state within the historical boundaries of the Western Sahara and agree to accept the results of a referendum. In return, the Polisario could perhaps become the dominant element in a Saharan Zone. This zone would share the economic wealth from Bu Craa phosphates, and it could become an independent Saharan state with an enlarged territory.

Mauritania would give up an area of land in the northern part of the country that amounts to about 15 percent of its national territory. In return, Mauritania would benefit from two small border rectifications in its favor and would gain a protective buffer against both Morocco and Algeria. In addition, the Mauritanians would share in the economic wealth from mineral deposits in Rio de Oro and would enjoy an enhanced security position. Additional inducements might take the form of economic largesse from wealthy oil-producing states in the Arabian peninsula, such as Saudi Arabia and the United Arab Emirates, both strong supporters of Morocco.

A Saharan Zone offers several other attractions:

1. It would have some flexibility stemming from referendum options and a transition period.

2. The zone could be a pole of attraction for Sahrawis living outside the Western Sahara, a kind of national homeland for those Sahrawis who preferred to emigrate from the surrounding countries (and from Sakiet al-Hamra).

3. It would go a long way toward promoting and achieving regional stability.

4. The zone would correspond, more than does the Western Sahara, to the areas formerly controlled by the Reguibat tribe, whose members dominate the Polisario movement.

5. The referendum would satisfy the strong international consensus in favor of self-determination for the Sahrawi population.

Any compromise proposal, by definition, will fail to satisfy all the demands of the contending parties. Morocco would object to the potential removal of Rio de Oro from its claimed territory, and the Polisario would hesitate to accept a settlement that leaves Sakiet al-Hamra under Moroccan control. Another drawback would be the changes involved in former colonial boundaries, a violation of an important OAU principle. The 1963 border rectifications between Mauritania and Mali suggest that this need not be a stumbling block.[15] In addition, it is unlikely that the OAU would oppose a settlement acceptable to the parties to the conflict.

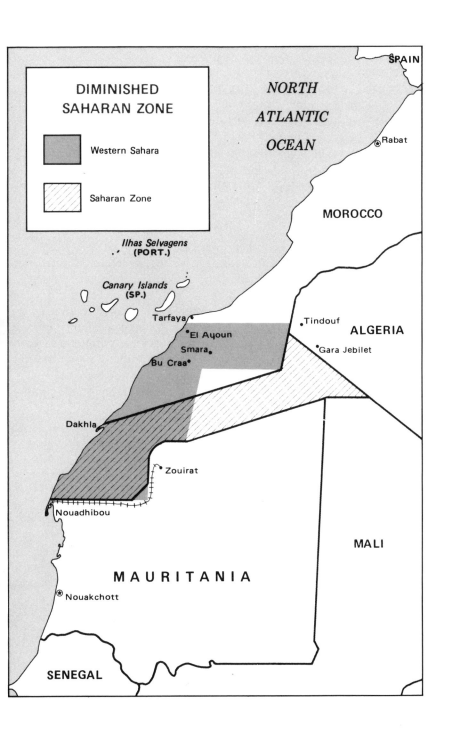

DIMINISHED
SAHARAN ZONE

Western Sahara

Saharan Zone

NORTH
ATLANTIC
OCEAN

SPAIN

⊛ Rabat

MOROCCO

Ilhas Selvagens
(PORT.)

Canary Islands
(SP.)

Tarfaya

•Tindouf   ALGERIA

•El Ayoun

Smara•

Bu Craa•

•Gara Jebilet

Dakhla

•Zouirat

Nouadhibou

MALI

MAURITANIA

⊛ Nouakchott

SENEGAL

Certain changes in perception are necessary before a Saharan Zone will be acceptable to the key parties. Morocco will need to view the military conflict as essentially unwinnable over the long term and will need to realize the diplomatic cost of its increasing international isolation. Algeria will need to appreciate the long-term advantages accruing from a regional settlement with Morocco, to the extent that it is willing to push the Polisario toward a political compromise. The Polisario will need to perceive its military fortunes on the decline over the long term and to see in the Saharan Zone an opportunity to achieve its basic goals.

Perceptions in the other direction—especially a sense of "victory is possible" on the part of Morocco or the Polisario (or both)—ensure a continuation of the Western Sahara conflict. In addition to regional destabilization, continued conflict poses specific dangers to Morocco—internal strains over time, both economic and political, and diplomatic isolation, especially within the OAU.

The concept of a Saharan Zone is an approach that contains several key elements of a viable settlement. At the appropriate moment, it is a concept that the parties to the conflict might want to examine seriously. At that point, an Enlarged Saharan Zone may represent maximum Polisario concessions, while a Diminished Saharan Zone may represent maximum Moroccan concessions. This difference, at least, could establish the parameters of serious negotiations.

The Regional Context of a Settlement

In the fall of 1982, prospects for settlement of the Western Sahara conflict were poor. The seating of the SDAR delegation at the OAU Council of Ministers meeting in Addis Ababa in February had the effect of hardening the Polisario Front's diplomatic position. In the following months, the Polisario and Algeria asserted that the SDAR had become a full member of the OAU and bilateral negotiations with Morocco should now be pursued. In the front's view, no further special OAU meetings to deal with the Sahara issue were necessary. This position effectively ruled out further cooperation with the OAU Implementation Committee. The proposed shuttle by OAU Chairman Moi among the interested and concerned parties to get their agreement to the Nairobi III decision was dead. Following the successful boycott of the OAU summit in Tripoli in August, Morocco reaffirmed the "definitive and irrevocable" decisions taken by the Nairobi summit in June 1981 and declared that the admission of the SDAR to the OAU was null and void. The OAU itself was going through the worst crisis in its history, with members split—and split rather evenly—over the issue of the SDAR's admission.

Even if the work of the Implementation Committee somehow resumes, prospects for holding a referendum as called for by the OAU are poor. King Hassan has made it clear in his public statements that he views the referendum as an opportunity for the Sahrawi population to confirm once and for all Moroccan sovereignty in the Sahara and has said that he will not accept a negative vote. Morocco refuses to withdraw its army and administration from the Western Sahara prior to the referendum and also rules out any discussions with the Polisario Front. Given the considerable differences among public positions, there appears little likelihood that the opposing parties will be able to agree on the eligibility of voters, the places and conditions of voting, or the supervising and controlling authorities for the referendum.

Thus, formal positions on the diplomatic front still remain quite rigid. With the exception of the two tactical compromises made by Morocco, no party to the conflict is ready as yet to state publicly that it is willing to negotiate on the basis of less than its maximum demands. And Algeria, even though it grants assistance and asylum to the Polisario, continues to insist that it is not a necessary party to negotiations. Meanwhile, the military conflict continues as a costly war of attrition. Neither side has won, nor can reasonably expect to win, a decisive advantage on the battlefield.

The need for a broader approach to settle the Western Sahara dispute remains. An approach that centers on such problems as a cease-fire and referendum limited to the Western Sahara itself is unlikely to succeed. These problems, though important and immediate in their own right, need to be linked to broader regional issues in order to come to grips with the underlying dynamics of the Sahara conflict. Unless a solution of the Sahara dispute is part of a broader Moroccan-Algerian (and, to a lesser extent, Mauritanian) accommodation — as suggested in the preceding proposal for a Saharan Zone — the solution is unlikely to be a lasting one. In particular, a solution forced on Morocco by international diplomatic and economic pressures is unlikely to be tolerated over the long run by the Moroccan population. In this regard as in others, the regional context of the Sahara conflict is a critical factor in the search for a settlement.

Outside parties can assist in the search for a solution, especially in a region like northwest Africa where the actors have such difficulty in resolving their own disputes. On the international level, care must be taken that the festering Western Sahara conflict does not escalate into major hostilities between Morocco and Algeria. If this occurs, the Sahara conflict could become internationalized, a polarization of forces could occur in what is essentially a regional dispute, and a proxy confrontation between the United States and the Soviet Union over the Sahara could ensue. Both superpowers would be dragged, against their will, into a conflict over which they had no control.

The Soviet Union's restrained behavior on the Sahara issue strongly suggests that Moscow has no interests in an escalated conflict. The United States has a vested interest in a negotiated solution that is responsive to the basic needs of all the parties to the conflict. This interest can best be served by a judicious mixture of diplomatic support and defensive arms for Morocco, provided in ways that encourage Rabat to be flexible diplomatically and forthcoming in negotiations. The United States and France, each in its own way, strive to maintain good relations with both Morocco and Algeria. Furthermore, both Washington and Paris share a common interest in the survival of moderate states in Africa and the Arab world. This commonality of interests could form the basis of greater U.S.-French coordination of policy toward the Sahara dispute — a policy coordination that could strengthen the Western alliance in a region where the Soviet Union has little incentive to promote conflict.

Appendixes

Appendix A | Tripartite Agreement Among Spain, Morocco, and Mauritania Signed at Madrid on November 14, 1975*

At a meeting in Madrid on November 14, 1975, the representatives of the governments of Spain, Morocco, and Mauritania reached agreement on the following principles:

1. Spain reaffirms its decision, repeated countless times at the United Nations, to decolonize the territory of the Western Sahara by putting an end to the responsibilities and powers that it holds as the administrative authority;

2. In view of this decision, and in conformity with the negotiations among the interested parties recommended by the United Nations, Spain will proceed immediately to set up an interim government in the territory with the participation of Morocco and Mauritania and the collaboraton of the Jemaa. The responsibilities and powers referred to in the previous paragraph will be transferred to this government.

To this end, it has been agreed that two deputy governors will be appointed, one proposed by Morocco, the other by Mauritania, to assist the

---

* Source: The official text of this agreement, released by the Moroccan Ministry of Information on November 21, 1975, was published in *Le Monde*, November 23–24, 1975, p. 4.

governor-general of the territory in the execution of his duties.

The Spanish presence in the territory will come to a final end before February 28, 1976;

3. The views of the Sahrawi population as expressed through the Jemaa will be respected;

4. The three countries will inform the secretary-general of the United Nations of the measures taken under the heading of the present document as a result of negotiations that took place in conformity with Article 33 of the United Nations Charter;

5. The three countries party to the agreement declare that they reached the preceding conclusions in the best spirit of understanding, brotherhood, and respect for the principles of the United Nations Charter and as their own contribution to the preservation of peace and international security;

6. This document will become operative on the day of publication in the Official State Bulletin of the law relating to the decolonization of the Sahara, which authorizes the Spanish government to carry out the undertakings contained in this document.

Appendix B | Peace Treaty Between the Polisario Front and the Islamic Republic of Mauritania Signed in Algiers on August 5, 1979*

On 3, 4 and 5 August 1979, a Mauritanian delegation...and a Saharaoui delegation...met in Algiers...and, after negotiations have agreed on the following:

1. Considering the strict observance by the two parties, Mauritanian and Saharaoui, of the Sacred Principles of the OAU and the U.N. Charters regarding the right of peoples to self-determination and the inviolability of the frontiers inherited from colonial times.

2. Considering the urgent need for the two parties to find a global and final solution to the conflict which guarantees full national rights for the

* SOURCE: U.S., Congress, House, Committee on Foreign Affairs, *Arms for Morocco? U.S. Policy Toward the Conflict in the Western Sahara*, Report of a Study Mission to Morocco, the Western Sahara, Mauritania, Algeria, Liberia, Spain, and France, August 5–18, 1979, for release in January 1980 (Washington, D.C.: Government Printing Office, 1979), pp. 18–19.

Saharaoui people and stability and peace throughout the region.

I. (A) The Islamic Republic of Mauritania solemnly declares that it does not have and will not have territorial or any other claims over Western Sahara.

(B) The Islamic Republic of Mauritania decides to withdraw from the unjust war in Western Sahara in accordance with the modalities agreed upon jointly with the representative of the Saharaoui people, the Polisario Front.

II. The Polisario Front solemnly declares that it does not have and will not have territorial or any other claims as regards Mauritania.

III. The Polisario Front, on behalf of the Saharaoui people, and the Islamic Republic of Mauritania decide to sign between them, a final peace agreement.

IV. The two parties have decided to hold periodic meetings with each other to look after the implementation of the modalities mentioned in the paragraph I, paragraph B.

V. The two parties will transmit this peace treaty immediately after its signature to the Acting President of the OAU, to members of the Ad-Hoc Committee, the Secretary-General of the OAU and the U.N., as well as the Acting President of the Non-Aligned.

Secret Part: Modalities of the Peace Agreement

1. Considering the public part of the present agreements.

2. Considering the necessity of a just and final peace based on total respect for the respective territorial integrity and sovereignty of the two brotherly Saharaoui and Mauritanian peoples, the sole guaranty of the establishment of a climate of comprehension, understanding and cooperation between the two peoples.

3. Considering that the Polisario Front is the sole legitimate representative of the people of the Western Sahara.

I. The Islamic Republic of Mauritania undertakes to put an end to its presence in the Western Sahara and to hand over directly to the Polisario Front the part of the Western Sahara that it controls within 7 months from the date of the signing of the present agreement.

Appendix C | Decision of the OAU Implementation Committee on Western Sahara*

The OAU Implementation Committee on Western Sahara, meeting in its First Session in Nairobi from 24 to 26 August 1981, pursuant to Res.AGH/ Res.103 (XVIII).

Having heard the concerned and interested parties;

Having taken into consideration the results of the consultations held by the Ministers for Foreign Affairs of the countries, members of the Implementation Committee;

Taking note of the views expressed by the various delegations of the Implementation Committee;

Expressing satisfaction at the positive participation of the parties to the Conflict;

Conscious of the need for all the parties concerned to cooperate for the successful implementation of Resolution AGH/Res.103 (XVIII), of the Eighteenth Ordinary Session of the Assembly of OAU Heads of State and Government, held in Nairobi, so as to attain the objectives laid down in the resolution and make the parties concerned agree on the steps to be taken in the context of that resolution;

Taking into consideration the need for the United Nations to participate in the Referendum and Cease-fire by virtue of Resolution AGH/Res.103 (XVIII), adopted by the Eighteenth Ordinary Session of the Assembly of OAU heads of State and Government, held in Nairobi, in June 1981:

DECIDES to organise and conduct a general and free Referendum in the Western Sahara, establish and maintain the Cease-fire, as follows:

a) *Referendum*

    I. The Referendum shall be one of self-determination which will enable the people of Western Sahara to express themselves freely and democratically on the future of their territory.

    II. The Referendum shall be held in the Western Sahara (ex-Spanish Sahara), the maps of which were deposited with the United Nations.

    III. All Saharawis listed in the Census conducted in 1974 by the Spanish authorities who have attained the age of 18 or above, shall be eligible to vote in the Referendum. In determining the Saharawi refugee population in the neighbouring countries,

---

* SOURCE: U.N. Doc. A/36/512-S/14692, annex; and OAU Doc. AHG/IMP.C/ WS/DEC.1(I) Rev. 1.

reference should be made to the records of the UNHCR. In establishing the population of the Western Sahara, account shall be taken of the internationally-recognised rate of population growth.

    IV. The voting shall be by secret ballot on the basis of one person one vote.

    V. The people of the Western Sahara shall be given the following choice:

        (a) Independence, or

        (b) Integration with Morocco.

b) *Structural Requirements*

    I. The referendum shall be organised and conducted by the Implementation Committee in collaboration with the U.N.

    II. For a fair and impartial organisation of the Referendum, an impartial Interim Administration supported by Civilian, Military and Police components shall be set up.

    III. The Interim Administration shall work in collaboration with existing administrative structures in the area.

    IV. The Interim Administration shall also be assisted by an adequate number of OAU and/or U.N. Peace-keeping Force.

c) *Cease-Fire*

    I. The Committee urges the parties to the conflict to agree on a cease-fire through negotiations under the auspices of the Implementation Committee.

    II. All the parties concerned shall undertake to respect the cease-fire and maintain it after the proclamation of the date fixed by the Implementation Committee.

    III. For the fair conduct of the Referendum and the strict observance of the Cease-fire, troops of the parties to the conflict should be effectively confined to their bases in conformity with the recommendations of the Fifth Session of the Ad Hoc Committee of Heads of State on Western Sahara held in Freetown, Sierra Leone, from 9 to 11 September, 1980.

    IV. The Peace-keeping Forces shall be stationed in the area so as to guarantee the cease-fire.

d) *Financing of the Implementation of the Decision*

The OAU Current Chairman shall consult the U.N. in order to determine the U.N. involvement in the implementation of this decision including its financing.

e) *General Principles*

    I. All the parties undertake to respect the results of the Referendum.

II. Neighbouring countries undertake to respect the results of the Referendum and to abstain from interfering in the internal affairs of other countries.

III. The Implementation Committee shall announce the results of the Referendum.

Appendix D | United Nations Resolution 3646 on the Question of Western Sahara. Adopted 76 Votes to 9, with 57 Abstentions, by the General Assembly on November 24, 1981*

The General Assembly,

Having considered in depth the question of Western Sahara,

Recalling the inalienable right of all peoples to self-determination and independence in accordance with the principles set forth in the Charter of the United Nations and in General Assembly resolution 1514 (XV) of 14 December 1960, containing the Declaration on the Granting of Independence to Colonial Countries and Peoples,

Recalling its resolution 35/19 of 11 November 1980 on the question of Western Sahara,

Having considered the relevant chapter of the report of the Special Committee on the Situation with regard to the Implementation of the Declaration on the Granting of Independence to Colonial Countries and Peoples,

Having heard the statements made on the question of Western Sahara, in particular the statements of the representative of the Frente Popular para la Liberación de Saguia el-Hamra y de Río de Oro,

Recalling its resolution 35/117 of 10 December 1980 on co-operation between the United Nations and the Organization of African Unity,

Taking note of the decision of the Assembly of Heads of State and Government of the Organization of African Unity at its eighteenth ordinary session, held at Nairobi from 24 to 27 June 1981, to organize throughout

---

* SOURCE: U.N. Doc A/36/677, November 17, 1981, pp. 10–11.

the Territory of Western Sahara a general and free referendum of the people of Western Sahara on self-determination,

Taking note of the decision adopted by the Implementation Committee on Western Sahara of the Organization of African Unity at its first ordinary session, held at Nairobi from 24 to 26 August 1981, concerning the establishment of appropriate machinery to enable the people of Western Sahara to express themselves freely and democratically on their future,

1. *Reaffirms* the inalienable right of the people of Western Sahara to self-determination and independence in accordance with the Charter of the United Nations, the Charter of the Organization of African Unity and the objectives of General Assembly resolution 1514 (XV), as well as the relevant resolutions of the General Assembly and the Organization of African Unity;

2. *Welcomes* the efforts made by the Organization of African Unity and its Implementation Committee on Western Sahara with a view to promoting a just and definitive solution to the question of Western Sahara;

3. *Takes note* of the decision of the Assembly of Heads of State and Government of the Organization of African Unity at its eighteenth ordinary session to organize throughout the Territory of Western Sahara a general and free referendum of the people of Western Sahara on self-determination;

4. *Welcomes* the steps taken by the Implementation Committee with a view to organizing and conducting the referendum;

5. *Appeals* to the two parties to the conflict, Morocco and Frente Popular para la Liberación de Saguia el-Hamra y de Río de Oro, to observe a cease-fire in accordance with the decisions of the Organization of African Unity and its Implementation Committee;

6. *Urges*, to that end, Morocco and the Frente Popular para la Liberación de Saguia el-Hamra y de Río de Oro to enter into negotiations with a view to establishing an immediate cease-fire and concluding a peace agreement permitting the fair conduct of a general, free and regular referendum on self-determination in Western Sahara;

7. *Reaffirms* the determination of the United Nations to co-operate fully with the Organization of African Unity in the fair and impartial organization of the referendum;

8. *Requests*, to that end, the Secretary-General to take the necessary steps to ensure that the United Nations participates in the organization and conduct of the referendum, and to report to the General Assembly and the Security Council on this subject, and on the measures requiring a decision by the Council;

9. *Urgently requests* the Secretary-General to co-operate closely with the Secretary-General of the Organization of African Unity with a view to the implementation of the decisions of the Assembly of Heads of State and Government of the Organization of African Unity and of its Implementation Committee, and of the present resolution;

10. *Requests* the Special Committee on the Situation with regard to the Implementation of the Declaration on the Granting of Independence to Colonial Countries and Peoples to continue to consider the situation in Western Sahara as a matter of priority and to report thereon to the General Assembly at its thirty-seventh session.

Notes

Chapter One

1. "The Sahara," *An-Nahar Arab Report: Backgrounder*, part 1, July 28, 1975, p. 1.

2. Sieur Le Maire, *Voyages aux Isles Canaries, Cap-verd, Sénégal* (Paris, 1695); quoted in John Mercer, *Spanish Sahara* (London: George Allen & Unwin, 1976), p. 17.

3. André Dessens, "Le Problème du Sahara occidental trois ans après le départ des Espagnols," *Maghreb-Machrek*, no. 83 (January–March 1979): 76; and Virginia Thompson and Richard Adloff, *The Western Saharans: Background to Conflict* (London: Croom Helm; Totowa, N.J.: Barnes & Noble Books, 1980), pp. 104, 123.

4. Robert Rézette, *The Western Sahara and the Frontiers of Morocco*, trans. Mary Ewalt (Paris: Nouvelles Editions Latines, 1975), p. 25.

5. *Le Monde*, February 12, 1976, p. 4. The two deposits extend for about forty miles. The Spanish subsequently raised their original estimate of Saharan phosphate deposits from 1.7 billion tons to more than 3.0 billion tons. The Madrid journal *Ya* of December 9, 1969, for example, contained estimates of 1.715 billion tons for the reserves of the Bu Craa deposit and 1.562 billion tons for the reserves in the neighboring region. This higher figure of nearly 3.3 billion tons is not widely accepted. It is quite possible, however, that in addition to Bu Craa there are other deposits of phosphate as yet undiscovered in the Western Sahara. The significance of the phosphate factor for Moroccan policy is assessed in Chapter Two.

6. *Middle East Economic Digest* 101, no. 31 (August 4, 1978): 4–5.

7. *Middle East*, no. 54 (April 1979): 106; and testimony and statement of Anne Lippert, in U.S., Congress, House, Committee on Foreign Affairs, Subcommittees on Africa and on International Organizations, *U.S. Policy and the Conflict in the Western Sahara: Hearings*, July 23–24, 1979 (Washington, D.C.: Government Printing Office, 1979), pp. 18, 22.

8. This account draws especially on John Mercer, *The Sahrawis of Western Sahara* (London: Minority Rights Group, 1979), p. 5; and idem, *Spanish Sahara*, p. 71.

9. Probably Muhammad ibn Idris (826–836); quoted in *Corriere della Sera* (Milan), April 23, 1979, p. 3.

10. Mercer, *Sahrawis of Western Sahara*, p. 5; and idem, *Spanish Sahara*, pp. 74–75.

11. Useful accounts of the Reguibat may be found in David M. Hart, "The Social Structure of the Rgībāt Bedouins of the Western Sahara," *Middle East Journal* 16 (1962): 515–27; F. Beslay, "Un Etat sahraoui?" *Le Monde*, January 6, 1976, p. 3; and Mercer, *Spanish Sahara*, pp. 132–33. Hart argues that the only element distinguishing the Coastal and Eastern Reguibat is the camel brand that each group uses. Because of their common ancestry, shared values and traditions, and the great coherence and tightness of their social system (they have never feuded among themselves or raided each other's camels), Hart contends that the Reguibat, though divided into six major clans, should be considered a single tribe rather than a group, aggregation, or confederation of tribes (pp. 515, 523–25).

12. Attilio Gaudio, *Sahara espagnol: Fin d'un mythe colonial?* (Rabat: Arrissala, 1975), divides 21 nomadic tribes of the Western Sahara into three categories: warrior, Maraboutic, and tributary. Of the total he considers 8 the most important: Tekna, Coastal Reguibat, Eastern Reguibat, Ulad Delim, Ulad Bu Sba, Barikallah, Arrusiyyin, and Ahl Ma al-Ainain. Gaudio's listing, plus a more detailed tribal breakdown for the main regions within Sakiet al-Hamra and Rio de Oro, is reproduced in Elsa Assidon, *Sahara occidental: Un Enjeu pour le Nord-Ouest africain* (Paris: François Maspero, 1978), pp. 149–53.

13. Mercer, *Spanish Sahara*, pp. 124, 127; and Assidon, *Sahara occidental*, p. 39, *n*17. An intriguing example of sharply conflicting figures appears in the work of a single author, Attilio Gaudio. In his 1975 study, *Sahara espagnol*, Gaudio states: "The 60,000 inhabitants of Rio de Oro and Sakiet al-Hamra thus represent today only a weak part of the real population, a third or a fourth." But in a 1978 study, *Le Dossier du Sahara occidental* (Paris: Nouvelles Editions Latines), Gaudio argues for the validity of the 1974 Spanish census with its much more modest figure of 73,500 and omits any reference to his earlier estimate. This clear discrepancy with its obvious political implications is revealed in Assidon, *Sahara occidental*, p. 150.

14. The results of the 1974 Spanish census are summarized in *Le Monde*, February 19, 1976, p. 5; and "Mauritanie: Sous le signe de l'unité," supplement to *Jeune Afrique*, no. 857 (June 10, 1977): 22–23. These results appeared in a 158-page document, *CENSO-74*, which contains computerized breakdowns of the data into a

wide variety of categories. The census, taken on a village-by-village basis, was very detailed and lists tribal, subtribal, age, and occupation groups.

15. Quoted in Mercer, *Spanish Sahara*, p. 106.

16. This combined offensive involved a French campaign, called Ecouvillon ("mop-up"), with five thousand troops, six hundred vehicles, and seventy aircraft, and a Spanish campaign, named Ouragan, of nine thousand troops and some sixty aircraft (Assidon, *Sahara occidental*, pp. 1, 16). For a detailed account of the two-week operation, see Christine Garnier and Philippe Ermont, *Désert fertile: Un Nouvel Etat—la Mauritanie* (Paris: Hachette, 1960), pp. 191-203. The March 1958 Spanish-Moroccan Agreement of Cintra, in which Spain returned Tarfaya to Morocco the following month, was an important factor in ending the hostilities. Nevertheless, some irregular forces and nomadic tribesmen, unimpressed by the retrocession of Tarfaya, continued to fight. For a dissident Moroccan view that the monarchy, aided by French and Spanish forces, repressed the 1957-1958 popular uprising in the Sahara, see Ahmed Rami, "Malaise dans l'armée: Un Officier parle...," *Afrique-Asie*, no. 99 (December 29, 1975-January 11, 1976): 14.

17. John Gretton, *Western Sahara: The Fight for Self-Determination* (London: Anti-Slavery Society, 1976), p. 18; and Mercer, *Spanish Sahara*, pp. 123-24.

Chapter Two

1. Robert Rézette, *The Western Sahara and the Frontiers of Morocco*, trans. Mary Ewalt (Paris: Nouvelles Editions Latines, 1975), pp. 41-42. Yusuf ibn Tashfin adopted the title *amir al-mu'minin* ("commander of the faithful"), which acknowledged his religious as well as political authority. This title has been adopted often by Moroccan rulers since the time of the Saadian dynasty (1554-1659), including King Hassan II, and is explicitly mentioned in the Moroccan constitution.

2. For an elaboration and critique of al-Fassi's argument, especially as it relates to the Western Sahara, see Lewis B. Ware, *Decolonization and the Global Alliance in the Arab Maghrib: The Case of Spanish Sahara* (Maxwell Air Force Base, Ala.: Air University Institute for Professional Development, December 1975), pp. 20-22.

3. Quoted in Elsa Assidon, *Sahara occidental: Un Enjeu pour le Nord-Ouest africain* (Paris: François Maspero, 1978), p. 16.

4. Quoted in Virginia Thompson and Richard Adloff, *The Western Saharans: Background to Conflict* (London: Croom Helm; Totowa, N.J.: Barnes & Noble Books, 1980), p. 223.

5. Georges Salvy, "Le Grand Jeu politique dans le désert," *Le Monde*, January 31, 1976, p. 2; and Rézette, *Western Sahara*, pp. 11-12.

6. For a detailed examination of this complex subject, see Frank E. Trout, *Morocco's Saharan Frontiers* (Geneva: Droz Publishers, 1969), pp. 286-392.

7. See, for example, *Le Monde*, January 30, 1976, p. 4.

8. The Moroccan chief of staff, Gen. Driss Benomar Alami, reportedly was furious when, with Tindouf in sight and poorly defended, King Hassan ordered a withdrawal. In an emotional scene after returning to Rabat, Benomar angrily threw his hat on the king's desk and told Hassan to find some other commander to do his dirty work for him.

9. I. William Zartman, "Conflict in the Sahara," in idem, *Ripe for Resolution: Conflict and Intervention in Africa* (New Haven, Conn.: Yale University Press, forthcoming), pp. 14–15.

10. Jerome B. Weiner, "The Green March in Historical Perspective," *Middle East Journal* 33 (1979): 21.

11. Colonel (later General) Ahmed Dlimi, who succeeded Gen. Mohamed Oufkir in 1972 as the military strongman of the Moroccan regime, comes from this part of the Ulad Delim (*Le Monde*, February 3, 1976, p. 2, *n*2).

12. Weiner, "Green March," p. 23.

13. Allal al-Fassi, for example, makes this argument. See his *Livre rouge*, part 1, published as *Perspectives Sahariennes*, no. 15 (Tangier, January 1960): 14.

14. The examples in the text are taken from Attilio Gaudio, *Le Dossier du Sahara occidental* (Paris: Nouvelles Editions Latines, 1978), pp. 261–62; and Trout, *Morocco's Saharan Frontiers*, p. 158.

15. The activities of Shaikh Ma al-Ainain and his relations with Moroccan sultans are discussed in some detail in Gaudio, *Le Dossier du Sahara occidental*, pp. 65–81; and Trout, *Morocco's Saharan Frontiers*, pp. 156–61.

16. The relevant diplomatic materials were reviewed by the International Court of Justice in 1975 during its consideration of certain aspects of the Western Sahara question. This World Court case is discussed in Chapter Three.

17. Assidon, *Sahara occidental*, p. 18.

18. Quoted in *Le Monde*, October 24, 1975, p. 3.

19. In the West Irian case, the act of free choice organized by the Indonesian government in an environment it tightly controlled was accepted by the U.N. General Assembly as a valid act of self-determination (see Thomas M. Franck, "The Stealing of the Sahara," *American Journal of International Law* 70 [1976]: 700–701).

20. These events are treated in more detail in Chapter Three.

21. Tahar Ben Jelloun, "Une Certitude, des questions...," *Le Monde*, March 3, 1976, p. 6.

22. Editorial by Ahmed Alaoui, political director of *Le Matin du Sahara*, April 20, 1979, p. 1. Alaoui is a cousin and confidant of King Hassan and a minister of state. For a detailed official statement of the Moroccan position, see Morocco [Kingdom], Ministry of Foreign Affairs, *The Legitimate Decolonization of Atlantic Western Sahara and the Plots of Algerian Rulers Aiming at Hegemony in North-Western Africa*, U.N. Doc. E/CH. 4/Sub. 2/391, June 15, 1977.

23. See, for example, John Gretton, *Western Sahara: The Fight for Self-Determination* (London: Anti-Slavery Society, 1976), pp. 22–24, 48; W. Michael Reisman, "African Imperialism," *American Journal of International Law* 70 (1976):

801-2; and Pauline Lalutte, "Sahara: Notes Toward an Analysis," in *The Struggle for Sahara*, MERIP Reports, no. 45 (Washington, D.C.: Middle East Research & Information Project, March 1976), pp. 8-9. This popular conception is found frequently in newspapers and weekly periodicals.

24. Gretton, *Fight for Self-Determination*, p. 21.

25. These figures are from W. F. Stowasser, "Phosphate Rock," preprinted from U.S., Department of the Interior, Bureau of Mines, Bulletin 671, *Mineral Facts and Problems*, 1980 ed. (Washington, D.C.: Government Printing Office, 1980), p. 4. Stowasser's table gives a single figure for Morocco and the Sahara, from which I subtracted 2.2 and 5.2 billion tons for Saharan phosphate reserves (1) at 1978 costs and prices and (2) with different assumptions about prices and technology.

26. Gretton, *Fight for Self-Determination*, pp. 22-23; Assidon, *Sahara occidental*, pp. 130-31.

27. Peter Hallock Johnson, "Phosphates: The Next Cartel?" *Fletcher Forum* 1 (1976/77): 154-55; Assidon, *Sahara occidental*, pp. 130-31; and Thomas A. Blue and Roberto Portillo, *Phosphate Rock*, CEH Marketing Research Report (Menlo Park, Calif.: SRI International, March 1980), p. 760.0005 H.

28. Blue and Portillo, *Phosphate Rock*, p. 760.0005 H-I; and *New York Times*, October 30, 1977, p. 7. It is difficult to present a precise account of Moroccan phosphate prices because different grades of phosphate rock, ranging from 68 to 77 percent bone phosphate of lime, are sold at different prices, and OCP often has sold phosphate below the list price. In retrospect, it is clear that OCP leaders failed to anticipate the high elasticity of world demand for phosphate and the large supply response from U.S. producers. It is hard to avoid the conclusion that Morocco would have benefited economically in the long run if its decision makers had heeded the counsel of the younger voices in OCP who advocated a more gradual policy of phosphate price increases.

29. W. F. Stowasser, "Phosphate Rock," preprinted from U.S., Department of the Interior, Bureau of Mines, *Bureau of Mines Minerals Yearbook, 1977*, vol. 1, *Metals and Minerals* (Washington, D.C.: Government Printing Office, 1980), p. 2.

30. Ware, *Decolonization and the Global Alliance*, pp. 29-30; and Bertrand Fessard de Foucault, "Et la Mauritanie?" *Le Monde*, November 9-10, 1975, p. 2.

31. *Le Monde*, June 2, 1979, p. 4.

32. Paul Balta, "La Crise du Sahara: Une Grande Partie de poker," *Le Monde*, November 28, 1975, p. 7. For an English translation of Balta's two-part series of articles, see "Spanish Sahara: A Highly Coveted Prize," *Manchester Guardian Weekly*, December 7, 1975, pp. 13-14.

33. For a more detailed account of the Mauritanian position, both under Ould Daddah and the succeeding military regime, see U.S., Department of Defense, Defense Intelligence Agency, *Struggle and Stalemate in the Western Sahara*, DDB-2300-4-79 (Washington, D.C., January 1979), pp. 21-23.

34. Gretton, *Fight for Self-Determination*, p. 38.

35. *Middle East*, no. 54 (April 1979): 14; and *New York Times*, September 10, 1980, p. 2.

36. Gretton, *Fight for Self-Determination*, p. 25.

37. *Le Monde*, October 24, 1975, p. 3. In interviews with the author in Algiers in September 1981, Algerian mining officials outlined a large-scale project involving (1) the mining of forty million tons a year of iron ore from Gara Jebilet; (2) the construction of a railroad from Gara Jebilet to the Mediterranean coast, west of Oran; and (3) the development of an industrial complex in western Algeria, especially steel mills that would produce for internal use twenty million tons of steel a year from the forty million tons of ore. Studies for this project were nearly completed, although the basic decision on the undertaking will not be made before 1985, that is, after the current 1980–1984 Five-Year Plan. If undertaken, the project would not be completed until 1990–1992.

38. See, for example, Ould Daddah's account in Mokhtar Ould Daddah, "Sahara: La Genèse d'un affrontement," *Jeune Afrique*, no. 790 (February 27, 1976): 24; and Daniel Junqua, "La Mauritanie prise au piège: La Faute à l'Espagne!" *Le Monde*, February 16, 1978, p. 7. For an English translation of Junqua's three-part series of articles, see "The Trap Springs on Mauritania," *Manchester Guardian Weekly*, March 5, 1978, p. 12, and March 12, 1978, p. 12.

39. *Le Monde*, October 24, 1975, p. 3.

40. For concise statements of the official Algerian position, see the letters to the editor from Algeria's ambassador and chargé d'affaires in Washington, Abdelaziz Maoui and Slim Tahar Debagha, *New York Times*, June 14, 1979, p. A28; and *Christian Science Monitor*, May 24, 1979, p. 22. See also, among many examples, M. Tareb, "Sahara occidental: La Répose appartient au peuple sahraoui," *El Djeich*, no. 146 (July 1975): 46–47. *El Djeich* is an Algerian Army publication that mirrors official government positions. For a detailed exposition of the Algerian government's position, see Algeria [Democratic and Popular Republic], *Memorandum on the Western Sahara Affair* (Algiers, September 1977).

41. Ahmed-Baba Miské, *Front Polisario: L'Ame d'un peuple* (Paris: Editions Rapture, 1978), pp. 121–28; John Mercer, *Spanish Sahara* (London: George Allen & Unwin, 1976), p. 227; and *Le Monde*, November 27, 1975, p. 5. The full name of the MLS was "Vanguard Organization for the Liberation of the Sahara," called "The Muslim Party" by the Spanish colonial administration. Miské (p. 129) states that Spanish sources claimed that Bassiri was held only for a brief period before being released to Moroccan authorities. A French source, however, says that Bassiri was seen last in 1974 at the beach resort of Fuerte Ventura, in the Canary Islands (Raoul Weexsteen, "La Stratégie du Front Polisario face à ses adversaires directs et à leurs protecteurs," *Le Monde Diplomatique*, no. 281 [August 1977]: 5, *n*29).

42. Mercer, *Spanish Sahara*, p. 228.

43. According to the records of the Moroccan Ministry of Interior, SDAR Prime Minister Mohamed Lamine was born in 1948 in Tan Tan, where his father still lives; Minister of Information Mohamed Salem Ould Salek was born in Tarfaya in 1950; and Omar Hadrami, an important Polisario official, is from Bou-Izakar, near Goulimine (*Le Monde*, April 8, 1981, p. 5). See also "Western Sahara: Who Is Polisario?" *Africa Confidential* (London) 22, no. 2 (January 14, 1981): 4.

44. Weexsteen, "La Stratégie du Front Polisario," p. 5.

45. *Le Monde*, November 27, 1975, p. 5; and Ould Daddah, "La Genèse d'un affrontement," p. 27.

46. Gretton, *Fight for Self-Determination*, p. 31.

47. David Lynn Price, *The Western Sahara* (Beverly Hills, Calif., and London: Sage Publications, 1979), p. 28.

48. Much of the material in the remainder of this section is based on a January 1979 visit to Algiers and the Polisario camps in the Tindouf region. Meetings were held with a number of Polisario officials, including Omar Hadrami, a member of the Executive Committee and Revolutionary Council, and Ibrahim Hakim, the foreign minister of the government-in-exile. For a more recent account of the Polisario refugee camps, see Barbara Harrell-Bond, *The Struggle for the Western Sahara*, Part 3, *The Sahrāwī People*, American Universities Field Staff Reports, Africa, no. 39 (Hanover, N.H.: AUFS, 1981), pp. 1–10.

49. Assidon, *Sahara occidental*, pp. 66–67.

50. See, for example, Raoul Weexsteen, "La Question du Sahara occidental," *Annuaire de l'Afrique du Nord* (Paris: CNRS, 1978) 16 (1977): 429–30; and Gretton, *Fight for Self-Determination*, p. 32.

51. Assidon, *Sahara occidental*, p. 67.

52. Gretton, *Fight for Self-Determination*, p. 33.

53. See *Le Monde*, February 29–March 1, 1976, p. 3.

54. The text of the SDAR constitution is given in Harrell-Bond, *The Sahrāwī People*, pp. 12–13.

Chapter Three

1. Robert Rézette, *The Western Sahara and the Frontiers of Morocco*, trans. Mary Ewalt (Paris: Nouvelles Editions Latines, 1975), p. 128; and Thomas M. Franck, "The Stealing of the Sahara," *American Journal of International Law* 70 (1976): 701.

2. Elsa Assidon, *Sahara occidental: Un Enjeu pour le Nord-Ouest africain* (Paris: François Maspero, 1978), p. 46.

3. John Gretton, *Western Sahara: The Fight for Self-Determination* (London: Anti-Slavery Society, 1976), p. 35.

4. Ibid., p. 26; and *Le Monde*, February 16, 1978, p. 7.

5. *Le Monde*, February 16, 1978, p. 7; and Bertrand Fessard de Foucault, "Et la Mauritanie?" *Le Monde*, November 9–10, 1975, p. 2.

6. Mokhtar Ould Daddah, "Sahara: La Genèse d'un affrontement," *Jeune Afrique*, no. 790 (February 27, 1976): 26; and André Pautard, "L'Enjeu mauritanien," *L'Express*, May 16–22, 1977, p. 55.

7. *Le Monde*, February 16, 1978, p. 7.

8. Franck, "Stealing of the Sahara," pp. 703–4.

9. Colin Legum, ed., *Africa Contemporary Record: Annual Survey and Documents, 1974–1975* (New York: Africana Publishing Co., 1975), p. B81.

10. Quoted in *Le Monde*, November 27, 1975, p. 1.

11. Legum, *Africa Contemporary Record, 1974–1975*, pp. B82, B137.

12. *Le Monde*, November 27, 1975, p. 5.

13. Rézette, *Western Sahara*, pp. 147–48.

14. This version was given in late June 1975 by Algerian authorities to Paul Balta, the *Le Monde* correspondent in Algiers, who duly reported the information in *Le Monde*, July 1, 1975, p. 3. According to Gretton, the Algerian government chose to reveal this well-kept secret in mid-1975 because it was exasperated by Morocco's diplomatic success among Third World countries (*Fight for Self-Determination*, p. 37, n11). John Mercer states that the joint occupation of the Sahara was planned at a secret meeting between Moroccan and Mauritanian representatives in New York in October 1974 ("Confrontation in the Western Sahara," *World Today* 32 [1976]: 230). Since such an arrangement would require the participation of the two heads of state, the *Le Monde* account is probably accurate.

15. Quoted in Pautard, "L'Enjeu mauritanien," p. 55. The Moroccans made a tape recording of this statement and provided Mauritania with a copy.

16. *Le Monde*, February 16, 1978, p. 7; and Ould Daddah, "La Genèse d'un affrontement, p. 26.

17. See "Western Sahara: Advisory Opinion of the International Court of Justice" (hereafter "Advisory Opinion"), U.N. Doc. A/10300, October 17, 1975, pp. 13–14.

18. Ibid.; for the text of UNGA Resolution 3292, see pp. 2–4. Despite the advisory opinion approach, some observers have argued that the Western Sahara questions at the ICJ were treated very much like a contentious case. See, for example, Maurice Barbier, "Un Droit intangible: L'Autodétermination," *Le Monde*, March 3, 1976, p. 6.

19. For a thorough treatment of the Spanish presidios question, see Robert Rézette, *The Spanish Enclaves in Morocco*, trans. Mary Ewalt (Paris: Nouvelles Editions Latines, 1976).

20. Mercer, "Confrontation in Western Sahara," p. 231.

21. *Le Monde*, July 1, 1975, p. 3.

22. The text of the Moroccan-Algerian joint communiqué of July 4, 1975, appeared in the Algerian government-controlled daily *El Moudjahid*, July 5, 1975, p. 1.

23. For discussions of Algeria's 1975 change of position, compare André Dessens, "Le Problème du Sahara occidental trois ans après le départ des Espagnols," *Maghreb-Machrek*, no. 83 (January–March 1979): 77; and I. William Zartman, "Conflict in the Sahara," in idem, *Ripe for Resolution: Conflict and Intervention in Africa* (New Haven, Conn.: Yale University Press, forthcoming), p. 18.

It is reasonable to assume that there was an internal debate among Algerian leaders during the summer and fall of 1975 over the regime's Sahara policy. Although the precise details of this debate have not (and may never) become known publicly, one can imagine that Boumediene, who was known to be personally committed to opposing a Moroccan takeover, and Minister of Interior Mohamed Abdelghani eventually prevailed over Bouteflika, Minister of Industry and Energy Belaid Abdessalam, Minister of Finance Ismail Mahroug, and Minister of Information and Culture Taleb Ibrahimi, who probably favored an accommodation with Morocco for economic and pragmatic reasons. In May 1982, Ibrahimi became foreign minister following the death of Mohamed Benyahia, who perished in a plane crash while trying to mediate the Iraq-Iran war.

24. U.N. Doc. A/10023/Add. 5, November 7, 1975, p. 11.

25. "Advisory Opinion," pp. 64-65.

26. Franck, "Stealing of the Sahara," p. 711.

27. Abdelaziz Dahmani, "L'Autre Affaire de Zouerate," *Jeune Afrique*, no. 854 (May 20, 1977): 30.

28. Virginia Thompson and Richard Adloff, *The Western Saharans: Background to Conflict* (London: Croom Helm; Totowa, N.J.: Barnes & Noble Books, 1980), p. 172.

29. A prime example of this interpretation is Franck, "Stealing of the Sahara," pp. 709-11.

30. Quoted in *Africa Report* 25, no. 5 (September-October 1980): 51.

31. The symbolic significance of the color is twofold: green is closely associated with the Prophet Mohammed, and in Islamic tradition is the color of peace. The figure of 350,000 volunteers was selected because it represents the annual number of births in Morocco. For a discussion of how the Green March drew upon, and was consistent with, Moroccan religious and historical traditions, see Jerome B. Weiner, "The Green March in Historical Perspective," *Middle East Journal* 33 (1979): 20-33.

32. The five-man planning group was composed of King Hassan; Dr. Mohamed Benhima, minister of court; Gen. Moulay Hafid of the royal household; Col. Ahmed Dlimi, head of security; and Ahmed Bensouda of the royal cabinet (Robert G. Neumann, "Morocco and the Sahara," [Transcribed interview, Oral History Program, University of California, Los Angeles, August 2, 1976], p. 31).

33. A detailed breakdown of the provincial distribution of marchers is given in Weiner, "Green March," p. 28. Weiner (p. 27) points out that the rural areas of Morocco, where King Hassan's strength and depth of support are much greater, were overrepresented. The rural provinces of Khenifra and Ksar as-Souk were asked to volunteer 4-6 percent of their population, whereas urbanized Oujda province and industrialized Khouribga, both troublesome areas for the government, had their volunteer quotas limited to 0.26 percent and 0.76 percent of their respective populations.

34. Neumann, "Morocco and the Sahara," pp. 44-45.

35. Abdellatif Rahal, quoted in "Secretary-General Given Mandate on Sahara Issue," *UN Monthly Chronicle* 12, no. 10 (November 1975): 10.

36. Gretton, *Fight for Self-Determination*, p. 36; and *New York Times*, December 3, 1975, p. 12.

37. Mercer, "Confrontation in Western Sahara," p. 237.

38. *Le Monde*, February 4, 1976, p. 7.

39. Franck, "Stealing of the Sahara," pp. 712–14. The argument that the United States worked to prevent effective Security Council action at the time of the Green March is supported by Daniel Patrick Moynihan, then-U.S. ambassador to the United Nations (see Moynihan, with Suzanne Weaver, *A Dangerous Place* [Boston: Little, Brown, 1978], p. 247).

40. *Le Monde*, October 30, 1975, p. 7.

41. Dessens, "Le Problème du Sahara occidental," p. 82; and Franck, "Stealing of the Sahara," p. 716.

42. Neumann, "Morocco and the Sahara," p. 35.

43. Ibid., p. 45.

44. According to Franck, a Moroccan-Spanish agreement on the Green March had been reached in Madrid around November 4, following two days of talks between Moroccan Prime Minister Ahmed Osman (King Hassan's brother-in-law) and the Spanish "ultras" led by Arias. Juan Carlos, it would appear, "had been overruled or made to back down." This scenario called for a token march that would stop short of the Spanish "dissuasion line," thus allowing both governments to save face. Further, the march would serve as a smoke screen, behind which Moroccan Army units would enter the Sahara and begin operations against Polisario Front forces ("Stealing of the Sahara," p. 716). While Franck's version approximates the actual sequence of events in the Sahara, it is not at all clear that this drama was played out quite so neatly following the script of a prior agreement.

45. This quotation, or perhaps paraphrase, of Boumediene was given by Ould Daddah to André Pautard and appears in Pautard, "L'Enjeu mauritanien," p. 56.

46. For this "sellout" argument, see, for example, Franck, "Stealing of the Sahara," p. 715; and Mercer, "Confrontation in Western Sahara," p. 233.

47. Dessens, "Le Problème du Sahara occidental," pp. 82–83. This parliamentary inquiry revealed that the Council of Ministers had decided to "abandon" the Sahara to Morocco on October 25, 1975, at least two weeks earlier than is generally thought.

48. For varying accounts of a Spanish-Algerian-Polisario "secret" agreement or treaty, see ibid., p. 77; *Le Monde*, December 2, 1975, p. 7, and February 16, 1978, p. 7; and David Lynn Price, *The Western Sahara* (Beverly Hills, Calif., and London: Sage Publications, 1979), p. 17. The existence of such an agreement is suspect. It is more likely that elements within the Spanish government gave assurances to Algeria and the Polisario Front that subsequently were nullified by the Tripartite Agreement. It is known, for example, that in September 1975 Spanish officials were negotiating with the Polisario Front, with the Algerian government acting as a

middleman, for the release of 20-30 Spanish soldiers captured and held prisoner by the Polisario.

49. Quoted in Dessens, "Le Problème du Sahara occidental," p. 77.

50. *Jeune Afrique*, no. 872 (September 23, 1977): 24; *Le Monde*, November 27, 1975, p. 5; and Gretton, *Fight for Self-Determination*, p. 33.

51. Quoted in *Le Monde*, December 12, 1975, p. 6.

52. Price, *The Western Sahara*, p. 28; and interview with Omar Hadrami, member of the Polisario Front Executive Committee and Revolutionary Council, Algiers, January 7, 1979. See also the account by a Polisario spokesman in *Le Monde*, November 20, 1975, p. 3. Dessens argues that the Spanish Army in the Sahara, humiliated and bitter that civilians in Madrid were "abandoning" the territory to the Moroccans, knowingly allowed the three thousand Sahrawis who had received military training to take their weapons and vehicles and swell the ranks of the Polisario Front ("Le Problème du Sahara occidental," p. 83). In a dissenting view, Raoul Weexsteen suggests collusion between the disengaging Spanish forces and the occupying Moroccan forces in late 1975. What appeared as collusion, however, may well have been a question of timing. The Moroccans may simply have moved in on the heels of the departing Spanish. For the collusion argument, see Weexsteen, "Le Sahara occidental aux prises avec ses voisins: Ces Hommes qui se battent dans le désert...," *Le Monde Diplomatique*, no. 263 (February 1976): 10; for an excerpted English translation of Weexsteen's article, see "Fighters in the Desert," in *The Struggle for Sahara*, MERIP Reports, no. 45 (Washington, D.C.: Middle East Research & Information Project, March 1976), pp. 3-6.

53. *Le Monde*, December 27, 1975, p. 2.

54. Dessens, "Le Problème du Sahara occidental," p. 78.

55. Interview with Omar Hadrami, Algiers, December 26, 1978.

56. See, for example, *Le Monde*, December 14-15, 1975, p. 4.

57. See the account by Ahmed El Gharbaoui in *Al Bayane* (French-language daily of the Moroccan [Communist] Party of Progress and Socialism), December 31, 1975; quoted in *Le Monde*, February 19, 1976, p. 5, *n*1.

58. *Le Monde*, February 20-21, 1976, p. 2.

59. Ibid., February 27, 1976, p. 2; and *New York Times*, February 28, 1976, p. 6.

60. *Le Monde*, February 27, 1976, pp. 2, 4; and Mercer, "Confrontation in Western Sahara," p. 238.

61. Quoted in *Le Monde*, December 9, 1975, p. 3.

62. Ibid., December 9, 1975, p. 3, December 18, 1975, p. 10, and January 16, 1976, p. 4; Thompson and Adloff, *The Western Saharans*, pp. 134-35; I. William Zartman, "Conflict in the Sahara," mimeo., March 8, 1979, p. 9; idem, testimony, in U.S., Congress, House, Committee on Foreign Affairs, Subcommittees on Africa and International Organizations, *U.S. Policy and the Conflict in the Western Sahara: Hearings*, July 23-24, 1979 (Washington, D.C.: Government Printing Office, 1979), pp. 68-69; and Weiner, "Green March," pp. 29-30.

63. Zartman, "Conflict in the Sahara," p. 9; and idem, statement in U.S., Con-

gress, *U.S. Policy and the Conflict*, p. 31.

64. Quoted in *Le Monde*, February 29–March 1, 1976, p. 3.

65. At the Addis Ababa meeting, 17 OAU members reportedly favored recognition of the Polisario Front as a liberation movement, 9 were against, and 21 abstained (*Le Monde*, March 4, 1976, p. 2, *n*1).

66. See the account in *Jeune Afrique*, no. 872 (September 23, 1977): 24.

67. *Le Monde*, April 16, 1976, p. 5.

68. Price, *The Western Sahara*, pp. 38–39.

69. The material in this and the preceding paragraph is drawn from interviews with Moroccan officials in El Ayoun in December 1978; compare David Lynn Price, "Morocco: The Political Balance," *World Today* 34 (1978): 496–97. For an earlier account of the development program, see *Le Monde*, December 21, 1977, p. 3; for a more recent account, see *Le Monde*, April 8, 1981, p. 5.

70. See, for example, *Jeune Afrique*, no. 872 (September 23, 1977): 22–24.

71. *Le Monde*, February 26, 1981, p. 7.

72. *Washington Post*, August 30, 1977, p. A12; Tony Hodges, "Western Sahara: The Escalating Confrontation," *Africa Report* 23, no. 2 (March–April 1978): 5; *Jeune Afrique*, no. 857 (June 10, 1977): 24; and Price, *The Western Sahara*, p. 33.

73. The text of a proclamation of a new Mauritanian republic was found on the bodies of the Polisario guerrillas after the battle (Dahmani, "L'Autre Affaire de Zouerate," p. 30). Paul Balta states that El Ouali knew Ould Daddah well and appealed to the Mauritanian leader to renounce his alliance with Morocco and form a federated state with the Sahrawis. Only after failing in this appeal did El Ouali organize the fateful attack against Nouakchott, in the hope that the Mauritanian population would rise up and overthrow the Ould Daddah regime. (*Le Monde*, January 6–7, 1980, p. 5.)

74. Dessens, "Le Problème du Sahara occidental," p. 78. Raoul Weexsteen contends that the Polisario's attack against Zouirat on May 1, 1977, had two other objectives (in addition to dealing a heavy blow to the Mauritanian economy): to draw international attention back to the Western Sahara following Morocco's "diversionary intervention" in Zaire (where King Hassan had sent a military force to counter an invasion of mineral-rich Shaba province by Angolan-based rebels) and to create a climate of insecurity among the eight hundred French technicians working on the iron-mining operation. The latter objective, at least, was achieved when French women and children were evacuated from Zouirat shortly after the first Polisario attack. (Weexsteen, "La Question du Sahara occidental," *Annuaire de l'Afrique du Nord* [Paris: CNRS, 1978] 16 [1977]: 430.)

75. This and the preceding two paragraphs are drawn mainly from John Damis, "Mauritania and the Sahara," *Middle East International*, no. 71 (May 1977): 18; and idem, "Mauritania: Little Room for Manoeuvre," *Middle East International*, no. 89 (November 1978): 28. See also "Mauritanian Government Receives Substantial Aid

from Arab States," *Middle East*, no. 54 (April 1979): 104-5; John Mercer, *The Sahrawis of Western Sahara* (London: Minority Rights Group, 1979), pp. 15-16; and Thompson and Adloff, *The Western Saharans*, pp. 273, 306, n13.

76. See Damis, "Mauritania: Little Room for Manoeuvre," p. 27.

77. Price, *The Western Sahara*, p. 25.

78. *El Moudjahid*, March 12, 1979, p. 6.

79. Interview with Ibrahim Hakim, Algiers, December 31, 1978.

80. *Le Monde*, January 8, 1980, p. 9.

81. Quoted in *Africa*, no. 94 (June 1979): 40.

82. *Le Monde*, May 26, 1979, p. 4, June 2, 1979, p. 4, and June 3-4, 1979, p. 4.

83. *Christian Science Monitor*, August 17, 1979, p. 3; *Le Monde*, August 7, 1979, p. 1, and August 12-13, 1979, p. 1; *New York Times*, August 21, 1979, p. A5; and *The Economist*, August 11, 1979, p. 52.

84. *New York Times*, August 21, 1979, p. A5; and *Christian Science Monitor*, August 22, 1979, p. 9.

85. Non-Aligned Countries, Sixth Conference, "Final Declaration," Doc. 1/Rev. 2, Havana, September 3-7, 1979, par. 35.

86. *Washington Post*, July 3, 1980, p. A27.

87. *Le Monde*, July 5, 1980, p. 5.

88. The moderate African states that supported Morocco and opposed the SDAR's admission to the OAU included Senegal, Ivory Coast, Zaire, Gabon, Cameroon, and Guinea. At the time of the Freetown summit, Morocco claimed that twelve OAU members were prepared to walk out if the SDAR were admitted.

89. *Le Monde*, July 6-7, 1980, p. 4.

90. U.N. Doc. A/RES/34/37, December 4, 1979, pp. 2-3.

91. Quoted in U.S., Congress, House, Committee on Foreign Affairs, Subcommittee on Africa, *Current Situation in the Western Sahara—1980: Hearing*, December 4, 1980 (Washington, D.C.: Government Printing Office, 1981), p. 7.

92. U.N. Doc. A/35/596, November 17, 1980, pp. 14-16.

93. Caroline Tisdall, "A Death Trap in the Desert," *Manchester Guardian Weekly*, April 13, 1980, p. 6.

94. *Christian Science Monitor*, October 18, 1979, p. 9; and *New York Times*, November 12, 1979, p. A8.

95. *New York Times*, November 12, 1979, p. A8; Howard Schissel, "Stalemate in the Western Sahara," *Middle East International*, no. 143 (February 13, 1981): 14; *Christian Science Monitor*, January 22, 1980, p. 13; and *The Economist*, February 23, 1980, p. 40.

96. *Christian Science Monitor*, March 25, 1980, p. 10; and *Le Monde*, March 18, 1980, p. 6.

97. *Christian Science Monitor*, May 12, 1980, p. 14.

98. Schissel, "Stalemate in the Western Sahara," p. 14; and *Le Monde*, February 26, 1981, p. 7, and March 5, 1981, p. 3.

99. *Le Monde*, March 5, 1981, p. 3, April 8, 1981, p. 5, June 2, 1981, p. 7, and May 9–10, 1982, p. 3; and interview with Moroccan Southern Zone Commander Col.-Maj. Abdelaziz Bennani, Agadir, August 22, 1981.

100. *Washington Post*, April 26, 1981, p. A27; *Le Monde*, April 19–20, 1981, p. 3; and interview with Colonel-Major Bennani, August 22, 1981.

101. *The Economist*, October 24, 1981, p. 43; and *Le Monde*, December 17, 1981, p. 7.

102. *Le Monde*, June 28–29, 1981, p. 2, and June 30, 1981, p. 8. The seven states comprising the OAU Implementation Committee are Kenya (chairman), Guinea, Mali, Nigeria, Sierra Leone, Tanzania, and the Sudan. The committee's membership was formed from the heads of state who comprised the OAU ad hoc Wisemen's Committee plus Kenyan President Daniel arap Moi, the 1981–1982 OAU chairman. The text of the resolution adopted by the OAU summit in Nairobi is contained in OAU Doc. AHG/Res.103 (XVIII).

103. *Le Monde*, June 28–29, 1981, p. 2, July 4, 1981, p. 6, and July 7, 1981, p. 6.

104. U.N. Doc. A/36/512-S/14692, annex, pp. 1–3. For an account of the deliberations at Nairobi II within the Implementation Committee and an interpretation of the resulting decision, see *Jeune Afrique*, no. 1079 (September 9, 1981): 18–21.

105. See Algeria [Democratic and Popular Republic], *Referendum of Self-Determination for the People of the Western Sahara*, Memorandum presented to the OAU Committee of Implementation, Nairobi, August 1981 (n.p. [Algiers], 1981); this 91-page document was also published as an 8-page supplement to *El Moudjahid*, September 1, 1981.

106. Interview with Ali Habiballah, Polisario Front representative in Algiers, September 6, 1981.

107. U.N. Doc. A/36/677, November 17, 1981, pp. 10–11.

108. OAU Doc. AHG/IMP.C/WS/Dec. 2 (II) Rev. 2, February 8–9, 1982.

109. *Le Monde*, February 25, 1982, p. 1; and *New York Times*, March 14, 1982, p. 8. The nineteen African countries that walked out of the OAU meeting in Addis Ababa were Cameroon, the Central African Republic, Comoros, Djibouti, Equatorial Guinea, Gabon, Gambia, Guinea, Ivory Coast, Liberia, Mauritius, Morocco, Niger, Senegal, Somalia, the Sudan, Tunisia, Upper Volta, and Zaire.

110. *Le Monde*, July 23, 1982, p. 4; *New York Times*, August 7, 1982, p. 3; and *The Economist*, August 14, 1982, p. 29. In early July, for example, just a month before the Tripoli summit was to meet, President Milton Obote of Uganda accused Qadhafi of training Ugandans in Libya to overthrow the Obote regime (*Christian Science Monitor*, July 15, 1982, p. 7).

Of the nineteen African countries that had walked out of the OAU meeting in Addis Ababa in February, all boycotted the Tripoli summit except Mauritius, where elections in June had brought to power a Marxist-socialist coalition. In addition to this bloc of eighteen states, Uganda and Egypt joined the boycott because of their opposition to Qadhafi, while Sierra Leone joined because of the issue of SDAR membership. The boycott was complicated by the fact that five states (the Central African Republic, Djibouti, Niger, Tunisia, and Upper Volta) sent delegations to Tripoli to wait and see if an acceptable compromise could be worked out, but did not participate in any meetings. Curiously, the boycott included two states—Sierra Leone and Uganda—that had previously recognized the SDAR. In the end, a decision by Somalia, Djibouti, Tunisia, and Liberia—four potential swing states—not to attend the summit was crucial to the success of the boycott.

Chapter Four

1. André Dessens, "Le Problème du Sahara occidental trois ans après le départ des Espagnols," *Maghreb-Machrek*, no. 83 (January–March 1979): 76; and *Le Monde*, June 19, 1979, p. 5.

2. Dessens, "Le Problème du Sahara occidental," p. 76; and Robert A. Mortimer, "Western Sahara: The Diplomatic Perspectives," *Africa Report* 23, no. 2 (March–April 1978): 12–13.

3. Dessens, "Le Problème du Sahara occidental," p. 79; and *Washington Post*, May 26, 1977, p. A19.

4. *Le Monde*, March 4, 1976, p. 2; and Virginia Thompson and Richard Adloff, *The Western Saharans: Background to Conflict* (London: Croom Helm; Totowa, N.J.: Barnes & Noble Books, 1980), p. 151.

5. John Mercer, *The Sahrawis of Western Sahara* (London: Minority Rights Group, 1979), p. 15; Dessens, "Le Problème du Sahara occidental," p. 80; and David Lynn Price, *The Western Sahara* (Beverly Hills, Calif., and London: Sage Publications, 1979), p. 58.

6. *Le Monde*, June 14, 1979, p. 4, and October 4, 1981, p. 11.

7. Ibid., June 14, 1979, p. 4.

8. David Lynn Price, "Morocco: The Political Balance," *World Today* 34 (1978): 499; and Dessens, "Le Problème du Sahara occidental," p. 84.

9. *Le Monde*, June 19, 1979, p. 5; and *Middle East International*, no. 123 (April 25, 1980): 6–7.

10. *Middle East International*, no. 123 (April 25, 1980): 7.

11. *Le Monde*, April 2, 1981, p. 5; and *El País*, April 2, 1981, pp. 1, 47.

12. See, for example, the interview with Polisario Political Bureau member Lamine Bouhali in *Mundo Obrero Semanal* (Madrid), March 29–April 4, 1979, pp. 24–26.

13. *Le Monde*, June 19, 1979, p. 5. At the time of the visit of King Juan Carlos to Morocco, Hassan cautioned Spain that a mediator "always gets the end of his feathers burned by one side or the other."

14. Since 1974, the Qadhafi regime has purchased an estimated $20 billion worth of Soviet tanks, aircraft, artillery, military electronics, ammunition, and other

military hardware, making Libya the largest total purchaser of arms from the USSR. This huge arsenal, which includes MiG-23, -25, and -27 jet fighters and T-62 and -72 tanks, greatly exceeds the capacities of Libya's forty-thousand-man armed forces to absorb or use. For a discussion of Libya's acquisition of large stocks of Soviet weapons and their possible use, see John K. Cooley, "The Libyan Menace," *Foreign Policy*, no. 42 (Spring 1981): 77, 85–87. The types and numbers of all weapons possessed by Libya are listed in International Institute for Strategic Studies, *The Military Balance, 1981–1982* (London, 1981), p. 54.

15. *Le Monde* correspondent Paul Balta estimated that in the spring of 1981 Tripoli was providing nearly nine-tenths of the aid to the Polisario Front (*Le Monde*, April 10, 1981, p. 5). In May 1981, Gen. Ahmed Dlimi, commander of Morocco's southern zone, stated that 80 percent of the Polisario's military equipment was coming from Libya (ibid., June 2, 1981, p. 7).

16. *New York Times*, July 15, 1979, p. 14.

17. For a discussion of the inherent difficulties in Libyan-Algerian relations, see John K. Cooley, "Algeria and Libya: A Breath of Suspicion," mimeo., June 23, 1981, pp. 1–10, 14–16.

18. Thompson and Adloff, *The Western Saharans*, pp. 58–59, 259. Since 1979, Iraq, France, Saudi Arabia, and Kuwait have provided most of Mauritania's foreign economic assistance.

19. Dessens, "Le Problème du Sahara occidental," p. 82.

20. U.S., Department of Defense, Defense Intelligence Agency, *Struggle and Stalemate in the Western Sahara*, DDB-2300–4–79 (Washington, D.C., January 1979), p. 31.

21. *Le Monde*, May 22, 1981, p. 9.

22. Thompson and Adloff, *The Western Saharans*, p. 259.

23. See, for example, John Gretton, "Identifying the Polisario," *Middle East International*, no. 137 (November 7, 1980): 12.

24. Yearly breakdowns of French arms supplies and deliveries to Morocco are listed in the "Register of Arms Trade with Third World Countries" contained in Stockholm International Peace Research Institute, *World Armaments and Disarmament: SIPRI Yearbook* for the years 1976–1982 (Cambridge, Mass., and London: MIT Press; Stockholm: Almquist & Wiksell International, 1976–1977; London: Taylor & Francis, 1978–1980; London: Taylor & Francis; Cambridge, Mass.: Oelgeschlager, Gunn & Hain, 1981–1982).

25. *Le Monde*, June 10, 1977, p. 6; and Raoul Weexsteen, "La Question du Sahara occidental," *Annuaire de l'Afrique du Nord* (Paris: CNRS, 1978) 16 (1977): 432.

26. President Valéry Giscard d'Estaing, January 2, 1978; quoted in Dessens, "Le Problème du Sahara occidental," p. 84.

27. Ibid., p. 78; and *Le Monde*, October 24, 1979, p. 1.

28. Abdelfetah K., "Sahara occidental: La Coalition impérialo-réactionnaire," *El Djeich*, no. 177 (February 1978): 33.

29. See, for example, A. A., "Sahara occidental: La Désillusion des agresseurs," *El Djeich*, no. 176 (January 1978): 33.

30. *Marchés Tropicaux et Méditerranéens* 34 (1978): 73, 131–32.

31. Dessens, "Le Problème du Sahara occidental," p. 83. This view was also expressed to the author by SDAR Foreign Minister Ibrahim Hakim during an interview in Algiers on December 31, 1978.

32. *Le Monde*, October 28, 1977, p. 1.

33. Quoted in ibid., April 10, 1981, p. 5.

34. Ibid., January 6, 1981, p. 6, and January 11–12, 1981, p. 2.

35. Mercer, *Sahrawis of Western Sahara*, p. 20.

36. For a discussion of the general improvement in U.S.-Algerian relations since 1979, see John Damis, "Algeria Acquires a New Image," *Middle East International*, no. 142 (January 30, 1981): 6–7.

37. *Middle East International*, no. 76 (October 1977): 8; *Marchés Tropicaux et Méditerranéens* 34 (1978): 73; Mercer, *Sahrawis of Western Sahara*, p. 14; and U.S., Library of Congress, Congressional Research Service, Ellen B. Laipson, "Conflict and Change in North Africa: Emerging Challenges for U.S. Policy," Report no. 80-222 F (Washington, D.C., December 1980), p. 8.

38. Robert G. Neumann, "Morocco and the Sahara" (Transcribed interview, Oral History Program, University of California, Los Angeles, August 2, 1976), p. 16.

39. The conservative leaders of the Arabian peninsula have supported King Hassan with financial and diplomatic aid in the Sahara conflict both as a gesture of brotherhood among fellow monarchs and in return for Moroccan services: some two thousand French-trained Moroccan agents do security work in Saudi Arabia, while others form the personal bodyguard of Sheikh Zayed bin Sultan al-Nahayan, the ruler of Abu Dhabi and president of the United Arab Emirates federation (*Le Monde*, May 15, 1982, p. 5).

40. Statement and testimony of Deputy Assistant Secretary of State for Near Eastern and South Asian Affairs Nicholas A. Veliotes, in U.S., Congress, House, Committee on International Relations, Subcommittees on International Organizations and on Africa, *The Question of Self-Determination in Western Sahara: Hearing*, October 12, 1977 (Washington, D.C.: Government Printing Office, 1977), pp. 40–41. This hearing contains an appendix (pp. 66–82) of State Department responses to questions submitted by subcommittee chairman Donald Fraser; the responses set forth official U.S. government positions on issues and U.N. resolutions related to the Sahara dispute.

41. U.S., Congress, House, Committee on International Relations, Subcommittee on Africa, *Foreign Assistance Legislation for Fiscal Year 1979*, Part 3, *Hearings*, February 7–8, 14, and 28 and March 1–2, 1978 (Washington, D.C.: Government Printing Office, 1978), p. 159.

42. *New York Times*, July 7, 1979, p. 17; and *Washington Post*, February 11, 1979, p. A17. The contract for this commercial sale was signed in December 1977,

that is, before the Carter administration had decided to disapprove the sale of new weapons systems manufactured in the United States for use in the Western Sahara.

43. U.S., Congress, *Foreign Assistance Legislation for Fiscal Year 1979*, p. 177.

44. *Washington Post*, August 19, 1979, p. A13.

45. U.S., Congress, House, Committee on Foreign Affairs, Subcommittees on Africa and on International Organizations, *U.S. Policy and the Conflict in the Western Sahara: Hearings*, July 23–24, 1979 (Washington, D.C.: Government Printing Office, 1979), pp. 92–95, 154–57.

46. Robert Shaplen, "Eye of the Storm," part 1, *New Yorker*, June 2, 1980, p. 80. Shaplen (p. 83) suggests that the Moroccan arms issue underscored basic foreign-policy differences within the U.S. establishment between the "bold, aggressive approach" typical of the National Security Council and the "more judicious approach of the State Department." See also "Western Sahara: The Heat Is On," *Middle East*, no. 62 (December 1979): 43, 46; and William Safire, "The Road to Morocco," *New York Times*, October 25, 1979, p. A19. According to Safire, at the October 16 meeting of the Policy Review Committee at the White House, both Brzezinski and Defense Secretary Harold Brown strongly supported the Moroccan arms package on the grounds that King Hassan needed the offensive weapons, not to achieve a military victory, but to be sufficiently strong to negotiate for an autonomous region in the Sahara under Moroccan control. The committee dropped an earlier proposal to provide counterinsurgency training for Moroccan forces because such training was considered too provocative to Algeria (*New York Times*, October 19, 1979, p. A7).

47. See Stephen J. Solarz, "Arms for Morocco?" *Foreign Affairs* 58 (1979/80): 278–99. This article was reprinted in a report to the Committee on Foreign Affairs, House of Representatives, January 1980 (Washington, D.C.: Government Printing Office, 1979), pp. 1–15. Solarz continued the debate on U.S. arms sales to Morocco in replies to letters from Congressman Edward J. Derwinski and Professor I. William Zartman in *Foreign Affairs* 58 (1980): 962–66 and 59 (1980): 183–86.

48. U.S., Congress, House, Committee on Foreign Affairs, Subcommittees on International Security and Scientific Affairs and on Africa, *Proposed Arms Sale to Morocco: Hearings*, January 24 and 29, 1980 (Washington, D.C.: Government Printing Office, 1980), p. 3.

49. Quoted in U.S., Congress, House, Committee on Foreign Affairs, Subcommittee on Africa, *Current Situation in the Western Sahara—1980: Hearing*, December 4, 1980 (Washington, D.C.: Government Printing Office, 1981), p. 2.

50. U.S., Congress, *Proposed Arms Sale to Morocco*, pp. 2–3, 7–10.

51. Statement and testimony of Deputy Assistant Secretary of State for Near Eastern and South Asian Affairs Morris Draper, in U.S., Congress, House, Committee on Foreign Affairs, Subcommittees on International and Scientific Affairs and on Africa, *Arms Sales in North Africa and the Conflict in the Western Sahara: An Assessment of U.S. Policy. Hearing*, March 25, 1981 (Washington, D.C.: Government Printing Office, 1981), pp. 5, 14. In response to additional questions by committee chairman Clement Zablocki, the State Department declared that "the United States intends to be a reliable friend of Morocco in recognition of our shared

concerns including maintaining the integrity and independence of nations in Africa from outside aggression" (ibid., p. 39).

52. See, for example, *Defense Week* (Washington, D.C.), November 3, 1980, pp. 7-8; and *Boston Herald American*, November 11, 1980, pp. A1, A6.

53. Statement of Morris Draper, in U.S., Congress, *Arms Sales in North Africa*, pp. 5-6.

54. *Washington Post*, February 13, 1982, pp. A1, A28; and *New York Times*, February 12, 1982, p. A9.

55. *New York Times*, May 28, 1982, p. 3; and *Christian Science Monitor*, June 1, 1982, p. 5. The text of the agreement was not made public because of Moroccan sensitivities to the appearance of a return to the situation of the 1950s, when the United States had air bases in Morocco for use by the Strategic Air Command. The United States' use of these airfields, allowed by an agreement signed with France during the protectorate period, was sharply criticized by Moroccan political parties as an infringement of sovereignty, and in 1959, President Eisenhower reached agreement with King Mohammed V to close down the facilities by 1963.

56. *New Times* (Moscow) 80, no. 9 (February 1980): 15.

57. See, for example, A. Kapikrayan, "Algeria: Maturity of the Revolution," *New Times* 80, no. 26 (June 1980): 14-15; and K. Andreyev, "Algeria: Charting the Road Ahead," *New Times* 80, no. 27 (July 1980): 14-15.

58. *Le Journal Parlementaire*, no. 3 (February 1978): 24; and International Institute for Strategic Studies, *The Military Balance, 1981-1982*, pp. 48-49. In 1981, there were about twelve hundred Soviet military advisers in Algeria. According to the director of the Stockholm International Peace Research Institute, 55 percent of the arms delivered to Algeria in 1980 came from the Soviet Union (press conference in Stockholm, January 1982, reported in the *Guardian*, January 15, 1982, p. 6).

59. See, for example, Stockholm International Peace Research Institute, *SIPRI Yearbook, 1981*, p. 198, for a partial accounting of Algerian arms purchases from the Soviet Union from 1977 to 1980.

60. See, for example, *New Times* 79, no. 45 (November 1979): 27.

61. U.S., Central Intelligence Agency, National Foreign Assessment Center, *Communist Aid Activities in Non-Communist Less Developed Countries, 1979 and 1954-79*, ER 80-10318U (Washington, D.C., October 1980), pp. 21, 29. In 1981, some 4,500 Soviet technicians were working in the following sectors of the Algerian economy: education and training, 1,809; industry, 874; health, 550; and other activities, 1,273 (*El Moudjahid*, June 8, 1981, p. 3).

62. A summary of Soviet-Moroccan economic and commercial relations, including details of the 1978 Meskala phosphate agreement, is given in *Le Matin du Sahara*, February 10, 1978, pp. 1, 4. The 1978 phosphate and fishing agreements also are discussed in Abdelaziz Dahmani, "Mariage de raison," *Jeune Afrique*, no. 916 (July 26, 1978): 27-28, 30.

63. Dessens, "Le Problème du Sahara occidental," pp. 81, 86, *n*7.

64. See, for example, *Christian Science Monitor*, May 6, 1980, p. 6.

65. See, for example, the Soviet-Ethiopian joint communiqué published on September 18, 1979, during Prime Minister Alexei Kosygin's official visit to Addis Ababa, cited in *New Times* 79, no. 40 (October 1979): 14.

66. This consisted of lobbying on behalf of Algeria and a pro-Algerian statement on November 2, 1975, by Yakov Malik, the Soviet permanent representative to the United Nations and, at that moment, president of the Security Council (*UN Monthly Chronicle* 12, no. 10 [November 1975]: 10).

Chapter Five

1. *Le Monde*, February 6, 1976, p. 2; and I. William Zartman, "Conflict in the Sahara," in idem, *Ripe for Resolution: Conflict and Intervention in Africa* (New Haven, Conn.: Yale University Press, forthcoming), p. 34.

2. David Lynn Price, "Morocco: The Political Balance," *World Today* 34 (1978): 497; Zartman, "Conflict in the Sahara," p. 35; and André Dessens, "Le Problème du Sahara occidental trois ans après le départ des Espagnols," *Maghreb-Machrek*, no. 83 (January–March 1979): 85.

3. See, for example, *Le Matin du Sahara*, December 3, 1978, p. 1; and Dessens, "Le Problème du Sahara occidental," p. 85.

4. Elsa Assidon, *Sahara occidental: Un Enjeu pour le Nord-Ouest africain* (Paris: François Maspero, 1978), p. 8.

5. Quoted in Raoul Weexsteen, "La Stratégie du Front Polisario face à ses adversaires directs et à leurs protecteurs," *Le Monde Diplomatique*, no. 281 (August 1977): 5, *n*36.

6. The major opposition party in Morocco, the USFP, has been quite militant in its support of the government's Saharan policy. In 1977, for example, USFP leader Abderrahim Bouabid even proposed carrying the military struggle to Tindouf in southwest Algeria. (See *Jeune Afrique*, no. 858 [June 17, 1977]: 26.)

7. The USFP action marked the first break in the ranks of solid support among Moroccan political parties for the government's Sahara policy since the organization of the Green March in October 1975. The government reacted by arresting five members of the party's Politburo and charging them with disturbance of the peace for having published a communiqué that criticized the government's acceptance of OAU resolutions calling for a referendum in the Sahara. The five were convicted on September 24 and sentenced to prison terms ranging from one to two years. Three of the five, including party leader Abderrahim Bouabid, were imprisoned until pardoned by Hassan at the end of February 1982. The USFP's September 1981 criticism of the government illustrates how little maneuverability the king has on the Sahara issue.

8. See *Le Monde*, July 1, 1981, p. 6.

9. Reliable casualty figures are not publicly available. Both Morocco and the Polisario Front grossly exaggerate the other side's losses while understating their own. Prior to 1979, Morocco released no figures at all and refused to admit publicly

that a war was going on against the "so-called Polisario Front." Following the successful Polisario attack against Tan Tan in southwestern Morocco in January 1979, however, the Moroccan press began to provide more accurate news about the military side of the conflict.

10. "Quel avenir pour le Polisario?" *Jeune Afrique*, no. 1038 (November 26, 1980): 29–31.

11. According to some accounts, the Polisario Front has found it necessary to build up its military force, the Saharan People's Liberation Army (ALPS), through recruitment in the Algerian Sahara of "volunteers" from the Touareg tribes of Mali, Niger, and even southwest Libya (see, for example, *Marchés Tropicaux et Méditerranéens* 34 [1978]: 1905). For an account that stresses the lack of evidence of Touareg recruitment by the Polisario, see "Western Sahara: Who Is Polisario?" *Africa Confidential* (London) 22, no. 2 (January 14, 1981): 3.

12. *Le Monde*, February 13, 1976, p. 2; and Raoul Weexsteen, "La Question du Sahara occidental," *Annuaire de l'Afrique du Nord* (Paris: CNRS, 1978) 16 (1977): 427–28. Because the Algerian government would not permit representatives of the U.N. High Commission on Refugees to monitor the provision of relief supplies to Sahrawi refugees, the commission and several countries, including the United States, suspended their assistance to the refugees.

13. The discussion and accompanying map of the Sade plan are drawn from "Sahara occidental: Un Plan de plus?" *Demain l'Afrique*, no. 13 (October 1978): 32.

14. See Dessens, "Le Problème du Sahara occidental," p. 85.

15. See I. William Zartman, "A Disputed Frontier Is Settled," *Africa Report* 8, no. 8 (August 1963): 13–14.

Bibliography

Documents and Official Publications

Algeria [Democratic and Popular Republic]. *Memorandum on the Western Sahara Affair.* Algiers, September 1977.

————. *Referendum on Self-Determination for the People of the Western Sahara.* Memorandum presented to the OAU Committee of Implementation, Nairobi, August 1981. N.p. [Algiers], 1981.

Morocco [Kingdom]. *The Moroccan Sahara and the Reality Behind Algeria's Attitude.* London, July 1976.

————. Ministry of Foreign Affairs. *The Legitimate Decolonization of Atlantic Western Sahara and the Plots of Algerian Rulers Aiming at Hegemony in North-Western Africa.* U.N. Doc. E/CN. 4/Sub. 2/391. June 15, 1977.

Non-Aligned Countries. Sixth Conference. "Final Declaration." Doc. 1/Rev. 2. Havana, September 3-7, 1979.

Organization of African Unity. Secretariat. "Decision of the Implementation Committee on Modalities and Organizational Framework for the Referendum in Western Sahara." Doc. AHG/IMP.C/WS/Dec. 2 (II) Rev. 2. Nairobi, February 8-9, 1982.

Spain. Government General of the Sahara. *CENSO-74.* El Ayoun, 1976.

United States. Central Intelligence Agency. National Foreign Assessment Center. *Communist Aid Activities in Non-Communist Less Developed Countries, 1979 and 1954-79.* ER 80-10318U. Washington, D.C., October 1980.

————. Congress. House. Committee on Foreign Affairs. *Arms for Morocco? U.S. Policy Toward the Conflict in the Western Sahara: Report.* January 1980. Washington, D.C.: Government Printing Office, 1979.

180 | *Bibliography*

———. ———. ———. ———. *Regional Stability in Northern Africa: Report.* July 8, 1980. Washington, D.C.: Government Printing Office, 1980.

———. ———. ———. ———. Subcommittee on Africa. *Current Situation in the Western Sahara—1980: Hearing.* December 4, 1980. Washington, D.C.: Government Printing Office, 1981.

———. ———. ———. ———. Subcommittee on Europe and the Middle East. *Review of Recent Developments in the Middle East, 1979: Hearing.* July 26, 1979. Washington, D.C.: Government Printing Office, 1979.

———. ———. ———. ———. Subcommittees on Africa and on International Organizations. *U.S. Policy and the Conflict in the Western Sahara: Hearings.* July 23–24, 1979. Washington, D.C.: Government Printing Office, 1979.

———. ———. ———. ———. Subcommittees on International Security and Scientific Affairs and on Africa. *Arms Sales in North Africa and the Conflict in the Western Sahara: An Assessment of U.S. Policy. Hearing.* March 25, 1981. Washington, D.C.: Government Printing Office, 1981.

———. ———. ———. ———. ———. *Proposed Arms Sale to Morocco: Hearings.* January 24 and 29, 1980. Washington, D.C.: Government Printing Office, 1980.

———. ———. ———. Committee on International Relations. Subcommittee on Africa. *Foreign Assistance Legislation for Fiscal Year 1979,* Part 3, *Hearings.* February 7–8, 14, and 28 and March 1–2, 1978. Washington, D.C.: Government Printing Office, 1978.

———. ———. ———. ———. Subcommittees on International Organizations and on Africa. *The Question of Self-Determination in Western Sahara: Hearing.* October 12, 1977. Washington, D.C.: Government Printing Office, 1977.

———. ———. Senate. Committee on Foreign Relations. *Proposed Arms Sales to Morocco: Hearing.* January 30, 1980. Washington, D.C.: Government Printing Office, 1980.

———. Department of Defense. *Congressional Presentation: Security Assistance Programs, FY 1983.* Washington, D.C., 1982.

———. ———. Defense Intelligence Agency. *Struggle and Stalemate in the Western Sahara.* DDB-2300-4-79. Washington, D.C., January 1979.

———. Department of the Interior. Bureau of Mines. Stowasser, W. F. "Phosphate Rock." Preprint from *Bureau of Mines Minerals Yearbook, 1977,* vol. 1, *Metals and Minerals.* Washington, D.C.: Government Printing Office, 1980.

———. ———. ———. ———. "Phosphate Rock." Preprint from Bulletin 671, *Mineral Facts and Problems,* 1980 ed. Washington, D.C.: Government Printing Office, 1980.

———. Library of Congress. Congressional Research Service. Laipson, Ellen B. "Conflict and Change in North Africa: Emerging Challenges for U.S. Policy." Report no. 80-222 F. Washington, D.C., December 1980.

———. ———. ———. ———. "War in the Western Sahara: Issues for U.S. Policy." Washington, D.C., December 18, 1981.

"Western Sahara: Advisory Opinion of the International Court of Justice." U.N. Doc. A/10300. October 17, 1975.

Other Sources

A., A. "Sahara occidental: La Désillusion des agresseurs." *El Djeich*, no. 176 (January 1978): 30–34.

Alexander, Nathan [pseud.]. "The Foreign Policy of Libya: Inflexibility amid Change." *Orbis* 24 (1981): 819–46.

"Algeria's Clean-Up Campaign." *Middle East*, no. 60 (October 1979): 14, 16.

Andreyev, K. "Algeria: Charting the Road Ahead." *New Times* 80, no. 27 (July 1980): 14–15.

———. "Western Sahara: Difficult Search for Settlement." *New Times* 79, no. 34 (August 1979): 14–15.

Assidon, Elsa. *Sahara occidental: Un Enjeu pour le Nord-Ouest africain*. Paris: François Maspero, 1978.

Ben Madani, Mohamed. "The Western Sahara: An Historical Survey." *Maghreb Review* 1 (1976): 13–15.

Blue, Thomas A., and Portillo, Roberto. *Phosphate Rock*. CEH Marketing Research Report. Menlo Park, Calif.: SRI International, March 1980.

Borchgrave, Arnaud de. "Scènes de guerre au Sahara." *Jeune Afrique*, no. 854 (June 10, 1977): 24–25.

Cooley, John K. "Algeria and Libya: A Breath of Suspicion." Mimeo. June 23, 1981.

———. "The Libyan Menace." *Foreign Policy*, no. 42 (Spring 1981): 74–93.

Dahmani, Abdelaziz. "L'Autre Affaire de Zouerate." *Jeune Afrique*, no. 854 (May 20, 1977): 30–31.

———. "Mariage de raison." *Jeune Afrique*, no. 916 (July 26, 1978): 27–28, 30.

———. "Sahara: Pourquoi le sommet de Lusaka a été renvoyé." *Jeune Afrique*, no. 872 (September 23, 1977): 22–24.

———. "Sahara: Que s'est-il passé à Nairobi?" *Jeune Afrique*, no. 1079 (September 9, 1981): 18–21.

Dahmani, Abdelaziz, et al. "Révélations sur la crise du Sahara." *Jeune Afrique*, no. 880 (November 18, 1977): 76–81.

Damis, John. "Algeria Acquires a New Image." *Middle East International*, no. 142 (January 30, 1981): 6–7.

———. "Mauritania and the Sahara." *Middle East International*, no. 71 (May 1977): 17–19.

———. "Mauritania: Little Room for Manoeuvre." *Middle East International*, no. 89 (November 1978): 27–28.

———. "The Moroccan-Algerian Conflict over the Western Sahara." *Maghreb Review* 4 (1979): 49–57.

————. "The Moroccan Political Scene." *Middle East Journal* 26 (1972): 25–36.

————. "Morocco: Political and Economic Prospects." *World Today* 31 (1975): 36–46.

————. "The Role of Third Parties in the Western Sahara Conflict." *Maghreb Review* 7 (1982): 1–15.

————. "Western Sahara: A Critical Period." *Middle East International*, no. 169 (February 26, 1982): 6–7.

Daoud, Zakya. "Le Référendum au Sahara: La Bataille des modalités." *Lamalif*, no. 127 (July–August 1981): 12–16.

Dessens, André. "Le Problème du Sahara occidental trois ans après le départ des Espagnols." *Maghreb-Machrek*, no. 83 (January–March 1979): 73–86.

Fairmont, Robert. "Western Sahara: Morocco's Troubled Monarch." *Africa Report* 23, no. 2 (March–April 1978): 15–20.

Fassi, Allal El. *Livre rouge*, part 1. Published as *Perspectives Sahariennes*, no. 15. Tangier, January 1960.

Franck, Thomas M. "The Stealing of the Sahara." *American Journal of International Law* 70 (1976): 694–721.

Furlonge, Geoffrey. "Mauritania: Newest Member of the Arab League." *Middle East International*, no. 36 (June 1974): 20–22.

Garnier, Christine, and Ermont, Philippe. *Désert fertile: Un Nouvel Etat – la Mauritanie*. Paris: Hachette, 1960.

Gaudio, Attilio. *Le Dossier du Sahara occidental*. Paris: Nouvelles Editions Latines, 1978.

————. *Sahara espagnol: Fin d'un mythe colonial?* Rabat: Arrissala, 1975.

Gretton, John. "A Desert State That Vanished." *Geographical Magazine* 49 (1976/77): 155–60.

————. "Hassan's Last Trump?" *Middle East International*, no. 108 (September 14, 1979): 8–9.

————. "Identifying the Polisario." *Middle East International*, no. 137 (November 7, 1980): 12–13.

————. "An Open Letter to Polisario." *Middle East International*, no. 76 (October 1977): 6–8.

————. "Turning Point in the Sahara." *Middle East International*, no. 98 (April 27, 1979): 10–11.

————. "The Western Sahara in the International Arena." *World Today* 36 (1980): 343–50.

————. *Western Sahara: The Fight for Self-Determination*. Research report no. 1. London: Anti-Slavery Society, 1976.

Harrell-Bond, Barbara. *The Struggle for the Western Sahara*. American Universities Field Staff, Africa, Reports nos. 37–39. Hanover, N.H.: AUFS, 1981.

Hart, David M. "The Social Structure of the Rgībāt Bedouins of the Western Sahara." *Middle East Journal* 16 (1962): 515–27.

Hassan II. *The Challenge: The Memoirs of King Hassan II of Morocco.* Translated by Anthony Rhodes. London: Macmillan, 1978.

Hijab, Nadia. "Why Were the People Called to the Polls?" *Middle East,* no. 57 (July 1980): 26–27.

Hodges, Tony. "Restart of Phosphate Mining Faces Guerrilla Threat." *Middle East Economic Digest* 101, no. 31 (August 4, 1978): 4–5.

———. "Western Sahara: The Escalating Confrontation." *Africa Report* 23, no. 2 (March–April 1978): 4–9.

Hyman, Anthony. "Morocco: The Military Gamble." *Middle East International,* no. 114 (December 7, 1979): 10–11.

International Institute for Strategic Studies. *The Military Balance, 1981–1982.* London, 1981.

"Interview: Omar Hadrami, Polisario Representative." *Africa Report* 23, no. 2 (March–April 1978): 39–43.

Iseman, Frederick. "The War in the Sahara." *Harper's,* September 1980, pp. 41–56.

Jallaud, Thomas. "Western Sahara Conflict." In *New African Yearbook, 1980.* New York and London: I.C. Publications, 1980, pp. 54–56.

Joffe, George. "Morocco: An Experiment in Democracy." *Middle East International,* no. 123 (April 25, 1980): 7–8.

Johnson, Peter Hallock. "Phosphates: The Next Cartel?" *Fletcher Forum* 1 (1976/77): 154–63.

K., Abdelfetah. "Sahara occidental: La Coalition impérialo-réactionnaire." *El Djeich,* no. 177 (February 1978): 24–37.

Kapikrayan, A. "Algeria: Maturity of the Revolution." *New Times* 80, no. 26 (June 1980): 14–15.

Kapikrayan, A., and Bolmatov, A. "Algeria: The Chosen Road." *New Times* 79, no. 45 (November 1979): 26–27.

Kazadi, F. S. B. [pseud.] "Carter's Saharan Foray." *Africa Report* 23, no. 2 (March–April 1978): 44–46.

Kudryavtsev, A. "Mauritania: Now That the Guns Are Silent." *New Times* 80, no. 9 (February 1980): 14–15.

Kuhlein, Conrad. "Western Sahara: Standpoints and Compromises." *Aussenpolitik* 32, no. 1 (1st quarter, 1981): 59–72.

Lalutte, Pauline. "Sahara: Notes Toward an Analysis." In *The Struggle for Sahara.* MERIP Reports, no. 45. Washington, D.C.: Middle East Research & Information Project, March 1976, pp. 7–12.

Legum, Colin, ed. *Africa Contemporary Record: Annual Survey and Documents, 1974–1975.* New York: Africana Publishing, 1975.

Lewis, William H. "Western Sahara: Compromise or Conflict?" *Current History* 80 (1981): 410–13, 431.

Maclean, John. "State Department Divided from Within over Tank Sale to Morocco." *Defense Week* 1, no. 31 (November 3, 1980): 7–8.

Markham, James M. "King Hassan's Quagmire." *New York Times Magazine*, April 27, 1980, pp. 116, 118, 120–25.

"Mauritanian Government Receives Substantial Aid from Arab States." *Middle East*, no. 54 (April 1979): 104–5.

Mercer, John. "Confrontation in the Western Sahara." *World Today* 32 (1976): 230–39.

———. *The Sahrawis of Western Sahara*. Report no. 40. London: Minority Rights Group, 1979.

———. *Spanish Sahara*. London: George Allen & Unwin, 1976.

Miské, Ahmed-Baba. *Front Polisario: L'Ame d'un peuple*. Paris. Editions Rapture, 1978.

Morgan, Susan. "Morocco: Austerity and Sacrifice." *Middle East International*, no. 128 (July 4, 1980): 11–12.

———. "The OAU and the Sahara." *Middle East International*, no. 129 (July 18, 1980): 10–12.

———. "Saudi Plan Mooted for Sahara Conflict." *Middle East*, no. 57 (July 1979): 18–19.

Mortimer, Robert A. "Western Sahara: The Diplomatic Perspectives." *Africa Report* 23, no. 2 (March–April 1978): 10–14.

Neumann, Robert G. "Morocco and the Sahara." Transcribed interview, Oral History Program, University of California, Los Angeles, August 2, 1976.

Ould Daddah, Mokhtar. "Sahara: La Genèse d'un affrontement." *Jeune Afrique*, no. 790 (February 27, 1976): 26–27.

Pautard, André. "L'Enjeu mauritanien." *L'Express*, May 16–22, 1977, pp. 55–56.

"Peace Moves over Western Sahara." *Events* (Beirut), May 19, 1978, p. 26.

Price, D[avid] L[ynn]. "Morocco and the Sahara." *Middle East International*, no. 86 (August 1978): 19–20.

———. "Morocco: The Political Balance." *World Today* 34 (1978): 493–500.

———. *The Western Sahara*. Washington Papers, no. 63. Beverly Hills., Calif., and London: Sage Publications, 1979.

Rami, Ahmed. "Malaise dans l'armée: Un Officier parle...." *Afrique-Asie*, no. 99 (December 29, 1975–January 11, 1976): 13–15.

Reisman, W. Michael. "African Imperialism." *American Journal of International Law* 70 (1976): 801–2.

Rézette, Robert. *The Spanish Enclaves in Morocco*. Translated by Mary Ewalt. Paris: Nouvelles Editions Latines, 1976.

———. *The Western Sahara and the Frontiers of Morocco*. Translated by Mary Ewalt. Paris: Nouvelles Editions Latines, 1975.

"Sahara: La Partie visible de l'iceberg." *Lamalif*, no. 94 (January–February 1978): 10–11.

"Sahara: Le Guerre pour avoir la paix." *Lamalif*, no. 92 (November 1977): 14–17.

Schissel, Howard. "Changes in Algiers Invite Optimism on Sahara Conflict." *Middle East,* no. 53 (March 1979): 13–14.

———. "Mauritanian In-Fighting." *Middle East International,* no. 145 (March 13, 1981): 11–12.

———. "Stalemate in the Western Sahara." *Middle East International,* no. 143 (February 13, 1981): 13–14.

"Secretary-General Given Mandate on Sahara Issue." *UN Monthly Chronicle* 12, no. 10 (November 1975): 5–10.

Sehimi, Mustapha. "Sahara: 5 Scénarios pour 1978." *Le Journal Parlementaire,* no. 3 (February 1978): 15–24.

Shaplen, Robert. "Eye of the Storm," part 1. *New Yorker,* June 2, 1980, pp. 43–89.

Solarz, Stephen J. "Arms for Morocco?" *Foreign Affairs* 58 (1979/80): 278–99.

Stockholm International Peace Research Institute. *World Armaments and Disarmament: SIPRI Yearbook* for the years 1976–1982. Cambridge, Mass., and London: MIT Press; Stockholm: Almquist & Wiksell International, 1976–1977; London: Taylor & Francis, 1978–1980; London: Taylor & Francis; Cambridge, Mass.: Oelgeschlager, Gunn & Hain, 1981–1982.

The Struggle for Sahara. MERIP Reports, no. 45. Washington, D.C. Middle East Research & Information Project, March 1976.

Tareb, M. "Sahara occidental: La Réponse appartient au peuple sahraoui." *El Djeich,* no. 146 (July 1975): 46–47.

Tessler, Mark. *Politics in Morocco: The Monarch, the War, and the Opposition.* American Universities Field Staff, Africa, Report no. 47. Hanover, N.H.: AUFS, 1981.

Thompson, Virginia, and Adloff, Richard. *The Western Saharans: Background to Conflict.* London: Croom Helm; Totowa, N.J.: Barnes & Noble Books, 1980.

Trout, Frank E. *Morocco's Saharan Frontiers.* Geneva: Droz Publishers, 1969.

Ware, Lewis B. *Decolonization and the Global Alliance in the Arab Maghrib: The Case of Spanish Sahara.* Maxwell Air Force Base, Ala.: Air University Institute for Professional Development, December 1975.

Weexsteen, Raoul. "La Question du Sahara occidental." *Annuaire de l'Afrique du Nord* (Paris: Editions du Centre National de la Recherche Scientifique, 1978) 16 (1977): 425–37.

———. "Le Sahara occidental aux prises avec ses voisins: Ces Hommes qui se battent dans le désert...." *Le Monde Diplomatique,* no. 263 (February 1976): 10–11.

———. "La Stratégie du Front Polisario face à ses adversaires directs et à leurs protecteurs." *Le Monde Diplomatique,* no. 281 (August 1977): 4–5.

Weiner, Jerome B. "The Green March in Historical Perspective." *Middle East Journal* 33 (1979): 20–33.

Weinstein, Brian. "The Western Sahara." *Current History* 78 (1980): 110–14, 136–37.

"Western Sahara: The Heat Is On." *Middle East*, no. 62 (December 1979): 46–48.

"Western Sahara: Who Is Polisario?" *Africa Confidential* 22, no. 2 (January 14, 1981): 2–5.

Younger, Sam. "Ideology and Pragmatism in Algerian Foreign Policy." *World Today* 34 (1978): 107–14.

Zartman, I. William. "Conflict in the Sahara." In idem, *Ripe for Resolution: Conflict and Intervention in Africa*. New Haven, Conn.: Yale University Press, forthcoming.

———. *Conflict in the Sahara*. Middle East Problem Paper, no. 19. Washington, D.C.: Middle East Institute, 1979.

———. "Conflict in the Sahara." Mimeo. March 8, 1979.

———. "A Disputed Frontier Is Settled." *Africa Report* 8, no. 8 (August 1963): 13–14.

———. "Referendum and Negotiation in the Western Sahara." Mimeo. October 1, 1981.

Newspapers and Periodicals

Africa

Africa Confidential (London)

Africa Report

Afrique-Asie

American Journal of International Law

An-Nahar Arab Report

Aussenpolitik (Hamburg; English edition)

Boston Herald American

Christian Science Monitor

Current History

Defense Week (Washington, D.C.)

El Djeich (Algiers)

The Economist

L'Express

Fletcher Forum (Medford, Mass.)

Foreign Affairs

Foreign Policy

Harper's

Jeune Afrique

Journal Parlementaire

Lamalif (Casablanca)

Maghreb-Machrek

Maghreb Review

Manchester Guardian Weekly

Marchés Tropicaux et Méditerranéens

Le Matin du Sahara (Casablanca)

Middle East

Middle East Economic Digest

Middle East International

Middle East Journal

Le Monde

Le Monde Diplomatique

El Moudjahid (Algiers; French-language edition)

Mundo Obrero Semanal (Madrid)

New Times (Moscow)

New Yorker

New York Times

Orbis

El País

Perspectives Sahariennes (Tangier)

Sahara Libre (Algiers)

Times (London)

UN Monthly Chronicle

20 Mai (Algiers)

Washington Post

World Today

Index

HOOVER INTERNATIONAL STUDIES

South Africa: War, Revolution, or Peace?
L. H. Gann and Peter Duignan

Two Chinese States
Ramon H. Myers, editor

The Panama Canal Controversy
Paul B. Ryan

The Imperialist Revolutionaries
Hugh Seton-Watson

Soviet Strategy for Nuclear War
Joseph D. Douglass, Jr., and Amoretta M. Hoeber

Science, Technology and China's Drive for Modernization
Richard P. Suttmeier

Waiting for a "Pearl Harbor": Japan Debates Defense
Tetsuya Kataoka

The End of the Tito Era
Slobodan Stanković

Afghanistan: The Soviet Invasion in Perspective
Anthony Arnold

Communist Powers and Sub-Saharan Africa
Thomas H. Henriksen, editor

The United States and the Republic of Korea
Claude A. Buss

The Clouded Lens: Persian Gulf Security and U.S. Policy, 2d ed.
James H. Noyes

Communism in Central America and the Caribbean
Robert Wesson, editor

Ideology of a Superpower
R. Judson Mitchell

A U.S. Foreign Policy for Asia
Ramon H. Myers, editor

The ASEAN States and Regional Security
Sheldon W. Simon